DEDICATION

In Memoriam: To the souls lost; may they rest in peace.

In Solidarity: To the survivors; may they yet rise again.

In Celebration: To those who so love their neighbors that

they have ministered to them, giving physical, spiritual,

emotional, and financial resources toward recovery.

THE SKY IS CRYING

RACE, CLASS, AND NATURAL DISASTER

CHERYL A. KIRK-DUGGAN
EDITOR

Abingdon Press
Nashville

THE SKY IS CRYING
RACE, CLASS, AND NATURAL DISASTER

ISBN 0-687-33473-X
LCCN 2006026705

All scripture quotations unless noted otherwise are taken from the *New Revised Standard Version of the Bible*, copyright 1989, Division of Christian Education of the National Council of the Churches of Christ in the United States of America. Used by permission. All rights reserved.

Scripture quotations marked (NIV) are taken from the HOLY BIBLE, NEW INTERNATIONAL VERSION®. NIV®. Copyright © 1973, 1978, 1984 by International Bible Society. Used by permission of Zondervan Publishing House. All rights reserved.

Scripture quotations marked (NKJV) are taken from the New King James Version. Copyright © 1982 by Thomas Nelson, Inc. Used by permission. All rights reserved.

Scripture quotations marked (GNT) are from the Good News Translation in Today's English Version-Second Edition © 1992 by American Bible Society. Used by permission.

Excerpts from THE POWER OF NONVIOLENCE are reprinted by arrangement with the Estate of Martin Luther King, Jr, c/o Writers House as agent for the proprietor, New York, NY. Copyright 1958 Martin Luther King, Jr., copyright renewed 1986 Coretta Scott King.

Excerpts from WHERE DO WE GO FROM HERE: CHAOS OR COMMUNITY? reprinted by arrangement with the Estate of Martin Luther King, Jr, c/o Writers House as agent for the proprietor, New York, NY. Copyright 1967 Martin Luther King, Jr., copyright renewed 1995 Coretta Scott King.

Excerpts from PILGRIMAGE TO NONVIOLENCE reprinted by arrangement with the Estate of Martin Luther King, Jr., c/o Writers House as agent for the proprietor, New York, NY. Copyright 1963 Martin Luther King, Jr., copyright renewed 1991 Coretta Scott King.

"The Katrina Pledge" is reprinted with permission from *Sojourners* magazine, www.sojo.net, 1-800-714-7474.

The opinions expressed in this book are the authors' own, and do not necessarily represent those of Abingdon Press or The United Methodist Publishing House.

06 07 08 09 10 11 12 13 14 15—10 9 8 7 6 5 4 3 2 1

MANUFACTURED IN THE UNITED STATES OF AMERICA

CONTENTS

CONTRIBUTORS

Valerie Bridgeman Davis teaches Old Testament and Preaching and Worship at Memphis Theological Seminary. She also directs the Arts and Theology Institute for the seminary. An ordained minister, Bridgeman Davis is an award-winning published and performance poet and author of *In Search of Warriors Dark and Strong and Other Poems*.

Toni Dunbar is an associate pastor at City of Refuge United Church of Christ in San Francisco, California, and the charter chaplain at San Francisco's juvenile probation department. She is a former judicatory minister and the author of *Blessed: Sermons from the Edge*. Her interests are postcolonial religious theory and the potential for non-Christian, precolonial religious practice and thought to influence revitalization of the Christian church, particularly the urban inner-city church serving youth and the hip-hop generation. Her doctor of ministry project (Pacific School of Religion, 2007) is "Just Faith: Program, Policy, and Prayer in San Francisco's Juvenile Justice System."

Marcia L. Dyson is an ordained minister, stirring public speaker, and gifted writer. Rev. Dyson engages in a ministry of healing to wounded women, neglected children, and suffering men throughout America and around the globe. A contributing writer for *Essence* magazine, Dyson is working on several books, including a novel, *Don't Call Me Angel*, which explores the spiritual development of an African-American woman, and *Awakening Eve: Essays and Sermons to Arouse the Spiritual and Social Consciousness in Women*.

Cheryl Fries is a writer and documentary filmmaker who lives with her husband and daughter in Austin, Texas. She is currently writing a book about her award-winning film *In the Shadow of the Blade*, in which a restored combat helicopter flew to Vietnam veterans as a catalyst for cathartic storytelling.

Cecilia González-Andrieu is a doctoral candidate at the Graduate Theological Union in the area of art and religion and has been appointed to the theology faculty of Loyola Marymount University. Winner of first-place honors from the Catholic Press Association for her column of essays in *The Tidings*, she has recently contributed to *The Treasure of Guadalupe*, an anthology by Latina and Latino theologians.

Diana L. Hayes is Professor of Systematic Theology at Georgetown University, with a specialization in womanist and U.S. liberation theologies. She is the author or coeditor of six books and has written more than sixty articles and book chapters on black theology; womanist theology; issues of race, class, gender, and religion; and black Catholic theology.

Dwight N. Hopkins is a constructive theologian working in the areas of contemporary models of theology, black theology, and liberation theologies. He is interested in multidisciplinary approaches to the academic study of religious thought, especially cultural, political, economic, and interpretive methods. Author of more than ten books and editor of three volumes, Professor Hopkins is senior editor of the Henry McNeil Turner/Sojourner Truth Series in Black Religion (Orbis Books). He is an ordained American Baptist minister. His latest works include *Being Human: Race, Culture, and Religion* and *Loving the Body: Black Religious Studies and the Erotic* (coeditor).

Peniel E. Joseph teaches in the Department of Africana Studies at SUNY-Stony Brook. He has been awarded fellowships from the Woodrow Wilson International Center and Ford Foundation and is the author of *Waiting 'Til the Midnight Hour: A Narrative History of Black Power in America* and editor of *The Black Power Movement: Rethinking the Civil Rights-Black Power Era*.

Shari Julian holds a doctorate in public policy and has a clinical postdoctorate in counseling, with an emphasis in human systems, and more than twenty-two years experience in both the hospital and private settings. Her specialization in traumatic events and large-scale disaster response has involved her in work around the world as a clinician and consultant. She is a diplomate and fellow in forensic expertise and forensic medicine in the American College of Forensic Examiners International and a member of the faculty in the Department of Criminology and Criminal Justice at the University of Texas at Arlington.

Doll Kennedy is currently working on her PhD in Christian Ethics and Social Theory at Union Theological Seminary in New York. She is also an ordained itinerant elder in the African Methodist Episcopal Church and serves as the director of the ministries of hope and healing at Saint James AME (Newark, New Jersey).

Dorrance Kennedy is Assistant Professor of Social Work at Shaw University. He also serves as Associate Pastor of First Baptist Church (Fayetteville, North

Carolina) and is an ordained Baptist minister and licensed clinical social worker. He was recently selected to serve on the African American Advisory Board of CASA (Court Appointed Special Advocates). He is a native of New Orleans.

Cheryl A. Kirk-Duggan is Professor of Theology and Women's Studies at Shaw University Divinity School, Raleigh, North Carolina, and is an ordained elder in the Christian Methodist Episcopal Church. She is the author and editor of more than twenty books and numerous articles, and was named the 2001 Quintessential Womanist Scholar of the Year. Her forthcoming works include *Violence and Theology*.

Bishop Vashti Murphy McKenzie is the presiding bishop of the thirteenth Episcopal District of the African Methodist Episcopal Church, which comprises the state of Tennessee and the commonwealth of Kentucky. She was the first woman elected to Episcopal office in the two-hundred-nineteen-year history of the denomination and the first woman to serve as President of the Council of Bishops. Bishop McKenzie is the author of two books on leadership as well as *Journey to the Well*, which has appeared on several best-seller lists.

Eung Chun Park is the Robert S. Dollar Professor of New Testament at San Francisco Theological Seminary and the Graduate Theological Union in Berkeley. He is the author of *The Mission Discourse in Matthew's Interpretation* and *Either Jew or Gentile: Paul's Unfolding Theology of Inclusivity*. He was recently elected a member of the *Studiorum Novi Testamenti Societas*.

Sister Jamie T. Phelps is an Adrian Dominican Sister and refounder of the Black Catholic Theological Symposium. She is Professor of Theology and Director of the Institute for Black Catholic Studies at Xavier University of Louisiana in New Orleans. Previously, she ministered for more than forty years as an educator (from elementary through doctoral levels), a pastoral minister in several Chicago Archdiocesan parishes, a psychiatric social worker and community organizer, a spiritual director, retreat director, and administrator. She has also traveled nationally and internationally ministering as a theologian, lecturer, and preacher.

Anthony B. Pinn is the Agnes Cullen Arnold Professor of Humanities and Professor of Religious Studies at Rice University. He is the author or editor of sixteen books, including *Terror and Triumph: The Nature of Black Religion*, *African American Humanist Principles*, and *African American Religious Experience in America*.

Alton B. Pollard III is Director of the Program of Black Church Studies and Associate Professor of Religion and Culture at Candler School of Theology at

Emory University. His interests include religion and popular culture, religion and social change, sexuality and health, and Pan-Africanist religious thought. His published works include *Mysticism and Social Change: The Social Witness of Howard Thurman* and *How Long This Road: Race, Religion, and the Legacy of C. Eric Lincoln.*

Ferenc Raj holds a PhD in Near Eastern and Judaic Studies from Brandeis University and has served Reform congregations in Brooklyn, New York, and Belmont, Massachusetts, prior to his election as Senior Rabbi of Congregation Beth El in Berkeley, California.

Melva L. Sampson currently serves as Project Manager for the Sisters Chapel WISDOM (Women in Spiritual Discernment of Ministry) Center, Spelman College. Her research interests include the cultural and religious representation of the black female body. She is a former recipient of the Nolan B. Harmon Award and served as a Patricia Roberts Harris Public Affairs Fellow in Washington DC.

J. Alfred Smith Sr. is Senior Pastor, Allen Temple Baptist Church, Oakland, California, and Distinguished Professor of Preaching and Church Ministries, American Baptist Seminary of the West and the Graduate Theological Union, Berkeley, California. Dr. Smith is a past national president of the Progressive National Baptist Convention and a past president of the American Baptist Churches of the West. In August 2004 he was named one of *Ebony* magazine's most influential black Americans and was among the magazine's top fifteen greatest black preachers of 1993. A renowned scholar, an acclaimed preacher, and an accomplished author of sixteen books, his most recent work is his autobiographical *On the Jericho Road.*

Darryl M. Trimiew is chair of the Department of Philosophy and Religious Studies of Medgar Evers College. He is also the author of *God Bless the Child That's Got Its Own: The Economic Rights Debate* and *Voices of the Silenced: The Responsible Self in a Marginalized Community.*

INTRODUCTION

CHERYL A. KIRK-DUGGAN

T error, trauma, and tragedy erupted—and safety vanished. Since September 11, 2001, when aircraft loaded with high-octane fuel-turned-suicide-bombs rammed the twin towers of the World Trade Center in New York City, the Pentagon in our nation's capital, and the countryside of Pennsylvania, followed by the catastrophic impact of hurricanes Katrina and Rita in 2005, we citizens of the United States can no longer fantasize or have delusions of grandeur that we are secure or beyond the realms of violent assault—via humanity or nature. The notion that our geographic borders framed by great oceans and two other countries that comprise North America, our collective intellect, our financial coffers, and our weapons of mass destruction can keep us safe evaporated on 9/11, and again in the aftermath of August 29, 2005, when Lady Katrina—a tramp, not a lady at all, certainly minus the usual aplomb of Southern gentility, including those affable Georgia peaches—pummeled the shores on the southern Gulf Coast. Lady Katrina[1] played hide-and-seek for a while, vacillating up and down with the size of her visits. When Katrina did hit, she stole lives, hopes, dreams, and possessions. Katrina changed and rearranged the landscape and swallowed up plants, animals, buildings, businesses, churches, schools, and life as we had come to know it. From the coast of Florida to Texas, Katrina was devastating to the states of Alabama, Mississippi, and Louisiana, in between. While those in New Orleans breathed a sigh of relief after Katrina passed over, no one in that city was ready when the next day three levees broke, placing 80 percent of the city under water.

A few weeks later, Katrina's cousin Rita came through the Gulf and packed an equally powerful wallop, particularly to southwest Louisiana and Texas. She came through with a vengeance—destroying lives, property, dreams, and hopes; uprooting trees and downing power lines. The destruction of Katrina and Rita combined has been horrific. Even at this writing, in the first few days of January 2006, many survivors remain displaced. They cannot return home. For some, where their homes once stood only a concrete slab remains. For those whose homes may still be standing, the mold, bacteria, and standing oil-polluted water poisons their mosquito-infested land with a cesspool of the unintended consequences of inaction and a failure of leadership on the federal, state, and local governments.

This collection of commentary, *The Sky Is Crying: Race, Class, and Natural Disaster*, is a response of reflections, critical essays, and sermons by activists, scholars, and clergy to this cacophony of bad news, of tremendous loss in the wake of natural disaster and human incompetence. Moved by the Spirit a few days after Katrina hit, I contacted John Kutsko, the director of academic and professional publishing at Abingdon Press, to float my idea of doing this volume and received an overwhelming Yes! from John and his editorial team. I then began the process of sharing this dream with others across the country, inviting them to engage in scholarly, pastoral, activist, and communal response to such tragedy. In the pages that follow you will hear their voices and mine. This introduction reflects on the lens of theological ethics for reckoning with the event of natural disaster. A review of a litany of previous disasters moves toward a discussion of the sociocultural milieu in the United States that is framed by an attitude of arrogance and denial that makes us think we are exempt from catastrophe. The analysis continues by examining systemic, domestic problems unearthed and exposed by recent natural disasters. I conclude by naming the contributors who have so graciously given their time and creative gifts to write reflections, essays, and sermons for *The Sky Is Crying*; royalties will go to support the rebuilding of Dillard and Xavier Universities in New Orleans.

Peering through to See and Name

There were many ways we could begin to organize this project to wrestle with the problems surrounding natural disasters and how human beings think about such phenomena, particularly from a religious, theological, and ethical perspective. When we think about religion or religious matters we think of concepts of faith and systems of belief; about one's sense of the divine, the sacred, and related institutions such as churches, synagogues, mosques, and temples. Religions are closely related to the particular contexts or cultures, traditions, and rituals. Theology, from the Greek *theos* for God and *ology* for *study*, pertains to the study of how people think about, experience, and talk about the divine, or experience of God. Some like to expand this term to include the practice or discipline a person engages in as the primary discipline or rule that governs one's life and how one relates to others. Ethics is the discipline or study of morals; that is, thinking about how people behave, which translates as what they value and whether they act out of a sense of virtue, duty, and rights or a sense of "ends justify the means." Nine questions helped spark the thinking of the participants for this volume as we began to wrestle with the enormity of the loss and devastation.

1. What are the theological and ethical implications of historic, natural disasters? For example, Pompeii volcano (79 CE); Lisbon earthquake (1755); New Madrid, Missouri, earthquake (1811); Chicago/Peshtigo Fires (1871); Galveston, Texas, hurricane and flood (1900); San Francisco Fire (earthquake) (1906); Tokyo earthquake (1923); Tangshan, China, earthquake (1976); Kobe, Japan, earthquake (1995); Southeast Asia tsunami (2004); Hurricane Katrina (2005)?

2. What are the theological and ethical issues of intentional human-induced disaster, and how do these relate to environmental racism and classism? For example, Guernica, Spain, firebombings (1937); Coventry, England, bombing (1940); Hiroshima and Nagasaki, Japan, atomic bomb attacks (1945); Tokyo, Japan, firebombing (1945); Dresden, Germany, firebombing (1945); Three Mile Island nuclear power plant accident, Middletown, Pennsylvania (1979); Chernobyl nuclear explosion (1986); the Holocaust (1933–45); the Rwanda massacre/genocide (1994); Darfur, Sudan, massacre/genocide (2005)?

3. What are the theological dangers of framing these as questions of theodicy? In other words, how does theodicy let humans off the hook, as it were?

4. What are the dimensions of so-called civilized behavior (cloaked in a thin veneer of respectability) when threats to life reduce supposed

utopias to violence and chaos? For example, Plato's *Republic*; Augustine's *City of God*; Thomas More's *Utopia*; Thomas Hobbes's *Leviathan*; George Orwell's *1984*; and William Golding's *Lord of the Flies*?

5. How do we name, expose, and ultimately transform systemic, human evil that contributes to disaster, when race, class, and poverty result in those deemed "other" being scapegoated, often at the cost of their lives?

6. What are the issues concerning a disregard for ecology in the light of the theological notion of dominion versus stewardship, when the earth becomes a killing field or a cancer alley?

7. What is the role of faith communities before disaster strikes regarding the understanding of what it means to be human versus an objectified, commodified other?

8. How can sacred texts inform our understanding of divine providence and human responsibilities in the wake of natural or human-induced disasters?

9. In the aftermath of a tragedy, what is the role of the media and popular press, given "the people have a right to know," when that knowledge is presented subjectively? Specifically, what is the media's role when people with observable differences are portrayed as courageous, self-preserving, and resourceful while the same behavior by those deemed other is seen as criminal, stereotypical, and at fault?

And the Beat Goes On: Disasters and Theodicy

What are the theological and ethical implications of historic, natural disasters? Although we had Hurricanes Rita and Katrina, and the Southeast Asia tsunami at the end of 2004 and throughout 2005, natural disasters are not new phenomena. Here is a thumbnail sketch of some infamous natural disasters: Pompeii volcano (79 CE); Lisbon earthquake (1755); New Madrid, Missouri, earthquake (1811); Chicago/Peshtigo Fires (1871); Galveston, Texas, hurricane and flood (1900); San Francisco Fire (earthquake) (1906); Tokyo earthquake (1923); Tangshan, China, earthquake (1976); Kobe, Japan, earthquake (1995).

Not all of the damage that occurs is the direct result of the meteorological event, but may have more to do with human behavior in the wake of the event. Thus, we ask: What are the theological and ethical issues of intentional human-induced disaster, and how do these relate to environmental racism and classism? Many human-induced disasters connect with war. For example, the first time a decision was made to intentionally bomb a civilian population occurred in the Guernica, Spain, firebombings (1937), an event immortalized in the artistry of Pablo Picasso. Additional war-related disasters during the twentieth and twenty-first centuries include: the Coventry, England, bombing (1940); the Tokyo, Japan, firebombing (1945); the Dresden, Germany, firebombing (1945); and the Hiroshima and Nagasaki, Japan, atomic bomb attacks (1945). Some human-induced disasters include accidents around nuclear power where explosions and leaks resulted in the death of innocent people and the extreme pollution of the environment: Three Mile Island nuclear power plant accident, Middletown, Pennsylvania (1979); and Chernobyl nuclear explosion (1986). Some human-induced disaster is the calculated, intentional genocide of a particular group of people by another group who determine that they can objectify and therefore dispose of people because of what they look like, believe, or possess. The objectified persons, on some level, are viewed as a threat and then scapegoated. The objectified ones are blamed for the circumstances of those who dominate; millions of innocent people have been gassed, slaughtered, annihilated, raped as acts of war, and destroyed: the Holocaust (1933–45); the Rwanda massacre/genocide (1994); Darfur, Sudan, massacre/genocide (2005).

When these kinds of bad things happen to innocent people, we often wonder why. How do we make sense out of such nonsense? One survivor of the Indonesian earthquake of May 2006 wondered, "I do not know what we did. But we must have sinned for God to be angry like this."[2] We may want to theologize and look for symbols of divine judgment in various geological and meteorological phenomena that cause great loss and devastation. We must remember, however, that geologists state that we live on unstable ground—six to thirty-six slow-moving plates of rock that are powered by 4.5-billion-year-old, boiling, radioactive residue from earth's formation. These plates bump up against, slide, or plunge below one another in a kind of friction that freezes them for a time. When energy builds up in a sudden manner, the plates shift and energy gets discharged that may cause spasms around the world in the form of earthquakes, volcanoes, or tsunamis.[3] Sometimes scholars approach this question with the issue of theodicy: *theos* (God) and *dike* (justice). Placing the matter of God in dialogue with the question of justice—the question of why bad things happen to good people—scholars examine the issue of theodicy. Traditionally, the focus ends up being since God is good, just, and powerful, and bad things happen, there is a contradiction. Thus, the question shifts to proving the existence of God. There are two traditional answers to the theodicy question: (1) the Augustinian or free-will argument, where human beings make bad choices; and (2) the Irenean argument, where people are born in God's image and likeness, and, by imposing difficult times, the Holy Spirit perfects one to embrace the image of God (moral freedom and responsibility) and God's likeness (capacity to reflect the Creator's essence). Contemporary Christian philosopher and theologian Kenneth Surin argues against the way most scholars study and analyze evil and suffering. He says that one should not impose a single standard, some "timeless reality," upon a particular event that happens at a stated sociocultural and historically conditioned time.[4]

In seeking to answer the question Why? with regard to natural disasters, philosophers have pressed the question of theodicy. In dealing with the theodicy question after the 1755 Lisbon earthquake, not only did philosophers attempt to sort out moral evil from natural evil or disaster, but they also began to explore history as opposed to theology for answers, beginning with G. W. F. Hegel. With recent tragedies answers to theodicy have become more human focused as the fault of human agency: incompetence, poor planning, negligence, and incompetence. People look more to politics and science to discern the machinations of nature. Where the response was once divine retribution, now the answer seems to fall into the arena of political retribution for human ineptitude.[5]

Peter Steinfels catalogs the accepted reasons for the costs of recent hurricane tragedies: complacency about the consequences of disaster; sluggish, maladroit governmental response; harsh economic disparities; dire need for material resources; racial differences; and callous dislocations. Today, few blame God and instead see the answer within human agency, which telegraphs the belief in human responsibility and human freedom. In short, the can-do spirit of U.S. citizens seems to ignore the intricacy and catastrophe in exchange for "just suck it up" and move ahead with recovery and rebuilding. Thick denial does not admit that some things cannot be restored; some communities cannot come back again; some will not recover; and some will not be made stronger. Further, technology, resources, and organizational strategies may not solve all our problems.

Steinfels suggests that we might pause and ponder how such disasters came to happen, which might "lead to a more profound understanding of the human condition and the untidiness of reality generally."[6] Often when asking why things of such magnitude happen, we desire a simple answer for a complex scenario.

The theological danger of simple answers is that we may scapegoat and make someone or something other without fully grasping the entire situation. Sometimes in blaming God, karma, or bad luck we seek to let humans off the hook. At the end of the day, the reality is that if one lives on a fault, one will experience an earthquake; if one lives near a river, it will flood; if one lives near the Gulf, one will experience a hurricane and/or tsunami. For some situations and challenges in life, there are no satisfactory answers, though this does not mean we do not continue to ponder the parameters of the inevitable.

Katrina, A Perfect Storm Revisited: A Case Study

Because "tragedy has no walls," Katrina redrew the Gulf Coast shoreline, remapped its populations, and destroyed more than ninety thousand square miles from Florida to Louisiana, piling water as high as twenty-nine feet in some areas. Eighty percent of New Orleans, some parts that rest eight feet below sea level, ended up under billions of gallons of water and oil from ruptured storage facilities. Amid relentless heat, humidity, and apocalyptic squalor, more than twenty thousand people at one point were housed in the Superdome. Deaths there were because of poor sanitation. Houston's Astrodome housed more than eleven thousand weary evacuees.[7]

The destruction left in the aftermath of Katrina was inevitable, particularly for New Orleans. In analyzing why we build cities in dangerous, precarious places and live amid such impending jeopardy, Adam Kushner suggests that it is our "dysfunctional raison d'etre, [our] Pompeii redux." He writes that the draining of the backswamp "has meant a Sisyphean, 300-year death match between engineers and the elements. . . . The levee and flood-control systems . . . built in fits and starts since 1724 . . . were still not done when Katrina struck. The cost has been immeasurable, and the failures innumerable."[8]

About three hundred twenty miles of levees and floodwalls connected with a network of canals brace and protect New Orleans, which is below the levels of Lake Ponchatrain and the Mississippi River. As long as the outside waters stay calm, the city stays dry. Katrina's 145-mile-per-hour winds helped create a storm surge, causing water to break levees or overflow them; what had been a Category 1 storm over South Florida became a Category 4 hurricane when it hit land in Louisiana. Many scientists posit that recent hurricanes were turbulent because during the 1990s the cycle of ocean currents and temperatures shifted, causing increased warm temperatures in the Atlantic—enough to provide added power for forming hurricanes and tornados, perhaps a consequence of global warming. Various waters have always made the Delta region precarious to live in, given that the Mississippi drains roughly half of the United States, so the country needed a port at its mouth for shipping purposes. Although natural levees built up over time, A. Baldwin Wood invented a huge pump that helped drain the backswamp of New Orleans and dumped it in Lake Ponchatrain. Other levees were built to protect the city, yet at the same time the backswamp's drainage caused the city to sink further below sea level. The shrinking Delta had been a prime protection from hurricanes.[9]

Reading page after page of commentary on Katrina and Rita from various perspectives, and viewing page after page of special photographic editions from *National Geographic* and *Time*, magazines whose sales will support disaster relief, grieved my heart. Some of this tragedy was avoidable. As early as 2001, *Scientific American*; the New Orleans newspaper, the *Times-Picayune*; and *National Geographic* had all named the inevitability of the destruction, chaos, damage, and death that would occur to New Orleans with a Category 3 or above major hurricane, given New Orleans's topography (being a city set on sinking mud, below sea level, between Lake Ponchatrain and the Mississippi River), and the substandard levees that were sinking. Add to that mix an overbuilt coastline and diminished wetlands that no longer provided a safety barrier in part because of dredging for big ships; we were left with a perfect storm: a destructive dynamo. In addition, when we exploit our environment, we may gain short-term benefits, but we will pay dearly in the long term.[10]

Columnist George Will reminds us that a great deal of selfless heroism, displaying the human capacity to be noble, surfaced after Katrina, accompanied to a lesser extent by chaos, anxiety, and irrational behavior. This behavior reflected the Hobbesian notion of the tenuous, fragile nature of life, particularly when governmental structures collapse, civility disappears, and thus passions no longer held in check via socialization acquire force. As great a marvel as cities are, we exude hubris when we forget that the various infrastructures and dependencies of cities that make them so wonderful also make them quite fragile. Will reminds us that in all of this mix, "the first business of government, on which everything depends, is security."[11]

What Katrina did not demolish, she exposed, and one of the exposés was the incompetence, corruption, and autocratic behavior among local leadership, particularly the police force. Internal and external disrespect loomed over the New Orleans police. The racial nature and makeup of New Orleans is key to understanding the complexities of the city. Despite a New Orleans population that was two-thirds African American prior to Katrina, the police department was predominantly white until the 1990s. The police department's reputation has been one of corruption, crime, and brutality. There was also tension with the working-class tribes of African American men, who with their costumes, song, and participation in Mardi Gras parades honor Native Americans for helping escaped slaves. This tension intensified after police roughed up some of the tribes of African American men, and at a town meeting with the city council the celebrated Chief of Chiefs, Allison "Tootie" Montana, collapsed and died. This was an indication of the tension steeping right at the surface when Katrina hit, when the levees broke, when 80 percent of New Orleans rested below water.[12]

Amid the storm, local, state, and federal leadership evaporated: a mobile command center had been moved and was unavailable; an emergency evacuation plan had been designed but never rehearsed; thousands of people were left wet and terrified; and some at the convention center were without water, food, or power. With about five hundred police missing, the major issue was that the rules and protocols that usually keep police orderly disappeared during the hurricane crisis; and without commanders visible, cops can become renegades. New Orleans Police Department (N.O.P.D.) had no contact with the Federal Emergency Management Agency (FEMA) or with other emergency services. The stench of rotting garbage, decaying bodies, and spilled gasoline was everywhere. With only about a mile of dry land, all government representatives were absent; but, urban myths to the contrary, there was little actual looting, and the deaths at the Superdome were because of illness, not homicide. Even after being in inhumane conditions, without potable water, clean clothes, or working toilets, and in misery without air-conditioning, the evacuees were orderly when buses came to pick them up. Instead of being voices of calm, Mayor Ray Nagin and Police Superintendent Eddie Compass were often spewing incendiary remarks. The majority of the remaining white citizens armed themselves, anticipating an Armageddon-type race riot, given the rumors. The riots never happened. With no one really in charge the situation for the poor was even more precarious. Many of the evacuees had no idea where they were going when they boarded their buses! With local, state, and national law enforcement coming from all over the country, and the mayor's order to make everyone leave town, New Orleans became a ghost town under martial law. The race card again raised its ugly head. Blacks remained with no effective transportation and were often manhandled; it was *suggested* that whites in palatial, dry parts of town leave via their luxury cars. At the end of the immediate crisis, police were overwhelmed, exhausted, and burned-out. Many will leave the town where they never received respect.[13]

These domestic natural disasters of 2005 show that this country is not prepared for and has not gotten smarter about dealing with catastrophe, and we are not ready to respond systematically with efficiency and competency. As the deaths and devastation and the costs of damage mount and we can no longer measure suffering, often the problem becomes too large for us to contemplate. In many instances the private sector responded more effectively than did the inept public, political systems. With all its charm, corruption, poverty, murders, termites, and neglected infrastructure, New Orleans—a city half underwater, half under indictment—was not capable of coping. At its worst, it got hotter, and "the whole city was poached in a vile stew of melted landfill, chemicals, corpses, gasoline, snakes, canal rats."[14] People could not understand why they had been forgotten; why there was no food or clean water; why all they got from FEMA was a busy signal.

> Katrina was in the cards, forewarned, foreseen and yet still dismissed until it was too late. That so many officials were caught so unprepared was a failure less of imagination than will, a realization all the more frightening in light of what lies ahead. For if we couldn't help our citizens in an hour of desperate need, how well will we do in six months or a year, when many are still jobless and homeless, but no longer center stage?[15]

Perhaps we name storms out of our humility, arrogance, or defiance. We simply cannot believe that such doom, death, and havoc results from an "inanimate climatic force. A tempest with agency is something we can comprehend, and it allows us to absolve ourselves and our miscalculations of some hand in the destruction."[16]

A city of community and culture, New Orleans believes in miracles, but her belief did not protect her this time. Even when exhausted and out of food, water, and sanitary conditions, New Orleanians fall back on their culture, "the magic of song, prayer, ritual and superstition."[17] Through their festivals, they reenact old stories to connect the human world with the divine; they utter their grief and gratitude. Some of those stranded never knew the magic of cars. Minus the magic of air-conditioning and electricity most of us could not have survived as long as the poor in the New Orleans Convention Center and the Houston Astrodome. The divisions within the city by class, race, and neighborhood are complex, as poor and rich mix across the genes and share superstitious beliefs. As a result of Katrina and her aftermath, the pretense and veneer of civility and a never-ending party is now gone.

> Living under the gloss of tourist attractions, Hollywood films, hot real estate, and girls gone wild, there was found a humanity never seen before on America's increasingly shallow television screens. Beneath the thin gloss were the huddled masses of the city's poor with all their good and bad, their magic and superstition. Some, if not most, of these people had been living on government charity and were ignored by elected officials.[18]

The "Feds" came late to New Orleans and did not understand the community and culture. The historic buildings, which tourists come to see, have remained because the city was too poor to demolish them when other cities were modernizing. When money was found, historic buildings were then in vogue. In short, poverty saved historic New Orleans; will New Orleans save her poor?[19]

Poverty, Class, Race, Sex, and Disaster

Many of the poor have been on welfare or remain on some kind of government subsistence. Contrary to popular belief, many of those who get these checks do not take them for granted or see them as a sense of entitlement; they are just trying to make ends meet. Although many have been moved off welfare into jobs, often these poor have to work longer hours and have less time to supervise their children. Some still need housing support and food stamps to fill in the gap because the poverty-level, menial jobs they have secured do not pay a living wage. There are "layers of disadvantage [that] are too deep to overcome—and keep the American Dream cruelly out of reach."[20]

Worldwide, twenty thousand people die each day because of poverty. Throughout the globe, a billion people's lives are at risk because they are so poor. In many rural countries, where wars, genocide, and AIDS have decimated youthful male and female populations, there are no able-bodied men to build rainwater-collecting receptacles to collect water. Grandparents, guardians of their orphaned grandchildren, try to hold kith and kin together even as their simple plots of land are so depleted that even with ample rain the yield is often insufficient.[21] In many regions in Asia and Africa, the

> perfect storm of human deprivation . . . brings together climatic disaster, impoverishment, the AIDS pandemic and . . . other diseases. [To wit] the world community has so far displayed a fair bit of hand-wringing, and even some high-minded rhetoric, but precious little action. . . . [Today] more than 8 million people around the world die each year because they are too poor to stay alive.[22]

Though the United States has engaged in a budget-breaking war on terrorism, lasting peace necessitates focusing on a critical issue that perennially feeds global instability—the extreme poverty that destabilizes us, globally and domestically. Of the three levels of poverty—relative, moderate, and extreme—most of the impoverished victims of Katrina and Rita are in relative poverty, where the household income falls below a particular percentage of the national average; they are below the so-called "poverty level." Those in relative poverty do not have the capacity to have most things the middle class assumes or takes for granted. Prior to the industrial revolution, the vast majority of the world's populations were poor. The growth of modern economy was astounding for many countries that are wealthy today. Societies who dominate economically often assume a superiority complex in areas ranging from culture and race to institutions and religion. Such attitudes and theories fueled colonialism, which in turn justified gross exploitation. In recent history, poor countries have deteriorated because when they asked for help they were told to go to the International Monetary Fund, which has dumped more debt on their struggling economies. Economist Jeffrey Sachs believes that we can shift the devastation of poverty and engender sustainable development and growth if we embrace a multifaceted approach that considers all factors, from family structure and societal infrastructure to geography.[23] The question remains, if we in the United States have the technology and insight to help remote villages through *"known, proven, reliable and appropriate* technologies and interventions,"[24] why have we not devised similar plans for poverty-stricken areas in the United States?

For example, across the Gulf region, 650,000 people lived in locales that experienced moderate to catastrophic damage. Sociologist John Logan's statistical research shows that there are significant demographic disparities between that population and those who lived in undamaged zones. The population of the damaged areas was:

- nearly half black (45.8 percent, compared to 26.4 percent of the undamaged areas);
- living in rental housing (45.7 percent compared to 30.9 percent);
- disproportionately below the poverty line (20.9 percent compared to 15.3 percent);
- unemployed (7.6 percent compared to 6.0 percent).

In New Orleans's seventy-two neighborhoods and thirteen planning districts there are many variables, and generally blacks and poor residents are more likely to be in harm's way because they live in less desirable, low-lying areas.[25]

How do we name, expose, and ultimately transform systemic, human evil that contributes to disaster when race, class, and poverty result in those deemed "other" being scapegoated, often at the cost of their lives? From an ethical perspective, what difference does black political leadership make to the black poor? Ethicist Traci West posits that if Katrina is any lesson, black political leadership does not make a difference: "I hate to get into this familiar game of blame, but, it seems like this incident is proof that class trumps race."[26] That's the lesson: the class perspective of these leaders completely framed their sense of who mattered and who did not. One of the most heart-wrenching stories is of the men who were left in the jail, and the water was up to their necks! They were left for three days with water up to their necks; screaming, screaming, screaming; with no food, or drinkable water available. As a Christian ethicist, West is concerned with the folk that are the least amongst the least, such as these jailed criminals, regardless of their guilt or innocence. That the city forgot about them and abandoned them completely for three days is horrific. A big concern is that the federal government has to be held accountable. The suffering of the most isolated and socioeconomically deprived population was not a part of the moral concern of the black political leadership either.

One of the major problems was the failure of the federal government to see these citizens as citizens they had to serve with all available resources. And while New Orleans has a history of black mayors, and a city council filled with black folk, the black political leadership did not really see the black poor; they did not see themselves as having any particular responsibility to the black poor in this crisis. Otherwise, they would not have had a plan for persons to get in their cars and drive away as the primary plan of evacuation; nor would they have put people in the Superdome, as a means of guaranteeing a safe environment, without substantive supplies of water, food, medical care, and electricity.[27]

The visuals of the lifeless bodies—the stranded, poor, elderly, and infant black bodies televised during Katrina—begs the question about the systemic yet hidden realities of the matrix of race, racism, class, classism, and poverty in the United States, especially on the southern Gulf. With this picture painted across television monitors for days on end, and with the fact that many people are still homeless and have been termed "refugees" in their own country, have we finally come to a place where poverty has our attention, or will its urgency disappear since this face of destitution is no longer on our television screens 24/7? In response, Monya A. Stubbs and Nelson D. Taylor invite us, especially people of faith, to embrace the Pauline concept of indebtedness, where we, the strong, discern, and then take action to affirm our weak neighbors, naming the gift they are to us and what God has done in and through them. Viewing the situation through indebted love calls us to consider both our response and the historic sociocultural and systematic roots of racial and socioeconomic injustice.[28]

An experience of indebtedness has not been the experience of many who have gone back to the Gulf Coast to live. Returning to New Orleans in October 2005, one man experienced a great euphoria in reuniting with his artist friends and other displaced, exiled New Orleanians; but he also felt an infinite sadness in returning to the French Quarter. He had left town on a pirated Jefferson Parish school bus, the experience reminiscent of a rescue mission set in a Hollywood-South-bayou version of the movie *Hotel Rwanda*. On a second journey back during Halloween weekend, amid catastrophic devastation, a discomforting premonition weighed heavily upon him. This premonition was not so much about the celebration of the day of the dead, for death was still in the air, but death because "landlords" were overtaking the street conversations, as numerous evictions had occurred in the surviving communities of the historic Treme, Marigny, and Bywater neighborhoods.[29]

He had returned because his landlord had given him a notice of eviction only a day after Governor Kathleen Blanco had lifted the moratorium on evictions. Like many residents and artists he was facing the cruelest of predators after the storm—greedy landlords with an insatiable and perverse appetite who were looking to cash in on this tragedy; his landlord had demanded rent before Mayor Nagin had plans in place for the reinhabiting of the 70117 zip code. He had to find a lawyer and a new, affordable apartment in a hostile rental market with limited space and skyrocketing rents. When more random acts of kindness and community solidarity were important, he faced rampant and unfettered greed, a product of racial, sociocultural, and economic cleansing.[30]

On his third and final return to New Orleans he had to move all his artwork over Thanksgiving to an apartment he was fortunate enough to find. With criminal audacity his old landlord charged the gay couple living next to him for the two months when they were unable to occupy their apartment. Sadly, they paid the two months because they did not want their belongings to be thrown out into the street. Such a hostile culture smacks of injustice and landlords should be charged with criminal fraud for collecting rents for months when apartments were uninhabitable with no electricity or heat while simultaneously collecting loss-of-rent claims for the same months from insurance companies and FEMA. The man commented, "As artists, we will not allow our voices to be silenced—especially by property-owning piranhas abusing our rights."[31]

Traci West echoes these concerns. In thinking about transforming human evil, one must also include the issue of sexuality. In New Orleans, there was a large population of lesbian, gay, bisexual, and transgendered persons (LGBT). Some of West's blogs discussed how in the aftermath of Katrina many organizations refused to provide homosexuals relief services. Many of these individuals are black and Latino, and they are also marginal economically. There was a need for separate networks of support so that they would not be treated shamefully. At least poor black folk who were heterosexual did not have to worry about whether they would receive help from some church-based relief organizations. The fairly large transgendered population in New Orleans faced many obstacles. Even if people did not receive nasty responses from Christian organizations and other faith-based organizations, they were afraid to seek out help from them because they did not know how they would be treated. The black church now has the reputation of using gay-hating language and policies so that the church is no longer seen as a refuge.[32]

When envisioning the various populations traumatized by Katrina, I am reminded of René Girard's *scapegoat* theory: when things go wrong, there is a need to blame someone or something. Again, despite September 11 realities, the terror around the world, and even the earlier tsunami, somehow citizens of the United States continue to think that they are safe. In many circumstances, through the fabric of society and our lives, we are *not* safe. Life circumstances and institutions we once took for granted either no longer exist or are quite fragile. There are few guarantees. With the many dysfunctional systems and personal relationships, the breakdown in our socioeconomic realities, and in some instances the diminishing interest in church and faith, we need a tangible, concrete group to blame. The LGBT community fits this bill for some.

For West, we need to find out more about how gay and transgendered people were treated by Christian organizations, as well as discover how LGBT people perceived Christian and faith-based organizations. That the church has lost its credibility as a place where *anyone* can come for help is a profound link with Katrina. Not only have the organized churches lost their credibility; many have lost the center of their faith: to embody Jesus Christ. The obsession with heterosexual superiority has allowed society to deify heterosexuality to such an extent that Jesus is no longer there. By definition, in the church anybody should be welcome—especially anybody who needs help. And now, because of their aggressive homophobia, the church and faith-based organizations are suspect as trusted community resources.[33]

Amid all of the trauma and dislocation, persons who are lesbian, gay, bisexual, or transgendered or who have HIV/AIDS face further stress of prejudice, some of it legal. The hardest hit states constitutionally ban same-sex marriages; the federal government has a Defense of Marriage Act (DOMA).[34] These laws make it tremendously difficult for surviving gay partners to get any kind of relief support from government relief agencies. Katrina displaced about eight thousand people with HIV/AIDS. "Tragedy does not discriminate and neither should relief agencies," said Lambda's executive director. Lambda Legal Defense, working with other LGBT advocacy groups, has helped change policies at relief agencies and state governments after the 9/11 catastrophe in the more liberal Northeast.[35]

Generally, gay people trying to find their domestic partners are not getting support from local or federal aid organizations, and FEMA is citing DOMA as the cause. One minister, in the company of Texas governor Rick Perry, claimed God sent Katrina to "purify our nation." He added, "This may have nothing to do with God being offended by homosexuality. But it possibly does."[36] Another pastor said, "Thank God for Katrina. New Orleans, symbol of America, seen for what it is—a putrid, toxic, stinking cesspool of fag fecal matter."[37]

The issue of recognition of same-sex couples and their families after disasters is a familiar one for LGBT people. After 9/11, the Red Cross recognized the same-sex partners of victims in the attacks only after heated criticism from the LGBT community. This time the community has been proactive, and the National Youth Advocacy Coalition (NYAC) has organized a coalition of about thirty-five national and regional LGBT groups to look out for LGBT survivors. The coalition includes Human Rights Campaign (HRC), National Gay and Lesbian Task Force, Family Pride Coalition, Lambda Legal, and the National Center for Transgender Equality (NCTE), among others.[38]

There have been few reports thus far of discrimination against LGBT people. In one case, a preoperative transsexual was arrested for using the women's bathroom at a shelter at Texas A&M University, after escaping from New Orleans. Texas A&M police arrested her and a cousin of hers, who was also a preoperative transsexual and a minor, after the pair used a women's shelter. The older individual was thrown in jail, and LGBT groups only found out about her case four days later via a local student newspaper. The reporter stumbled across the case while going through arrest reports for information on another case. In an interview with the *Washington Blade*, the transsexual said officials told her that she would be in prison for at least six months to a year because the courts had a backlog. After several gay and lesbian activist groups learned of the case, they lobbied the university to drop the charges. Although the LGBT communities in Louisiana and Mississippi were already under attack from anti-gay forces before the storm, the states also have vibrant LGBT communities.[39]

The storm, like a thief in the day and the night, exposed shattered race relations and socioeconomic disparities, yet many unsung heroes on the Gulf helped others, and thousands of people across the country, of all races and all classes, helped evacuees settle in, in their towns and cities. Congregations of all denominations and faiths have raised funds and sent work teams to the Gulf to help rebuild, clean debris, and repair buildings, lives, and communities.[40]

Traci West reminds us that even the most liberal politicians now talk only about the middle class. No one talks about the need for better public policy to respond to the needs of the poor, only about the needs of the middle class. Problematically, there is dependence on the media for identifying what moral issues matter. There is ineffective black political leadership that is complicit. The black political leadership also dismissed the needs of the black poor. These politicians had a nonworkable plan that was completely dismissive of the poor of their city, who made up a huge segment of their community. How could they ignore them?[41] What have we heard from the media?

West asks, in the aftermath of a tragedy, what is the role of the media and popular press, given "the people have a right to know," when that knowledge is presented subjectively? Specifically, what is the media's role when people with observable differences are portrayed as courageous, self-preserving, and resourceful while the same behavior by those deemed other is seen as criminal, stereotypical, and at fault? Another issue that concerns West is the way in which the media gave this event attention. The Katrina crisis is one of the few times that the conditions and voices of the black poor were seen on prime-time television. This raises the broader issue of how, absent a catastrophe of this magnitude, the poor remain invisible. When was the last time there was a news story on the plight of the poor? The reporters were listening to the particular circumstance of poor people's lives, and it took a cataclysmic event such as Katrina to get the national media to consider the details of poor people's lives. The public is more dependent than ever on whom the media presents. And that is something to note: one has to be seen, and one has to get the media to allow one to be seen, for a moral claim on society to even exist. The public is dependent on the media culture, the national corporate media, to depict what is morally wrong. Some leaders are liars and manipulators who are quoted uncritically by the corporate media. There is a new state of affairs when the media is needed to recognize that poverty exists. We, the public, have reacted with surprise that suffering is part of what occurs as a result of poverty. This is news, in part, because we have not seen it before on television news. In doing ethics, part of our commitment is to help people see what is morally viable and help people build a critique of what our media shows us.[42]

One can imagine the answers to the questions of the role of media amid massive public tragedy and the connection between poverty, suffering, and public concern when thinking of Michael Moore's docudrama *Fahrenheit 911*. The insignificance of the poor to the head of our national leadership is chronicled when, dressed in an after-five, cutaway, white tuxedo, President Bush celebrates his "have and have more philosophy," the philosophy of an elite group he is happy to be a part of. This mindset and the tax cuts to the wealthy have diminished funds for social programs, an intentional agenda of the Reagan and Bush administrations. With increased technology the shifts in the U.S. economy, with outsourcing jobs and services, NAFTA, and so forth, articulate the shift of the poor to the underclass and the strain and tension felt by the current socioeconomic impact on the middle class. Many of the poor and ever-dwindling middle class are only two paychecks away from bankruptcy and homelessness.

What is the economic fallout of Katrina? Not living up to a promise to rebuild the infrastructure of levees cost lives in Katrina. The only way such devastation could have been avoided was to have built the levees higher, but the Bush administration cut the budget. Engineers designed COAST 2050, a mass public-works project. When Louisianans turned to the federal government for help, they got little response when asking for the suggested cost of fourteen billion dollars. When one examines the social and environmental issues for the coast, how can one put a cost on it, given the lives lost and the families broken and dislocated? The cost to society is immense; the cost to the economy, staggering. Truth be told, the quest for more economic prestige triggered the geographic and ecological situation that made the devastation after Katrina logical, a disaster waiting to happen.[43]

When Katrina tore through the southern Gulf Coast, it also tore through the U.S. economy—agriculture, oil—as it crossed the pathways where what we grow and produce meets the world. Oil production is

central to the region's economy. The first oil field was discovered in
Louisiana in 1901. At the lower end of the Mississippi River, where
explorers planted New Orleans, rests all of the sediment, the organic
debris that travels from Minnesota to the Gulf; it cooks and eventually
becomes oil and gas, nature's moonshine. In 1947, companies set up off-
shore oil rigs on floating barges. Today drilling is sophisticated. Engineers
drill in ten thousand feet of water off the Gulf of Mexico. Oil fields off the
Gulf generate one quarter of the U.S. oil supply. There are many rigs,
refineries, and a workforce of sixty thousand people. Shipped to refineries, the oil is changed to gas and then sent over the United States in
pipelines, barges, and trucks. Katrina stopped eight refineries in their tracks
because there was no electricity to power the refineries and pipelines. Gas
prices soared and consumers felt the pinch. Such a catastrophe has an
economic ripple effect throughout the economy. Tampering with the
crude-oil market affects many other products; plastics, soda, some computer components, and medical equipment will go up in price.[44]

When Katrina hit, it paralyzed a main shipping channel, the fourth
largest port moving coffee and seafood. Acquiring the New Orleans port
was the most significant reason, given by Thomas Jefferson, for the
Louisiana Purchase. Half the grain the United States sells to the world
moves through this port. Now barges that carry this grain have no place
to go. The United States has never had to deal with the destruction of a
major city, ever. (Even the Chicago/Peshtigo fires of 1871 did not demolish Chicago, and the San Francisco earthquake and fire of 1906 left San
Francisco whole, yet wounded.) Recovery will take a long time for New
Orleans, the state, and the Gulf Coast. Katrina is the most intensive
natural disaster to hit the United States. Economic impact will probably
hit one hundred twenty-five billion dollars. What can be done to keep it
from happening again?

Engineers needed almost a week to plug the gaps in the levees while
New Orleans became a toxic stew. There were three-hundred-foot
breaches in the 12th Street and London canals. Then engineers could
start the centuries-old pumps. Hundreds of thousands were left homeless,
and cleaning up the entire Gulf Coast will take years. The question
remains, Is the country willing and able to invest the amount of capital
needed to build a large seawall across Lake Ponchatrain; to reconstruct
levees, seawalls, floodgates, and dams like the sea gates in the
Netherlands to hold back the North Sea? The Netherlands system short-
ened the coast by four hundred miles and took twenty years to build.[45]

The Katrina and Rita hurricane devastation erased more than five hundred thousand jobs; killed one thousand people; left two million people without power; and left probably hundreds of thousands without homes, personal goods, and a net of safety.[46] Amid FEMA's fumbling, contractors, prospectors, entrepreneurs, and investors were rushing to the Gulf Coast to get a piece of the reconstruction action of rebuilding. Questions of ethics and protocol cause one to pause. Even before New Orleans had pumped out all the water, cronyism and well-heeled political connections allowed some companies to acquire no-bid contracts worth one hundred million dollars. Halliburton, with continuing ties to its former CEO, Vice President Dick Cheney, secured a five-hundred-million-dollar contract to repair naval bases.[47] At the same time, FEMA was as clumsy as ever. For example, a national pet-supply company got the runaround, with the contract being changed, canceled, reinstated, and put on hold over a four-day period; and at the time of delivery, the truck driver drove 152 miles around the base trying to deliver 970 wire pet crates for housing starving animals in New Orleans. Under another FEMA contract, seventy-five ice trucks carrying forty thousand pounds of ice never arrived at the Gulf, because military officers turned them away. In late September, some fourteen hundred ice trucks all over the United States were still waiting for instructions from FEMA. There was even a "pissing contest" between FEMA and Kenyon Worldwide Disaster Services, when the latter almost pulled out of New Orleans because FEMA could not get its act together to iron out details for disaster mortuary services. The Louisiana State Health Department finally had to step in and take over.[48] New Orleans and the Gulf Coast are a long way from renewal, rebuilding, and restoration. There is much for us to think about, and much work for us to do in the name of justice.

Speaking for Those Who Cannot Speak for Themselves

The Sky Is Crying: Race, Class, and Natural Disaster celebrates the lives of the living and those who did not survive the trauma of Katrina. We honor their legacy and see this volume as an invitation for each of us to work for justice. The reflections, critical essays, and sermons are invitations to ponder our understandings of community, cosmology, God/Spirit, justice, responsibility, discrimination, pain, suffering, and restoration.

The volume begins with "Ruminations on Human Experience: Essays and Reflections." Opening with Valerie Bridgeman Davis, in "Retribution as First Response: Did God Punish New Orleans?" she speaks to various ways in which many theologians, religious leaders, and others wrestle with the why questions. This section follows with Cecilia González-Andrieu's contribution, "*Mañana* Is Too Late to Learn How to Love," which lifts up the concept of voice as a lens for contrasting beauty and ugliness as she gives witness to liberation and justice for the neighbor and the church. Shari Julian, a clinician who has been at ground zero of many natural and human-constructed disasters, relates the story of her connections with New Orleans and the need for us to create training for practitioners to deal with posttraumatic stress disorders and mass victimology in "Came the Hard Rain." "Hello Kitty: Reflections of a Katrina Volunteer" recounts Cheryl Fries's experience of being an activist volunteer at the Austin, Texas, convention center, then being turned away, all while being awakened to the impact of race in the face of a doll. Sister Jamie T. Phelps, who now makes her home in New Orleans and is head of a major university program, deals with the nature of good, evil, morality, relationships, and the future in "Hurricane Katrina and the Flood Waters of New Orleans: A Reflection." J. Alfred Smith Sr., who has many relatives on the Gulf Coast, speaks about ministering to a community and making sense of the theoretical and practical implications of answering the question of theodicy and the import of dealing with poverty in "Pastoral Reflections on Hurricanes Katrina and Rita." Dwight N. Hopkins, in "New Orleans Is America," offers a critique of the intersection of capitalism and poverty as they relate to the war in Iraq and the recovery efforts for New Orleans and the Gulf Coast. Diana L. Hayes ponders the impact of Katrina on black people in the southern Gulf, paying particular attention to the face of women in this tragedy, in "We, Too, Are America: Black Women's Burden of Race and Class." Doll Kennedy explores the triple oppressions of racism, classism, and sexism that moved a natural disaster to a sociocultural, political, and physical nightmare in "Myths and Media: A Socioethical Reflection on Hurricane Katrina." In "Questions of Calamity and Justice in Luke 13:1-5," Eung Chun Park offers an interpretation of two Jesus sayings in Luke as he explores the nature of experiencing and overcoming suffering. "Shouting at an Angry Sky: Thoughts on Natural Disaster as Theological Challenge" is Anthony B. Pinn's analysis of natural disasters from a humanist perspective, which challenges traditional theological anthropology. Toni Dunbar's "Crossing

Many Waters" constructs a myth of self-discovery to frame her compara-
tive analysis of the African holocaust, the *Maafa*, to the sociopolitical disenfranchisement of African Americans in the governmental response to
flood victims. Peniel E. Joseph muses over the impact of globalization in
the United States in concert with the marginalization of the black poor
in "Left Behind: Backdrop to a National Crisis." Marcia L. Dyson's contribution, "My Sister's Keeper: Reflections on Hurricane Katrina and
Black Female Activism," shares her experience of ministering to displaced women of New Orleans, particularly those exiled in Houston,
Texas. Cheryl A. Kirk-Duggan, in "'The Sky Is Fallin', the Dam Has
Broken': Violence, Chaos, and Oppression in Literature," uses literature
to explore the scope of so-called civilized behavior or respectability when
this behavior disintegrates into chaos amid natural disaster.

The second section of this volume, "Registering Indignation and
Intimacy: Poems," opens with a poem by Cheryl Fries, "Everything Is Wet
and Gone." This interlude continues with Valerie Bridgeman Davis's
poem "I Weep on a Slanted Rooftop" and concludes with the poem "Eyes
That Don't See" by Cheryl A. Kirk-Duggan.

The concluding section of this volume, "Righteousness in Context:
Sermons," opens with "'Wade in the Water': A Meditation on Race,
Class, and Katrina," where Alton B. Pollard III utters a brooding liturgy
as he helps us engage in moral and civic examination amid the devastation of a flood. Vashti M. McKenzie's sermon "Strong at the Wounded
Places (Esther 5:9-14)" explores bringing closure to events that challenge
us amid traumatic experiences. "Natural Disasters, Unnatural Neglect: 'It
Be's That Way Sometimes' (1 Kings 19:11-18; 1 Kings 18:36-39)" is
Darryl M. Trimiew's reading of 1 Kings to explore how one makes sense
of deep tragedy, particularly when most of the answers are never satisfactory. Melva L. Sampson wrestles with individual and communal salvation
given the fragile, wounded state of many, framed by the story of the good
Samaritan in "After Katrina and Rita: What Must I Do to Be Saved?
(Luke 10:25-37)." Dorrance Kennedy, a New Orleans native, exegetes
Job 1:7-11 to explore the complexities and dynamics of what we learn
about God, ourselves, and life amid the notion of trouble in "When
Trouble Comes (Job 1:7-11)." Ferenc Raj invites us to think about the
pain of those affected by Katrina and Rita and how their experiences
have been mythologized in the media, framed by systemic racism, in
"Questions, Enlightenment, and Stradivarius." Cheryl Kirk-Duggan
posits that pimping Jesus or prostituting the gospel for political mammon

destroys community and fails to follow the edicts of the ministry of Christ to the poor, the disinherited, the widow, the orphan, and our neighbors in "Pimping Jesus for Political Gain: Casting Stones at Our Neighbors (Luke 10:25-28)."

These reflections, essays, sermons, and poems are a lens through which the reader can think back over experiences of the natural disasters recent and historical, notions of cause and effect, and of theodicy and human responsibility. We essayists have cried out for those in the wilderness, whose voices have been silenced; who were omitted, disregarded, and made into objects. The reader now has an opportunity to be willing to ask hard questions about society, oppression, and the nature of freedom and responsibility, to make the way for justice and peace.

Notes

1. Note that Katrina is not so vicious because of her female name; Andrew was just as vicious in 1992.

2. Jodi Riwono, survivor of an earthquake measuring 6.2 on the Richter scale that struck near the Indonesian city of Yogyakarta killing thousands of people and flattening entire villages. AFP, "Verbatim," *Newsweek*, June 5, 2006.

3. George Will, "Where the Faults Lie," October 11, 2005, http://www.newsobserver.com.

4. Kenneth Surin, *Theology and the Problem of Evil* (New York: Basil Blackwell, 1981), 2-3.

5. Edward Rothstein, "Seeking Justice, of Gods or the Politicians," *New York Times*, September 8, 2005, http://www.nytimes.com.

6. Peter Steinfels, "Scarcely Heard Question: How God Could Have Allowed Catastrophe to Occur," *New York Times*, September 10, 2005.

7. *National Geographic*, Special Edition, 2005, 1-20, 41, 77.

8. Adam B. Kushner, "After the Flood," *The New Republic Online*, September 12, 2005, http://www.tnr.com.

9. Pierce F. Lewis, "Katrina's Lesson: Toward a New New Orleans," *National Geographic*, 29-35, 101.

10. *National Geographic*, 53, 67.

11. George F. Will, "Leviathan in Louisiana," *Newsweek* CXLVI, no. 11 (September 12, 2005): 88.

12. Dan Baum, "Deluged: The New Orleans Police During Hurricane Katrina," *New Yorker* 81, no. 43 (2006): 50-54.

13. Ibid., 54-63.

14. Nancy Gibbs, "New Orleans Lives by the Water and Fights for It," *Time* 166, no. 11 (September 12, 2005): 46.

15. Ibid., 49.

16. Kushner, "After the Flood."

17. Andrei Codrescu, "City of Ghosts: 'Ain't No Drownin' the Spirit,'" *National Geographic*, Special Edition, Fall 2005, 22.

18. Ibid., 23.

19. Ibid.

20. Weston Kosova, "Welfare as They Know It," *Newsweek* CXLV, no. 2 (January 10, 2005): 54.

21. Jeffrey D. Sachs, "The End of Poverty," *Time* 165, no. 11 (March 14, 2005): 4, 42.

22. Ibid., 46.

23. Ibid., 49.

24. Ibid., 50.

25. "Hurricane Katrina: Who Was Hit? Who Will Return? The First In-Depth Demographic Analysis of the Strike Zone," http://www.topica.com/lists/e-drum. See also, www.s4.brown.edu/Katrina/report.pdf.

26. Phone interview with Traci West, Associate Professor of Ethics, Drew University, Madison, NJ, December 6, 2005.

27. Ibid.

28. Monya A. Stubbs with Nelson D. Taylor, "Reflection: On Issues of Class, Race, and Faith," *Windows* (Winter 2006): 9-10, 22.

29. Jose Torres Tama, "The Culture of Evictions in the Wounded Pueblo of Post-Katrina New Orleans," http://www.torrestama.com.

30. Ibid.

31. Ibid.

32. Traci West interview.

33. Ibid.

34. The Defense of Marriage Act, or DOMA, is a federal law of the United States passed by Congress and signed by President Bill Clinton on September 21, 1996. First, it allows each state (or similar political division in the United States) to deny any marriage-like relationship between persons of the same sex that has been recognized in another state. Second, it explicitly recognizes for purposes of federal law that marriage is "a legal union of one man and one woman as husband and wife" and states that spouse "refers only to a person of the opposite sex who is a husband or a wife." *Wikipedia*, http://en.wikipedia.org/wiki/Defense_of_Marriage_Act.

35. "Gay, Aids Discrimination in Katrina's Wake," http://www.gaycitynews.com/gcn_437/gayaidsdiscriminationin.html.

36. Ibid.

37. Ibid.

38. Ibid.

39. Ibid. The 2004 Gay and Lesbian Atlas, published by the economic and social policy research organization the Urban Institute, based on the 2000 Census, shows that Mississippi has the highest concentration of same-sex couples raising children among its total population of same-sex couples, and Louisiana has the fifth highest concentration. Within the states' total populations Mississippi has the highest concentration of African American same-sex couples and Louisiana has the second highest. In addition, New Orleans is home to one of the country's most diverse and active LGBT communities and every year thousands of people pour into the city for the annual Southern Decadence Festival, the city's gay Mardi Gras.

40. Donald R. Frampton, "Reflection: New Orleans's Untold Stories," *Windows* (Winter 2006): 8.

41. Traci West interview.

42. Ibid.

43. *Katrina: American Tragedy*, TV: History Channel, December 26, 2005.

44. Ibid.

45. Ibid.

46. Randall Whittington, "Out of Chaos, Hope," *Windows* (Winter 2006): 3.

47. Keith Naughton and Mark Hosenball, "Cash and 'Cat 5' Chaos," *Newsweek* CXLVI, no. 13 (September 26, 2005): 34-36.

48. Ibid.

RUMINATIONS ON HUMAN EXPERIENCE: ESSAYS AND REFLECTIONS

Retribution as First Response: Did God Punish New Orleans?

Valerie Bridgeman Davis

There are hurricanes in the world as well as lilies.
—Abraham J. Heschel[1]

On August 29, 2005, Hurricane Katrina, as a Category 4–strength storm, took a brutal sideswipe at the coastal region of Louisiana, Mississippi, and Alabama. Except for a last-minute turn, the storm would have hit the city of New Orleans dead-on. For a brief few hours, a sigh of relief filled the news that, although the coast would be devastated, the city had not completely come to ruin. But then unrelenting rains came. And those who could not or would not evacuate the city found themselves in the midst of cataclysmic—some might say apocalyptic—death throes. The storm surge and ensuing floodwaters that breached the levee and caused other damage "made Katrina the most destructive and costliest natural disaster in the history of the United States."[2] Eighty percent of the city of New Orleans lay underwater. More than one million people were displaced by the storm. The effects of the storm, including tornadoes that spawned from it, were reported in as many as seven states.

In this essay, I examine the ways in which theologians, religious leaders, and others spoke about the *why* of the hurricanes in the weeks immediately following them. I categorize these conversations into the historic theological language regarding theodicy and retribution. Examining the rise of a pietistic faith that is less justice oriented among some African American Christians, I raise questions about the implications of such faith as it relates to theological understandings about God's behavior in the presence of natural disasters. Finally, I seek to offer a biocritical, womanist response that stands in resistance to any systems of thought or belief that blame victims, or that hold the deity culpable without rigorous pursuit of justice.

Setting the Stage: The Emerging Sermon in Context

The Sunday after the floods settled water and woe into New Orleans and all our lives, I was scheduled to preach at my home congregation in Memphis, Tennessee. Because I do not preach regularly, I had been working on a sermon a couple of weeks; but Hurricane Katrina and the ensuing floods, and bumbling governmental and rescue agencies' responses, meant the sermon had to change. What would I preach? What would anyone else preach? I teach preaching and worship, and in both my Preaching from the Prophets and my Introduction to Theology of Preaching and Worship courses, I scrapped my lesson plans and talked with students about the coming Sunday morning. I wanted to know how worship and sermons were going to be shaped in the face of the twenty-four-hour, nonstop pictures of misery and pain or ineptitude and insensitivity that were unfolding before our eyes on CNN, Fox News Channel, and other news outlets. Like most of the people I know, I was glued to the television and to Internet sites. I stayed in contact with family and friends who were directly affected by the storm and its aftermath. Feelings of helplessness gave way to feelings of frustration, fear, and outright anger. Hearing United States citizens referred to as "refugees" incensed me long before someone said that I should be angry.[3] I was shell-shocked and traumatized; and I was miles away from the epicenter of the traumatic drama. I can only imagine, and not very well, what people in the midst of the sorrow and suffering experienced.

I eventually wrote a sermon based on Psalm 11 titled "What Can the Righteous Do?" I decided the sermon needed to help people lament and address the displacement and disillusionment that the storm blew into our hearts and lives. I believed deeply that people needed permission to question and to curse, if need be; to help us ritually, and really allow us to cry and address the feelings of despondency and despair. I gave voice to what we were actually seeing: black, poor, older faces staring back at us from video clips. I lifted up stories I had heard or read of black men, especially those who were protecting and providing for their friends and families in the face of the worst of worst situations, in antithesis to visuals of looting or "thugging" young black men. I pointed out that storms were washing to the surface this country's blighted record of dealing unjustly with poor people, with elderly people, with people of color. Along with my godson, I sang "Come Ye Disconsolate" after the sermon. We prayed with people from the coastlines who were present, or with family members of people in the area. After the sermon, several of these "evacuees" came up to me and thanked me for both validating their feelings and for giving them hope. Such responses are what preachers hope for after they preach.

Calling for the Question: Why?

The devastation begged a question: why? Why were the seas, the weather, and Mother Nature turning on the Gulf Coast? Why was God angry enough to decimate the area and to start the massive migration of humanity, the likes of which have not been seen in the United States since the Great Depression? Efforts to make sense of the devastation and the human misery, and the poverty and lack uncovered by the storm, began almost as soon as the storm hit. Official websites, bloggers, denominational mission leaders, and others sought ways to help people cope. The loss was not just that of those on the coastline, but of those who had friends, colleagues, and family members in the region. For many African Americans whose roots are in the South, it was an assault on history and memory. Black faces peopled newscasts and suddenly the story was not just about the devastation of the storm, but about the slow response of federal, state, and local governments and the seeming indifference to poor people who could not evacuate the city for various reasons. There were reports of disparities in treatment between white New Orleans citizens and people of color; reports of surrounding cities refusing New Orleans residents entry into their towns; the displacement and separation of family members from one another; and the horrific pictures from the Superdome and the city convention center. How could we know the difference between reality and urban legend? Conversations about race and class took center stage as the television images showed face after face of poor, elderly, black people in New Orleans. A city built on jazz, food, and tourism, had—for the most part—been adept at hiding its poverty and its racial divide. But by mid-September, Katrina and its aftermath had swept away all the hiding places.

In that milieu, questions about God's wrath, of theodicy, and of human sinfulness as causative agents for these natural disasters (the hurricane and the flooding) emerged. Was God repaying evil for human evil? Was the deity giving an eye for an eye? If Walter Brueggemann is right that retribution is "the assumption or conviction that the world is ordered by God so that everyone receives a fair outcome of reward or punishment commensurate with his or her conduct,"[4] the people who believe such must concur that everyone who suffered because of Hurricane Katrina deserved what he or she got. This belief holds that there is always reasonable order in creation, or what Brueggemann calls "moral coherence." This system is evident in prophetic rhetoric, and in the Torah and historical books of the Hebrew Bible, and to some extent, in the Christian Scriptures. This system of reward and punishment assumes that the "evil" are completely and always "evil," and that the "good" are completely and always "good." Giving assent to retribution means that we must believe that suffering is connected to human behavior, for example, no one is sick except that person who has had a part in his or her illness. The other system that pulses through the biblical record is corollary and recognizable in the book of Proverbs, in which deeds always are followed with predictable consequences (if, then).

The problem, of course, with these systems of belief is that our lived experience testifies against closed systems of reward and punishment. Human experiences and human history testify that "in fact, the disobedient often prosper and the obedient often suffer. Any claim for retribution inescapably leads to a crisis of theodicy, whereby lived experience contradicts neat explanatory systems."[5] Life is complicated. Natural phenomena come and innocents are slaughtered. Poor, elderly people are trapped in nursing homes as the water rises and the staff abandons them to the elements.

At issue is the very nature of the deity: is God always good, completely powerful, or does God participate in and use evil for God's own purposes? These questions are as old as the record of Jeremiah's words: "Why does the way of the guilty prosper? Why do all who are treacherous thrive?" (Jeremiah 12:1). Yet every attempt to twist the biblical record into a sustained, consistent answer fails. Job's attempt to get God to answer the why question resulted in God's recital of God's handiwork (Job 38–41) and an ultimate admission to Job's friends that Job was right about God (Job 42:7). The biblical account answers the question on God in the midst of evil and suffering in a relationally dynamic and dangerous way. The record "never permits that lively relationship to be reduced to such cold rationalities as Western theology has preferred."[6]

Such conversations about God among scholars and theologians work to absolve the deity implicitly and sometimes explicitly. God as terrorist is a terrifying thought. But the biblical record is not interested in explaining the power of natural phenomenon apart from God,[7] and we are called to make a decision about whether the worldview of the texts matches what we now know about God and about the created order, or whether we must be locked into a belief system that assaults our sensibilities; in other words, may we say no to the texts?

Hebrew Bible scholar Abraham Heschel would answer that we may not disagree with the texts; we may only acknowledge the mystery of God and the very human tendency to assign human behavior to the Divine.[8] Quoting the ancient philosopher Philo, Heschel notes that we know God is not human, even as we use anthropomorphic language that is a "monstrosity."[9] Heschel argues that God's anger is not God's primary or overriding emotional attribute. According to Heschel, God's anger is retributive when it responds to human injustice and may be displayed in earthquakes, fires, and whirlwinds. Despite the several articles on websites insisting that God is not in the wind, fire, or earthquake, but in the still small voice, Elijah's experience in the text actually is the minority report (see 1 Kings 19:11-12). As Heschel notes, though God's anger is not a ruling passion, God's anger cannot be compared to human response to the same injustices.

> [Humanity's] sense of injustice is a poor analogy to God's sense of injustice. The exploitation of the poor is to us a misdemeanor; to God, it is a disaster. Our reaction is disapproval; God's reaction is something no language can convey.[10]

Heschel quotes Jeremiah's experience of the divine in 23:19-20 to further make clear his point.

> Behold the storm of the Lord!
> Wrath has gone forth,
> A whirling tempest;
> It will burst upon the head of the wicked.
> The anger of the Lord will not turn back
> Until He has executed and accomplished
> The intents of His mind.
> In the end of days you will understand it clearly.

Such comparisons of God's anger with natural phenomena to get across a supernatural message have led scholars to describe God as arbitrary and abusive. Heschel and Brueggemann would disagree. The biblical record is clear that God speaks in the storms for very specific sins of the people. Heschel, then, believes that "the anger of the Lord is a tragic necessity, a calamity for man and grief for God" in which innocent people suffer as much as the wicked once God's anger and/or wrath is unleashed.[11] But Jeremiah says much more about God, including that anger is an outburst; yet the deity practices kindness, "justice, and righteousness in the earth, for in these things I delight, says the LORD" (Jeremiah 9:23).

These competing statements about God in the book of Jeremiah are repeated throughout the biblical record. New Orleans and the coastal region of the United States became the laboratory in which every theory was tested. As Clarice J. Martin, New Testament womanist scholar, has noted, "The nature of the 'kind' of God and the 'character' of God one believes in comes to the forefront of theological and moral reflection, discourse, and debate when individuals broach the subject of theodicy, or suffering and evil in the human condition."[12] Martin notes that theodicy questions must be addressed in the context of specific evil and suffering and may not be unmoored from history. The prevailing question becomes: what is operative in this situation, "divine causation" (Is it God's hand and will?) or "human freedom" (Is it because of human action and/or sin?)?

The devastation of New Orleans made the question especially poignant as race and class overlapped and interplayed so that they were almost inseparable. Perhaps womanist sociologist and scholar Cheryl Gilkes Townsend said it best in an unpublished essay she wrote the week immediately after the storm: if people refused to see race in the context, they were not actually seeing the travesty.[13]

Varied Answers to the Why Question

The responses on the websites were all along the spectrum. There were several self-identified conservative evangelical people, such as Alabama Republican Senator Hank Erwin, who said:

> Warnings year after year by godly evangelists and preachers went unheeded. So why were we surprised when finally the hand of judgment fell? Sadly, innocents suffered along with the guilty. Sin always brings suffering to good people as well as the bad. We all need to embrace godliness and churchgoing and good, godly living, and we can get divine protection for that point.[14]

Senator Erwin concluded that the storms were God's appeal to us (the citizens of the United States) to get right. In response, William Willimon, bishop of the North Alabama Conference of The United Methodist Church, told the *News*, "I have no idea what sort of senator or politician Mr. Erwin is, but he's sure no theologian."

"I'm certainly against gambling and its hold on state government in Mississippi," Bishop Willimon said, "but I expect there is as much sin, of possibly a different order, in Montevallo as on the Gulf Coast. If God punished all of us for our sin, who could stand?"[15]

In contrast to Erwin's response, David Haggith, author of *End-Time Prophecies of the Bible* posted the following to one website:

> Would a God who is professed to be both just and loving, merciful and vengeful, have to resort to widespread, random killing? . . . This storm has most likely ended the lives of hundreds of *Christians* who lived in New Orleans who had no prophetic warning that they should flee New Orleans. . . . Does God have to kill all of these innocent people along with the not-so-innocent just to get a message through to a president who already craves the Lord's guidance? What kind of a God is that, which some people are so willing to put forward, who is unable to communicate to *one* who *wants* to listen, so he has to kill many? Whatever happened to God's ability to raise prophets *before* the big event to warn world leaders directly? . . . The image of God as one who speaks *through* the storm, not ahead of it, is one fomented by some Fundamentalist Christians today. Do they care that this view presents God as the ultimate terrorist—a fact to which they seem to be oblivious? . . . Both Christian Fundamentalist and Islamic Fundamentalists see the U.S. in this same light. But their vague pronouncements of impending judgment are like saying, "It's going to rain" without a time-table. When it eventually rains, they say, "See, we warned you."[16]

The rise within black communities of evangelical theologies and expressions of church that are disconnected from social action and social justice has also given rise to personal pietism that does not engage the culture, except as the culture offends moralistic beliefs (sin that is personal, not communal). This move away from a historic expression of black spirituality "sanctifies the state, worships the market, and genuflects before conservative government."[17] In addition, these expressions of church virtually foment an attitude that despises or pities poor people, but does not call the church to stand in solidarity with them over against policies and personalities that batter personhood and worth. With this wave of evangelical religiosity, poverty became a sin punishable by death; Christianity finds its best expression in social Darwinism.

I do not intend to say or imply that these were the best or only expressions of theology at work. But the pervasive pulse of "God's will" and "they deserved it for their sin" has been sickening. Like Michael Eric Dyson, I believe that "the black church must reclaim its legacy as a center of prophetic expression of outrage at the forces that make the lives of the poor and vulnerable hell. Otherwise, we forfeit our right to be called sons and daughters of a God whose first love is always those who are last."[18]

Postscript: The Realm of Mystery

So, did God punish New Orleans? In the end, there is no theologically satisfying answer. Theodicy is mystery, and retribution is an ethical decision. We must, in the presence of history, tradition, scripture, and experience determine what we most deeply believe about God and about the way the world works, and be prepared to live faithfully with our decisions. In the sermon I preached on September 4, 2005, I ultimately said, "No, this catastrophe is not God's punishment." Katrina was a hurricane, born and bred in the Caribbean waters, like hurricanes have been for thousands of years before, following the Gulf Stream of the storms before it. There may be corporate sins such as global warming, indiscriminate oil drilling, and destruction of coastal marshlands that contribute to the strength of the storms.

If the storms are the deity's punishment, we will have to explain why the people dying and caught in the maelstrom of pain are mostly all poor, mostly of color, and mostly very young and very old. Do we really believe that the God who claims to defend widows and orphans, and who stands with the poor, would "punish" New Orleans by causing their deaths? I want my faith and my theology to "make sense" on some level, even as I accept a certain level of mystery and inscrutability. Like most people, I approached the crisis with what I most deeply believe about God and what my own experiences about loss, grief, and suffering have taught me through the years. I did not allow the texts or historical theology to ultimately determine what I believe about this storm or any other.

My eyes were *not* watching God in the hurricane, and in that regard I had to read against the text, and to a larger extent, against the tradition.

I took a reformed Jewish stance with the text, a hermeneutic of struggle. Let's wrestle with God; let's lament; let's argue with God on the side of human dignity and human life. Let's rail against natural destruction and devastation; let's rail against death; let's cry out against unjust social structures that defy human life and dignity. Syndicated talk-show host Rabbi Shmuley Boteach expressed this stance, although he noted that for many of the faithful, "The closer they come to G-d, the more they become enemies of [humans]."[19] I found that I always want to be on the side of life and human thriving, with great hope and faith that in the end God, too, is on that side of the equation.

Notes

1. Abraham J. Heschel, *The Prophets* (New York: HarperCollins, 2001), 358.

2. "Hurricane Katrina," *Wikipedia*, http://en.wikipedia.org/wiki/Hurricane_Katrina. Hurricane Katrina was actually the third most powerful storm of the 2005 season behind two storms that followed it, Hurricanes Wilma and Rita. It was the eleventh named tropical storm of the season and the sixth most powerful storm recorded in the Atlantic basin.

3. The Immigration and Nationality Act of the United Nations defines *refugee* in Sec. 101(a)(42) as: "Any person who is outside any country of such person's nationality or, in the case of a person having no nationality, is outside any country in which such person last habitually resided, and who is unable or unwilling to return to, and is unable or unwilling to avail himself or herself of the protection of, that country because of persecution or a well-founded fear of persecution on account of race, religion, nationality, membership in a particular social group, or political opinion." Very few of the poor and dispossessed people in the United States coastal regions after Hurricane Katrina (and Rita) fit this definition. See "Hurricane Katrina: Local Effects and Aftermath," *Wikipedia*, http://en.wikipedia.org/wiki/Hurricane_Katrina#Local_effects_and_aftermath.

4. Walter Brueggemann, "Retribution," in *Reverberations of Faith: A Theological Handbook of Old Testament Themes* (Louisville: Westminster John Knox Press, 2002), 174. See also David R. Blumenthal, *Facing the Abusing God: A Theology of Protest* (Louisville: Westminster John Knox Press, 1993), and James L. Crenshaw, ed., *Theodicy in the Old Testament* (Philadelphia: Fortress Press, 1983).

5. Brueggemann, "Retribution," 176.

6. Brueggemann, "Theodicy," in *Reverberations of Faith: A Theological Handbook of Old Testament Themes* (Louisville: Westminster John Knox Press, 2002), 213.

7. See, for example, Psalm 97:5 for volcanic activity; Job 37:5 for God's voice as thunder; Micah 1:2-4; the plagues of Exodus 8; and so forth.

8. Heschel, *The Prophets*, 358.

9. Quoting Philo, *De Sacrificiis Abelis et Caini*, XXI, 96, in Heschel, 359, note.

10. Heschel, 365.

11. Ibid., 377.

12. Clarice J. Martin, "Biblical Theodicy and the Black Woman's Spiritual Autobiography: 'The Miry Bog, the Desolate Pit, a New Song in My Mouth'" in *A Troubling in My Soul: Womanist Perspectives on Evil and Suffering,* ed. Emilie M. Townes, (Maryknoll, NY: Orbis Books, 1993), 14.

13. Cheryl Gilkes Townsend in an essay sent to the womanist Listserv.

14. "Senator: God Judging U.S. with Disastrous Hurricanes; Alabama Republican Cites Culture of 'Gambling, Sin and Wickedness'" on http://www.worldnetdaily.com/ news/article.asp?ARTICLE_ID=46568, posted September 29, 2005.

15. Ibid.

16. "Why Did the Hurricane Katrina Happen? Some Reasons Given by Religious Conservatives," http://www.religioustolerance.org/tsunami04m.htm. Website maintained by Ontario Consultants on Religious Tolerance, post September 4, 2005. See, for very different responses, Tony Campolo, "Katrina: Not God's Wrath—or His Will," on http://www.beliefnet.com/story/174/story_17423.html; also see this website for a catalog of religious leader's responses to an Internet article titled "Deep Waters: A Spiritual Response to Hurricane Katrina," http://www.beliefnet.com/story/174/story_17418.html. The posts represent evangelical, Catholic, and Orthodox Christian responses, a Christian academic response, Jewish responses, and Islamic, Buddhist, and Hindu responses.

For a secular response, see Ross Gelbspan, "Katrina's Real Name," *Boston Globe,* August 30, 2005, http://www.boston.com/news/globe/editorial_opinion/oped/articles/ 2005/08/30/katrinas_real_name/.

17. Michael Eric Dyson, "God's Gonna Trouble the Water," http://www.beliefnet.com/ story/174/story_17474.html.

18. Ibid.

19. Shmuley Boteach, "The Defiant Man of Faith," http://www.beliefnet.com/story/ 174/story_17407.html.

MAÑANA IS TOO LATE TO LEARN HOW TO LOVE

CECILIA GONZÁLEZ-ANDRIEU

Night is the time of the moon and of luxuriant love, but it is also the hour when our aloneness addresses us with its own terrible voice demanding answers. Here I want to articulate, in a three-part reflection, the beginning of some answers to those questions in the dark that pierce our heart asking, *Why so much suffering* in the wake of Katrina and Rita? First, I examine the incredibly practical challenges that daily dehumanize our *semejantes*. Second, I reflect on the idea of past, present, and future and how this can either work to help us be actively prophetic or lull us into complacency. Finally, I conclude by introducing an efficient guide in the work of building a community of love through the liberation paradigm of Gustavo Gutiérrez.

Semejantes

I could write this in any of many voices. I could address you in the voice of a "refugee" child who lived with that word and the homelessness it meant until the day it became clear that I would never go back "home," because home had shifted. I could write as a mother who watches with eyes that sting like the images of the eyes of weeping parents, and who knows there are few things in life more frightening than the possibility of harm to my child. I could write as a veteran of hurricanes, earthquakes, urban riots, with tanks patrolling streets and helicopters in the air, adept at carrying my children everywhere for days with a backpack of supplies strapped to my back. I could write as a filmmaker who imagines the creation of scenes before they happen and can see my own street, my own home, and my church all reduced to rubble. I could write in any of these voices, because they are all mine, and in a way they are all yours. There are many "mes" who can tell these stories, and all of them become impatient with the search for that elusive rest that Augustine so beautifully described as only possible in God.[1]

I am not one simple me you will know and understand, and you are not one simple you I can even begin to define. We are not the sum total of all the voices of our experiences; rather we are their dialogue—sometimes coherent and at other times baffling conversations. We cannot be reduced to our own realities or personal selves; we are always in relationship with others, with ourselves, and with the universe, and this is what makes the process of loving and knowing most vexing. The failure to know and to love has become our corporate sin. What we do as a nation, and sometimes as a world; what we have institutionalized and made respectable; and the "isms" —racism, sexism, classism—are all based on this failure, this lack of engagement.

Semejante is the Spanish word that is normally used to translate "neighbor," yet it is much richer; it means someone who is just like me, who resembles me, who is an "other" me. *Semejante* is not used only for those who share my skin color, gender, nationality, or religion; it is used for every human being. *Semejante* is the most radically unifying concept we can employ, expressing that all humans are truly images of one another. Why, then, do we insist on separating and on breaking ourselves apart from one another?

First, the "isms" are based on not knowing ourselves; if we did, we would know ourselves irreducible to one category, one voice, one experience, one identity marker. The only way we can impute stereotypes on others is by believing in the one-dimensionality of the human being. If we knew and grasped the complex nature of ourselves, we would also know others as multilayered, intricate "worlds" of being and existence. We have underestimated our own persons, taken for granted that we are "this way" or "that," ensconced comfortably in a lack of growth and an absence of questions. Thus, the stereotypical reduction of others points directly back at us; it is our own humanity we do not understand.

Second, the "isms" are based on our fear and our misguided attempts at security. A blank piece of paper is controllable and discardable, but as soon as there is writing, pictures, figures, and complexity it interacts with us; it entreats us; it asks something of us. The "isms" try to remove the writing from the stories of human beings, making them blank and inter-changeable. In our terror of what is not clear or simple, we search for safety in erasing all ambiguity from others.

Finally, the "isms" thrive in an atmosphere of haste and instant results. Relationships take time to develop, and they require that we be willing to take a long-road approach to life instead of wanting everything to happen yesterday. If I minimize you into something resembling a three-word e-mail, I can move everything along much faster, can't I? Even writing this feels different. Here, there are no elaborated images of mothers or even crum-bling buildings; no hints of being or of doing. An e-mail of just a few words typed out on a screen is just utilitarian. Communication? Relationship? Neighbor? I have skipped all the steps of knowing you and I have gone straight to the results—to your utility and usefulness to me, as reader. If, in this short space, I determine you can add nothing to my needs, I can get nothing from you—and that (gulp!) you may actually need something from me is unthinkable—so in that instant, I label you "expendable." I label you in shorthand. You cease being for me, so I can get on with the important business of my own stuff. And in that moment, I forget all about you.

Now, my artistic voice, my poetic voice, the voice in me that notices the color of late-afternoon sunshine and the smell of rain, this voice wants to tell you that none of this is beautiful. To reduce you, to simplify you, to label you, to see how you are useful and if you are not, to discard you is "ugly."[2] The ugliness of it tells me it cannot come from God, it can-not reflect God's light, which is God's will. When I do what is ugly, I sin against the beauty of God and all God made. To exclude others from God's plentiful banquet is about as ugly as it gets.

Past/Present/Future

In the Christian tradition we engage a cognitive practice so much that we do it almost automatically—we routinely discern in the past the seeds of the future. We are accustomed to reading Isaiah's beautiful description of the suffering servant and see contained in those verses the figure of Christ (Isa. 53). This is the Christian relationship with scripture: seeing salvation history not as a series of unrelated events appearing randomly and lacking relationship, but rather as a telescope, where the next section that extends further into history is always contained in the past.

The Christian tradition is radically about the future, but it is not a future that lies exclusively distant somewhere and, like the proverbial bridge, we will "cross it when we get to it." The Christian witness is *a witness*; that means we have experienced, seen, understood, lived through, and been moved by a something—a glimpse—of what our future *must* be, *will* be, and in many ways now *is*. Our prayers express an understanding that as we witness to the possibility of a future filled with God and justice, we must actively be pulling it toward us, opening it up and recognizing it, in the midst of our present. "Your kingdom come" is about deep desire, which attracts and brings. Deep desire is beautiful.

If we understand in hindsight, with Isaiah and the prophets, that the future is contained within the past, that God's surprises build one upon the other through those willing to help make them manifest, then we must make the jump—and this is more difficult—to seeing the future as contained within our very present. Everything we are about today is already unfolding, and in many cases contains the seeds of events that will bear fruit much later. If the seeds we are sowing are ones of discontent and exclusion, the "isms" that break the human family, then discontent and exclusion will be the bitter fruit that awaits us in the future. *Mañana* will be too late to learn how to love; it will be too late to wring our hands and deplore the state of things. *Mañana* at that point will be today, and the consequences of all the pasts that contained that today will become manifest.

The promise of *mañana* is that if we take it seriously, as contained inside today, we can make it truly beautiful. Our pleading to our gracious God of "your kingdom come" will be not passive, but infused with our witness of its possibility because we know it, and because we are actively working toward its constant unfolding. When we reach out toward the future, in God's infinite generosity and our freedom, that beautiful future liberated from "isms" and selfishness can then embrace us gratefully back. How do we do this work of liberation?

A Guide: Gustavo Gutiérrez

Speaking recently at a meeting of U.S. Latino theologians about the assassination of Archbishop Oscar Romero (March 24, 1980), Gustavo Gutiérrez commented, "Romero's life could have been named after the famous novel *Crónica de una Muerte Anunciada* (*Chronicle of an Announced Death*). The work of speaking liberation is not always welcomed, but it must be done."[3] For Gutiérrez, the work of liberation has a number of features that I think can serve as guides as we pull toward a justice-filled future. I will begin with the liberation of scripture, continue with the liberation of the theologian and the liberation of the church, and conclude with Gutiérrez's central concept of the "liberation of the poor," which is embedded inside all of the other liberations to which he alludes.

The Liberation of Scripture

For Gutiérrez, the only subject of theology is God—nothing else. Theology is neither an ethical nor a sociological project; theology must be completely grounded in God and must be done for the benefit of the church. This groundedness in God makes scripture supremely important to Gutiérrez, as indeed his work shows, especially his magisterial study of the book of Job.[4] In his books, Gutiérrez encourages us to enter scripture with new eyes to see. He hopes we will discover that the Scriptures, and especially the Gospels, have a particular point of view, and discovering this point of view realize that as Christians our only authentic choice is to also make this point of view our own.

To illustrate this point-of-view dynamic Gutiérrez uses the parable of the widow's offering (Luke 21:1-4). Most Christians know this parable and generally understand that it says true charity is to give from our want and not from our surplus; the widow's generosity should shame us all. But Gutiérrez has a different purpose in bringing up this parable: he points sagely at the verses just before, which explain that Jesus had sat down by the door of the treasury in the Temple. There were many doors, Gutiérrez insists, and Jesus could have sat at any of them, but the very fact that he took a seat at the door of the treasury gave him a point of view he would not have had otherwise. For Jesus, that point of view brought into focus the issues of poverty among his people and led him to speak from that place. In his field of vision, he could see the economic struggles of his contemporaries, especially the most insignificant, to survive. Scripture has a point of view, Gutiérrez says, and that point of view has to do with the poor. I will expand on this later, but for now let us stay with the question of point of view, which leads us to the next form of liberation Gutiérrez addresses.

The Liberation of the Theologian

Having established that the biblical "witness" witnesses from a very particular space and a particular point of view, Gutiérrez encourages the theologian to do the same. He frankly puzzles over how some forms of theology are termed *teología* (theology), whereas others are termed *teología en contexto o contextual* (theology in context or contextual theology). What is the difference? According to Gutiérrez, the alleged difference is twofold.

First, in naming Western European and especially German theology just *theology*, the implication is that this theology is contextless, arising out of a human universality. This is just simply not the case, he insists. Just as Gutiérrez's own theology is born out of his confrontation with the concrete poverty of his parish in Lima, Peru, so Karl Barth's theology arose out of his experiences of war and the rise of Nazi ideology.[5] Both are contextual; both have a decided point of view. However, contemporary contextual theologies are honest and open about their social location and ideological commitments in a way that theologies from dominant groups and from the earlier part of the twentieth century are not. To liberate all theology from a misguided disguise of objectivity is one goal of liberation.

Second, the assignment of a contextual label to some theologies and not to others telegraphs an implicit message. Contextual theologies are only relevant to their contexts and not beyond these, thus *mujerista*[6] theologians would ostensibly have nothing to say to the rest of the church, as neither would African or Asian theologians. This is a scandalous impoverishment, Gutiérrez insists, of the theological conversation and of communities that can learn from one another. Until all theologies are understood as contextual and as relevant to communities beyond their borders, theology will continue a colonial pattern. The work of the theologian of liberation includes the need to call attention to this kind of linguistic and theological colonialism. This leads Gutiérrez to the community of reception of all theological work: the church.

The Liberation of the Church

Gutiérrez notes with some regret that the Christian church is among the last of the institutions in contemporary society that continues to refuse to see the relationship of cause and effect in relation to poverty. Critiquing his own Roman Catholic tradition, and in spite of what he terms "John Paul II's uniquely prophetic statements about poverty which already outnumber everything ever said by all his predecessors combined,"[7] the church structures from Rome all the way to the local parish have yet to take the connection seriously. The liberation of the church, Gutiérrez notes, is the prophetic word spoken to say that it is impossible today to be a faithful Christian and remain aloof to the causes of poverty and oppression in our world. In his characteristic style, Gutiérrez uses a story to illustrate this notion of liberation: the story of San Pedro Claver. Claver, Gutiérrez reminds us, is a canonized saint, and for Gutiérrez a saint embodies two key characteristics: (1) a marked poverty of spirit, by which he means an unquenchable thirst for God; and (2) standing as a model of Christian witness.[8] San Pedro Claver gets high marks on the first, having devoted his life to caring for sick slaves and dying from a contagion from one of his cares. Yet, Gutiérrez insists, he gets very low marks on the second, that of being a "model." Gutiérrez does not want to be anachronistic, and he readily admits that the time period did not allow for Claver to have a modern consciousness about the evils of slavery; however, he is very clear that pleading ignorance cannot be tolerated today. Liberation means not only working to alleviate the suffering of those who have been labeled insignificant; it also means that the very structures that cause this suffering have to be denounced and dismantled. Today, Gutiérrez says, Pedro Claver would have to protest loudly against slavery and do everything within his power to end its horror.[9] The Christian church, and each and every individual Christian, can do no less. This assessment takes me to the final liberation—the touchstone of Gutiérrez's theological work—the liberation of the poor.

The Preferential Option for the Poor

Gutiérrez's work has two salient features: the first is its coherence, since it begins and ends in God, and the Christian is bound to live according to God; the second is its concreteness. A Christian today, Gutiérrez says, has to bring into tension two realities: on the one hand the "world" and on the other hand the Christian witness as passed down to us in scripture and tradition. By correlating these realities, the phrase "the preferential option for the poor" traveled from Medellín and Puebla to the far reaches of the almost forgotten lands of Latin America.[10] There is no escaping the evidence of the scandalous poverty of much of the world, and, Gutiérrez insists, there is also no escaping the evidence that God, as witnessed to in scripture and in the life of the Christian communities throughout the centuries, has made and continues to make a preferential option for the poor. Just what does this mean concretely?

Gutiérrez believes the key to this phrase is the word *preferential*. To prefer is to put first, to have as the most important focus, to lift up. What *prefer* does not mean is exclusion; it does not mean an "exclusive" option for the poor. A preferential option for the poor is complicated business, Gutiérrez admits, with layers upon layers of liberation to be effected for its fulfillment.[11]

First, who are the poor to be liberated? Gutiérrez is very clear about three things:

1. The poverty we need to eradicate is not about "poverty of spirit," as some have historically implied. Poverty of spirit means sanctity, a need and hunger for God. This is the humility of acknowledging not having enough spiritual gifts, and of always feeling like there is a void within us that can only be filled by God.

2. Poverty is about "being insignificant." Thus, although material poverty certainly plunges human beings into insignificance, there are many other factors that can do the same: race, gender, sexual orientation, religion, and so forth. Insignificance is the most salient quality of the poverty to which Gutiérrez refers.

3. The poor themselves must embrace the preferential option for the poor. The poor, especially those who carry within them the wounds of colonialism, have internalized an attitude that both accepts poverty passively as their lot in life and has little compassion for those in a similar state. The process of *concientización* is one facet of liberation theology that addresses this problem head-on. The poor must become aware that God does not will their insignificance; rather, it is the opposite. The Christian God is one who wills their full and integral humanity: the process of becoming subjects.

Liberation theology has sometimes been accused of collapsing the coming kingdom of God into the present order, denuding the eschatological from the Christian witness and thus becoming nothing but a sociopolitical project. I believe Gutiérrez does not fall into this trap and that he remains wholly within the Christian eschatological tradition. Gutiérrez makes a distinction that I believe to be most helpful; he reiterates the orthodox position of the reign of God now and not yet, but he adds something else. Why do we think that eternity refers to what we call *future*? Why cannot eternity encompass all—our past, our present, and our future? As we have seen, this position makes it imperative that the reign of God announced by Jesus Christ break in constantly ever more fully, even now, "during the time of creatures."[12]

In one of the most striking phrases I have heard him utter, Gutiérrez encapsulated what I believe to be the key to the building of a loving community here and now. "We don't love the poor because they are good, this would give us all kinds of license to exclude, to qualify, to avoid. No, *we love the poor because God is good.*"[13] God is good in our yesterdays, our todays, and our tomorrows. We must question and dismantle the structures that in their ugly efficiency make human beings expendable. We must pull a different future into today; and we have a very helpful guide in Gustavo Gutiérrez. Liberation is the arduous and explosively dangerous work that anointed Romero's martyrdom. Liberation is the work of all, for all, because, as Gutiérrez always underlines, "God is for us." *Mañana* is contained in today; it will be as beautiful as we dare to dream and build it. Let's get to work.

Notes

1. Augustine, *Confessions*, bk. 1, chap. 1 (New York: Penguin, 1961).

2. See Toni Morrison's Pulitzer-Prize-winning novel *The Bluest Eye* (New York: Holt, Rinehart and Winston, 1970) and her rendering of ugliness when shaped by racism, classism, and sexism.

3. I am drawing here from my extensive notes of an intimate conversation session I participated in at the University of Notre Dame in October 2004 (Notre Dame conversation). The group gathered was all Catholic Latino doctoral students, and our time with Gustavo Gutiérrez was made possible by Notre Dame's Institute for Latino Studies and professors Virgil Elizondo and Timothy Matovina. This event is one of the most treasured memories of my theological education.

4. Gustavo Gutiérrez, *On Job: God Talk and the Suffering of the Innocent*, trans. Matthew J. O'Connell (Maryknoll, NY: Orbis Books, 1987).

5. See Karl Barth, *Church Dogmatics*, ed. and trans. G. W. Bromiley and T. F. Torrance (Edinburgh: T & T Clark, 1936–62).

6. The term *mujerista theology* has been put forth by Ada María Isasi-Díaz as a "Hispanic women's liberation theology." See especially, *En la Lucha = In the Struggle: Elaborating a Mujerista Theology* (Minneapolis: Fortress Press, 2004).

7. Notre Dame conversation.

8. Ibid.

9. Ibid.

10. *Medellín* refers to a regional synod of CELAM, the General Conference of the Latin American Episcopate, convened in Medellín, Colombia, in 1968 and its resulting documents. *Puebla* likewise refers to the second landmark general meeting of the Latin American Episcopate, this time in Puebla, Mexico, in 1979, as well as the documents produced from that meeting. For a detailed look at these events and the history of liberation theology, see *Mysterium Liberationis: Fundamental Concepts of Liberation Theology*, edited by Ignacio Ellacuría and Jon Sobrino (Maryknoll, NY: Orbis Books, 1993).

11. Notre Dame conversation.

12. Ibid.

13. Ibid.

CAME THE HARD RAIN

SHARI JULIAN

I heard the sound of a thunder that roared out a warning. . . .
Heard ten thousand whispering and nobody listening.
"A Hard Rain's A-Gonna Fall"—Bob Dylan

To maintain social progress, a nation must preserve all of its past as a reminder to its future citizens. The Gulf Coast's history is the nation's history: ours, unique and terrible, wonderful and sensual, cruel and struggling; a modern nation's story of economic growth and social development.

My Own Private New Orleans

The Gulf Coast, under the overlay of the recent gambling kitsch, is still languid and tropical. The cities along her shore were home to some of the most beautiful buildings of the antebellum South. Few understood the full scope of the loss of the wonderful buildings of Biloxi or of the fishing villages that have been home to generations of families still engaged in their ancestral occupations. When a nation loses its cultural, physical, and historical markers, it ultimately loses its direction.

Several months have passed since the waters and the hurricanes came like a biblical curse and wiped out an irreplaceable part of our southern Gulf Coast; within a day's drive of each other are sociohistorical artifacts of significant national history and the living reminders of distinct and unique cultures.

New Orleans had its own perfume: sweet olive and magnolia borne on a warm river breeze. Barely into my twenties, I moved there to teach at a university. Memories there form a corporeal collage: passion and mystery; leisurely exquisite meals; parties until dawn in elegant homes; costumes, dances, parades, festivals, and Carnival; spice-laden air; music and play. I can still see the fresh-washed streets of the French Quarter in the early mornings when, on my way to the university, I would stop to shop and pause to breathe deeply of air fragrant with fresh-baked bread and beignets and thick, dark, chicory coffee. New Orleans in the early morning light was a different city than the night city. In the mornings, vendors would stack their wares on heaping stands; spices and coffee would perfume the air; and mixed dialects exchanged the morning greetings over the sounds of zydeco, blues, and jazz.

This is the New Orleans I will always cherish. Like many others, I have known great love and great sorrow there. Before moving north at the dawn of the twentieth century, my family owned land and conducted commerce in the French Quarter. When I returned, those hundred-years-ago associations became my credentials into the private and ancient New Orleans social system. New Orleans's folk remember and live their past in their today. Dinner stories are told in the present tense about family exploits during the Civil War. When the rains and the wind came, it destroyed the city and the locus of thousands of lives both past and present.

The totality of loss is somewhat akin to the destruction of Pompeii. Some places will never return. Charity Hospital, one of the great American inner-city hospitals that served the poor and disenfranchised for more than a century, is gone. The lower Ninth Ward with its Mardi Gras traditions and exquisite soul food and Creole cafés was drowned. The shotgun houses and the streets that held thousands of stories of life and personal journeys left with the flood.

Since the time of its construction, the history of New Orleans and the history of the Louisiana black people have been inextricably woven. Slaves and later black labor built and maintained the levees that protected the city until the advent of the Army Corps of Engineers. Combined civil and political forces kept Louisiana blacks on plantations as sharecroppers and laborers and guardians of the levees. On swampy soil, in a harsh political climate, they built a unique U.S. city and region. These are indigenous people with a sacred, historical tie to an unrivaled land. Uprooting them to save them will result in the death of a city rebuilt by modern-day carpetbaggers.

An Invocation to the Community

Several weeks ago, I wrote an account of my experiences and observations while working at Dallas shelters for Hurricanes Katrina and Rita survivors. I noted that the system had failed. I shared my frustration at the chaos and lack of organization and my fears for the survivors' futures as they are dislocated repeatedly. I also recognized that the time is ripe, after three major disasters, to develop a program to train specialists in mass victimology.

I received many inquiries asking me to define *mass victimology* and *traumatology*. In my work here and elsewhere in the world, I have worked in many different situations with vast numbers of victims of various tragedies (for example, a natural disaster, an ethnic or racial cleansing, a terrorist act, a mass crime, or a transportation mishap). These tragedies have several elements in common. Most of the victims and the greatest long-term needs fall under the aegis of the mental health and social helping professionals. During the events, different modalities are needed than in individual or group therapy or in physical medical mediation. In advance of any event, preparatory work must be done, which includes the interventions of specialized agencies, organizational and individual training, and education. Each type of mass event must be prepared for and trained for differently. We have no international agency or accrediting body to handle such a transnational problem on a long-term basis. In our nation, we need an accrediting and long-term management organization, which should not be the Red Cross. The task of a nation's long-term safety and rehabilitation ought not to be dumped on a private agency that has to solicit emergency funding. Specialists in mass victimology have to come from eclectic backgrounds where they can cross-train in various disciplines to develop interdisciplinary and specific mass victim response plans. Without such an organizational and therapeutic framework to smoothly oversee and conduct reconstruction, relocation, crisis intervention, and therapy operations for the extent of the situation, I am convinced that the hospitality of emergency will rapidly devolve into terrible social displacement and racial abreaction.

Although my commentaries on Katrina received wonderful, encouraging responses, particularly from colleagues in the medical and social science fields with similar accounts and concerns, I was shocked to find myself the lightning rod for many hate mongers. The many respondents who voiced their frustration that the nation failed to use Katrina as a final solution for the "black problem" terrified me.

In shelters, I saw numerous white volunteers cradling babies, holding the elderly, cleaning the sick, and comforting the distraught. I saw love, charity, empathy, prayers, shared tears and hugs, concern, and mutual outrage at the plight of fellow citizens. I saw gratitude, appreciation, and connections between human beings who genuinely cared about one another. I came away with a wonderful sense of optimism about the dream of one America, black and white together.

Then came the letters, e-mails, and blog comments. This deluge of words was as destructive, hateful, and blind as the first tragedy. At first I thought it was an anomaly that I was hearing from the fringe element. They felt the words I wrote were so traitorous, dangerous, and toxic to the American way of life that I had to be silenced quickly by any means. They portrayed me as a godless, dangerous, radical liberal. My picture and address were posted on the Internet; my résumé was dissected along with the suggestion that a well-placed scalpel would be an appropriate response to me. One correspondent offered to hold me down for the carving.

What was my treason? Commenting on what I saw? Criticizing the response? Criticizing the complete lack of planning for the next phase of movement and resettlement? Commenting that the lack of planning would result in a racial blame reaction when the resettlement failed? My crime was telling the truth and presenting a reasoned opinion in a nation where dialogue is dead and ideologues grow fat, rich, and celebrated.

In therapy there is an axiom: a secret's only boundary is the imagination of others. In a nation built on secrets and suppression of truth, shaped by unchecked racism, classism, and prejudice, excuses for final solutions are all possible outcomes. Katrina did more than wash away cities and landscapes; she washed away the shiny veneer of one United States of America and exposed the knotted wood beneath. When the government refuses to openly, honestly, and impartially examine its mistakes and assign responsibility, truth is the victim. When miscreants are not punished and incompetents are rewarded, government ceases to be effective. When self-proclaimed prophets and readers of God's mind receive a platform to criticize others' orthodoxy and to legislate others' moral choices, great disaster looms close. When government does not respond to the poorest and least powerful, it is not compassionate; it is elitist and cruel. And when government is complicit in silencing truth and suppressing opposition, it is no longer a democracy. A democracy cannot exist without open dialogue, debate, and self-examination.

The readers must decide if the recounting of my experiences and observations are deserving of such venom. The accounts that follow were written right after Katrina and at the start of the emergency surrounding Rita and the Texas evacuation.

Katrina—My First Response

There are so many words that come to mind. As a scholar, I think diaspora, social displacement, systemic disruption, mass trauma, pandemic, and unbelievable chaos. As a clinician, I see something that we have never been trained to handle in this country—a level of victimization and its resultant psychosocial ripples that requires a new field of clinical practice: mass victimology. Katrina exposed a racist, social termite's nest, festering since Reconstruction. Many of these deeply religious survivors have lost God, faith, and hope. Hope has been replaced by magical thinking that augurs a second, more terrible level of social disruption and approaching anger.

Over and over, I kept hearing a framing of self that puzzled me until I realized that this is how it must have been for blacks after Reconstruction. Over and over, people said, "Everyone has been so wonderful. Thank you; thank you." When I said, "There is no need to thank us; you are our fellow citizens and we want to help you—American to American," there would be a long pause as if the idea of being the same never struck them before.

They are angry and it is growing. The system failed them. There is no system; there are no safeguards and preparations in place. I had been begging anyone who would listen for a program in mass victimology to prepare for the next tragedy after 9/11. Now it is here and the lack of organization, science, and preparation are resulting in awful consequences for our nation.

Imagine sending people who have been assimilated into a stable demographic population into cities and towns all over the United States; people who are as unprepared as the victims to understand their dislocation and their support needs. The lower Gulf states have a language, a history, a social dynamic, a faith, a societal structure, and a ritual system unlike any other. These people have been acculturated to this system for generations. When the dust settles and the mud dries we are going to see a nation that will lose patience with their needs. Abandoned once again, the fury and the trauma, momentarily quieted by the outpouring of empathy and support postcrisis, will arise larger and more terrible than we are equipped to handle as a nation. Over and over in the survivor stories I hear the loss of self, and the need to reclaim dignity and power.

Right now, numbness is being replaced by magical thinking. "People want me here—here is better. I think I'll stay here." What will happen when reality sets in? Most of the people who are planning to stay do not understand that the social construct is different here in Texas. Even though Louisiana and Texas are both southern states that share a border, we are vastly different. What will happen to the thousands being sent to Connecticut or Illinois or New Jersey? They are being offered free apartments, furniture, and so forth by generous and well-meaning people who have not thought through the long-term consequences. A lot of the apartments are where transportation and jobs are not readily available. What will happen when the magic wears off and the help fades? How about the holidays for a people who have thrived for generations on ritual, tradition, and celebration?

The trauma they are experiencing is so profound that we have no cultural term or machinery set up for it. The thousands of dead and nameless bodies rotting in the water, arriving dead on the buses, or dying in the shelters are a huge festering wound that no one dares mention. We have not seen this type of diaspora since Reconstruction. The immediate needs that are being addressed ignore the greater unspoken traumas. No governmental system can survive the number of wounded and disillusioned people that we will see sprouting up all over America. Something far greater and more organized has to be done.

Regarding the helpers, turf wars have already sprung up. In the name of "I know better than you do," chaos and wasted energy are multiplying. Initially, the Red Cross was in charge of certifying the therapists' credentials. After Oklahoma City and the pretenders who arrived there, this seemed like a wonderful clearinghouse. Everyone who wanted to help had to go through a brief orientation and a thorough checking of credentials. Only licensed professionals were allowed, and criminal checks were conducted. This seemed to be an excellent common-sense approach to thwart rapists, pedophiles, and other thugs from access to a vulnerable population. Actually, things ran pretty well at the beginning. Then came the special interest groups who I guess felt that their nonexistent coursework in this area qualified them to run things better. Immediate chaos, disorganization, and all sorts of ersatz "helpers" began running around. Some officious type grabbed our then current Red Cross badges and stopped us from going back on the floor to finish seeing our patients without the new badges, which they just happened to be out of. We had an optometrist with prescriptive lenses but no glasses or readers and no idea when he would ever see any. We had a booth for the deaf but no helpers. Amid all this chaos, generated by thousands and thousands of the walking wounded mixing with the powerless well intentioned, comes the whispered word pandemic. A lot of people are suddenly getting sick, and we have to have precautions. "Don't touch the patients, or eat or drink." "We only have one bottle of disinfectant in the mental health section, so come back here [the length of the convention center] after each patient." "What of the people who are being cycled out of here?" "What are we sending into the population?" "If people are sick and contagious, where are the precautions to separate the vulnerable?" "What of precautions such as masks and gloves to keep the medical professionals and first responders safe?" We asked these questions on the first day realizing: NO ONE IS IN CHARGE!

There is no consistent answer or approach or forethought. I am no infection guru but as soon as I heard on day one that people with no water were forced to drink water with bloated bodies, feces, and rats in it, the thought of cholera, typhoid, and delayed disease immediately came to me. With people fanning out across the United States and fears of disease, where is the Centers for Disease Control (CDC)?

In the age of computers, we are doing worse than the pencil squibs and the rolls of paper used to log the displaced after World War II. Literacy and computer access is unrealistically considered a given. Accessing the Federal Emergency Management Agency (FEMA) is through a website, not through interviews with warm, supportive counselors. People are in shelters waiting for FEMA to come "in a few days." "Be patient." The Lieutenant Governor of Louisiana pumped my hand and replied to my desperate queries about how to help people find their parents and babies, "Be patient—give us a few days."

The many mothers who have lost their children, and the children who have lost their parents, have had it with the "be patient" response. The shelters are surprisingly silent. The severely traumatized cry silently. One mother has been separated from her five-month-old for more than a week. Over and over, the mothers of the lost ask, "Do you think my baby has milk and diapers? Do you think they are being kind to my baby?" And then, so softly that I have to ask them to repeat themselves, "Do you think my baby is OK?" My response: the convenient lie. Every time I say, "Of course." I pray to God that it is true.

I am sure that there is a special circle of hell for the media: the survivor stories end on end for the titillation of the public. I heard one news anchor say something about the still unrecognized need to address the psychological trauma. I sent a response to the CNN tip line that there were hordes of every kind of mental health professional working 24/7. What was CNN's response? They ran an evening talk show with a pseudopsychologist as featured guest. I could just see the talk-show host and this psychologist down here gathering tales of the already exploited for their "Stories of the Survivors." A pop psychologist was representing the real unsung mental health heroes, counselors, psychologists, social workers and psychiatrists dealing with unmedicated psychosis and severe traumatic responses! Scream about accountability and point fingers for those who cannot. Where is the real help from the media? Help us find those babies and parents and missing family. We have a man in one shelter caring for four kids. They call him "Uncle." He is the cousin of the fiancé of the mother, who is probably dead. The children sit, play, and weep silently with open mouths that cannot scream. What media screams for them?

Finally, I say to hell with this no-blame game. The stories that I know to be true are enough to make me boil: the compassionate foreign doctors who cannot find anyone to validate their credentials; the expensive mobile hospital still sitting parked and waiting for federal paperwork to arrange transfer into Louisiana; the five C130s still sitting on the tarmac in San Diego since the night of Katrina, still waiting for orders to deploy. Where are the beds? We have some elderly people sleeping on hot plastic pool floats with no sheets. There were no showers for days for people who walked for hours through fetid waters. Their skin is breaking out in rashes. Where are the decontamination showers bought with Homeland Security money that can shower thirty people at a time? The Dallas Convention Center has no bathing facilities so the filth and skin reactions are getting worse. What of lice? There are no clothes for the really heavy and large. I was reduced to writing to the women I knew who went through weight-loss programs, so they could comb their closets and attics for "before" outfits. When I arrived with the sack of my gatherings, I had to engage in a full-scale battle, with all my red-headed-doctor fury, to get them distributed to the women still sitting in their stinking clothes.

The survivors are already exhibiting signs of posttraumatic stress disorder. They are terrified, insecure, and powerless. "If we tell the way we feel, maybe help will stop." They are furious at the state and federal government, but afraid to criticize too loudly for fear of adverse consequences and withdrawal of help. Repeatedly survivors say, "If they acted like a government, the body count would be less. The aid would be better managed. The days of filth and feces and death would end sooner." God help all of the poseurs in charge when these folk finally get in touch with their justifiable rage.

The tragedy is leavened by some moments of farce, such as when a man arrived with a case of expensive designer shoes in various sizes that he "saved" from his closet. A man appeared wearing twelve expensive watches up his arm. There are the too-poignant-for-words vignettes. I saw a lady sitting on a blanket holding a photo of two children, which she had pulled from the water. She kept crying and looking at it. She did not know them. They were losses and she mourned them.

Of course there are the criminals, thugs, and mobsters. One of the greatest indictments of the "spin machine" that will come from this situation will be the repeated characterization of victims as lawless and criminal. Over and over I hear people tell me how ashamed they are to be portrayed that way. Ninety-nine percent of these people are lawful, good citizens. To be reduced to taking food and water to survive in their most desperate hours and then to be lumped with television thieves and shooters is too shameful for most of them to bear. I heard from hospital employees who lived on a cup of watered grits twice daily so that the patients could survive. To keep up the morale of others they had to hide in closets the patients who did not live.

The people who survived this tragedy and the people who help them all know one truth. The help and love and care that have been extended to them have been on a citizen-to-citizen basis. The churches, doctors, therapists, and ordinary citizens who are giving all they can in time and resources are managing to mend at the most elementary level—neighbor to neighbor. The government has failed! We are more vulnerable now than before 9/11 because faith in the system is gone. No system can sustain itself as a viable entity when the citizenry are the walking wounded. Victims implode a system from within and expose its decay. This is the beginning of the end unless we can obtain a drastic change of philosophy and restore the government to a system that is "by the people, for the people." Right now nobody down here believes we have that.

Rita—Lessons Still Unlearned

Hurricane Rita arrived, and the e-mails calling for medical professionals and volunteers to be regularly scheduled and on alert again arrived. In the words of Yogi Berra, "It's déjà vu all over again."

In all fairness, the disasters keep arriving at a fast pace and all systems seem to be in crisis reaction rather than planning mode. However, some of the simpler fixes still are not in place. There are still no badges that say we are licensed mental health clinicians registered with the Red Cross. This will mean another big battle at the front door of the shelter with the guy who did not get the "just announce yourself memo." This may not seem to be an important fix, but when you encounter an evacuee weeping, after one of the "experts" who has somehow talked his way in has just told her that her homosexuality caused the floods, the urgency of limiting evacuee access to actual, trained clinicians assumes more importance.

My conversations with the local help agencies confirmed my earlier fears; it is getting harder to find therapists and other medical personnel available on a regular basis to service the needs of the evacuee population. This is not a lack of desire to help, but rather burnout related to negotiating the infrastructure confusion, and frustration with the lack of outcome planning. In the spirit of using words of the great social critic Jonathan Swift, I offer this immodest proposal.

Julian's Immodest Proposal

Treat this recurring situation as a systems theory problem. Break its components down into the simplest elements. Diagram how these elements affect one another, then create an action plan for each element. Systems theory says that each element affects other elements, and if you change one element, you change the system: figure out how to break this mess into workable elements. (1) Let people who have expertise establish the goals and criteria for best practices. (2) Report to the operational experts to weld the big pieces together. Do like football coaches: replay, refine, assign responsibility, accept responsibility, and then fine-tune. Make each individual in charge of the element responsible for the efficiency and functioning of the element.

Right now things are so contradictory and confused because nobody is in charge. A labyrinth of private agencies, public entities, charities, churches, and ersatz helpers all need to be negotiated, but without a map. Clinicians want to work directly with patients without having to wage operational battles with clueless functionaries. Give me a badge and let me do what I do best without having to fight to get to my patients and meet their needs.

In my preclinician life I also earned a doctorate in public administration at the University of Wisconsin. The progressives there taught me to let the experts do what they do best and to never forget that organizations exist to meet operational human needs in the most fair, efficient manner. To achieve this modest goal, my second suggestion is to get politicians and media out of the middle. If Vietnam and Iraq taught us anything, it was that waging any battle with an eye toward political gain or media posturing results in a bad plan with shackled generals.

Disasters like the ones we are currently experiencing involve every profession. No one is an expert in everything. If we are moving an entire city, such as Houston, north, get the traffic engineers to plan routes. Let them decide where to preplace water, fuel, food, toilets, and automotive and emergency medical support. Hundreds of thousands of cars sat still on baking highways headed north while two or three cars zipped south on an empty road. Finally, a day later, somebody got the idea to open the other half of the road to northbound traffic. Cars stalled, overheated, and broke down while their passengers sat for twenty hours in a metal hell. Surely an experienced traffic engineer could devise a solution to offset the chance of this happening again.

Traffic engineers have a professional association. Get them planning the routes and support needs prior to an evacuation, which will establish a set of principles for any situation. For example, so many cars can move so far in an hour using this particular flow; we can increase it by changing to this theoretical pattern. Based on those numbers, we need to station support at this and this point along the route. If things get fouled up, the engineers have the knowledge base to diagnose and fix it for next time, and that element of the operational plan is covered. The governor has someone to call for immediate knowledgeable input.

Mental health clinicians need to have each profession do what they do best. Again, this presupposes the suspension of turf wars and the ability to work together as professionals on a problem larger than individual egos. Let social workers assist with agency interfaces so that support needs can be coordinated faster. Let family therapists work on family stress needs and reunification issues. Let psychologists triage for severe psychological abreactions or disorders, thus leaving the psychiatrists to write prescriptions and to make critical care decisions. Let counselors deal with situational traumatic counseling and needs. Let child therapists and art therapists work with traumatized children to intervene as soon as possible. Set up prescribed teams to interface with the findings of each group.

Do some remedial charts so that problems do not get shipped out as an unpleasant surprise to some generous homeowner or some unsuspecting city. Have immediate triage so that vulnerable populations, such as the mentally handicapped, can be separated and protected, and opportunistic infections and medically vulnerable populations can be identified before the crisis grows. Make each professional organization related to its clinical grouping responsible for keeping the list of qualified emergency experts, for credentialing updates, and for issuing bona fides. Use only licensed professionals who are bound by codes of practice. This would cut down on the faux shrinks who offer counsel and comfort to vulnerable and frightened people. Have these professional groups interface this backup work with the current scheduling and operational group for each shelter. Thus, there would always be a psychiatrist on duty, rather than having to find a shanghaied blood-bank doctor who generously consents to writing drug prescriptions out of his field because unmedicated full-blown psychotic patients are running around a crowded shelter with no psychiatrist on duty. Finally, use infection protocols from the start.

Get the information technology professionals to develop a rapid registration system for everyone who is to be bulk lodged. A system of coding and number assignments would note exactly what the pressing issues are for each person. This would help eliminate the displacement and separation of families. Some people were determined not to leave the shelters because their missing loved ones would not know where to find them. Get personal bankers and financial experts to help them find and transfer lost or banked funds. These groups probably were not ever asked to give input.

Let the local real estate professional find possible FEMA campsites or easily adapted sites for bulk shelters, such as empty shopping centers or hospitals. Have a professional, salaried, coordinating staff move into each affected area to coordinate the efforts of these expert groups concerning scheduling, support, and access. Designate somebody in charge from the start to coordinate the input from the individual elements and have this person be responsible for seeing that the folk in charge of the assignment of public resources, personnel, and matériel have the most up-to-date information. Let the professional organizations handle operations.

Utilize the vast intellectual and professional resources of this country efficiently. Procurement professionals should not be sorting clothes and master schoolteachers should not be stocking shelves when problems in their specialty areas remain unaddressed. Let's use our best resource—

loving, caring, generous citizens—to the best advantage in a time of crisis. By developing registries, credentialing professionals, and optimizing information technology support before a crisis, we could avoid slow response, poor supply, and lack of personnel coverage. "Into the valley of Death rode the six hundred." Alfred, Lord Tennyson's poem "The Charge of the Light Brigade" is a cautionary tale about the consequences of poor planning and execution.

Here Comes the Sun

If the climatologists are correct, severe hurricanes are on the increase. Most think that global warming is responsible for this increase. If so, then we should take heed and put into place systems to help authorities allocate resources, credential responders, and respond in a timely manner. When human lives stand in the balance, is any price too steep?

Texas announced that it needs FEMA to require Louisiana to turn over its list of sexual predators and offenders. Some of the evacuated Katrina survivors sued the government for delays in payment and failure to provide housing and support services. The newspapers have reported evictions of evacuees from housing and apartments for nonpayment of rent, land in the affected region being sold to speculators for low prices, corporate interests buying up blocks of land for casinos and amusement parks, and scores of disenfranchised people without the resources to return home. Illegal aliens are pouring into the Gulf region to assist in the rebuilding process because they will work at subpar rates. Shady firms are hiring people and then absconding with the money. They are carpetbaggers, scalawags, and thieves replicating Reconstruction.

Stop the speculation on land sold at bargain prices by desperate people. Put a city plan with a sane ecological and levee policy into place that will rebuild and preserve this magnificent city. Offer as assistance to New Orleanians decent temporary housing and good wages so they can return home and rebuild the city they love. Evaluate the recipients of rebuilding contracts thoroughly and do not allow the use of illegal aliens or undocumented workers. There is a pool of undocumented workers who came for the wages and stayed because they were exploited or lack the resources to leave. Their presence guarantees another social problem, which further burdens this fragile ecosystem. Prepare an intelligent, coherent, supported plan to address further issues. Depoliticize the whole process and appoint professionals, not cronies, into key jobs and honor the needs of the state regardless of the political party in power. This preserves U.S. history and identity for all citizens and for future generations. A life without gumbo would be a dull life.

Local people who love and understand their land must lead rebuilding programs. All U.S. citizens have an obligation to make sure that when the floods washed away they did not leave with the souls and wills to prevail of thousands of indigenous people who will assimilate elsewhere and never return. New Orleans stayed alive through the combined exertions and breaths of a people tied to their land, and the extraordinary and unusual olio that they had made of its bounties. New Orleans had a pulse and a living vibrancy. New Orleans did not die from drowning; she lay mortally crippled from a heart attack.

Hello Kitty: Reflections of a Katrina Volunteer

Cheryl Fries

In eighty-seven years, Marjorie has never left New Orleans before today. "Baby, where we at again?" she asks as I wheel her to the triage area at the Austin Convention Center. This week Marjorie, dressed only in a faded cotton nightgown and pink slippers, has taken her first helicopter and airplane rides, both to convention centers. "Austin, Texas," I tell her. She shakes her head and snickers. "Well, isn't that something?"

As we maneuver through the crowds of arriving evacuees and harried volunteers, Marjorie orders me to stop in the loading zone where forklifts pull cartons of supplies from idling semi trucks. She bums a smoke off another evacuee and explains, "Sometimes I need a cigarette when I'm feeling stressed out." Now it is my turn to laugh. But for her skin color, she could be my own southern grandmother.

Until "The Stahm," as Marjorie calls it, I believed that my country was the greatest in the world; organized into well-equipped, solid services; able to respond with calm, kind efficiency to any disaster. In the past five days, as Marjorie was plucked from a boiling rooftop and dropped into the teeming and desperate crowds at the New Orleans Convention Center, I had realized the frailty of my illusion. Watching on television as the president joked about his fun past in New Orleans, as days went by and still FEMA did not respond, as families waved T-shirts from rooftop ovens, I not only saw the complete failure of the America I had once believed in; I knew as surely as I could see the sun shining outside my home in Austin that, were the waving arms and desperate faces covered with white skin, rescue would certainly have come sooner. In the room where my idealism once lived, anger moved in.

Marjorie is a gift to me, a way to channel the kinetics of my fury into something that will not eat me alive. I hover around her in the triage like an anxious relative as the EMT checks her pulse. Later, when I take her to the designated sleeping area for women and children, we talk of food, as many southern women do. "I bet you're a good cook," I say, and she laughs again. "Baby, one thing I can do is cook."

The night is long. After Marjorie is settled, there is Jesse, age five, who would really like to find a ball from the boxes of donated toys while his exhausted grandmother prepares a nest for the three children she has shepherded through this nightmare. There is the young couple with the sleeping baby whom I help to the phone bank to call relatives in Houston. There is the lone teenage boy with his head in his hands who refuses food, water, and questions; so I find a woman in a shirt that says "Victim Services" and hope for the best. I go to Marjorie's cot to say good night. "I'm glad you made it," I tell her. The paper-thin skin of her hand holding mine is soft as tissue. "Thank you, Baby." At midnight I leave with reluctance. My family will need me in the morning.

* * * * * * * *

Five thousand New Orleans evacuees were flown to Austin. All those I met were elderly, poor, disabled, or black. Many were all of these. I was proud of my city's response that day: truckloads teeming with donated clothes, toys, blankets, diapers; armies of volunteers; cheerful and compassionate nurses, doctors, firefighters, EMTs, and counselors on hand to help. Austin's Convention Center was the antithesis of the one in New Orleans where these people had spent the previous week: clean, cool, efficient, supplied; and kind. In the restroom two women embrace me. One says, "God has lifted us from the pit of hell into the arms of angels in Austin, Texas." We all cry.

The next morning I was turned away from the Austin Convention Center. The Red Cross had organized itself enough to require me to attend eight hours of training. "I just want to check on one woman I met last night," I begged. "She is elderly." They were very sorry, but it just could not be allowed. In the time I had been home to sleep, someone had found the book of regulations. Police officers had been posted at doorways. No one could enter without an armband, and there were no more armbands. My service, I am told, is no longer required.

In two weeks the convention center would be cleared, its new residents dispersed with one month's rent, a book of food stamps, and a sleeping bag. The truckloads of donations would be hauled to Goodwill, where evacuees would be welcome to buy whatever they needed. Almost as quickly as they came, the homeless of New Orleans were no longer available for television interviews. Hands were washed, floors were scrubbed, and convention centers were once again available for trade shows.

I would never see Marjorie again.

* * * * * * * *

When a New Orleans mother is hired at my mother's office, we jump at the opportunity to help her. Her family of four has sleeping bags and a change of clothes each. Both parents' jobs have washed away. Somewhere in the debris of New Orleans are scrapbooks she has made, documenting the lives from birth of her two children.

On the day we are to meet, I go to the store. It will be nice, I think, for my daughter and theirs to have new dolls to play with as the adults visit. I walk the doll aisle once, twice, then again. *Every doll is white. I've never noticed this before.* I cannot decide what is worse: that there are no black dolls or that I have never noticed. I settle for "Hello Kitty."

We collect for this family what we can—beds and sheets, towels, dishes, a sofa. E-mails to our friends bring generous gift cards from around the country. We invite them to join us at dinner or the park. Their gratitude is palpable, and yet it is clear to us all that no matter what is given, so much has been taken. They are welcomed, but not by their own choice. Our generosity is sincere, but still, the scrapbooks are gone.

* * * * * * * *

An Apache friend of mine warns me: "Compassion lives the shortest of lives." I think of the prophets who teach us to *be* our righteousness. And I know that in my own city there are many who are desperately poor; and that all through this great land and big world children die every day for reasons we can prevent. A strong hurricane hitting Texas's Rio Grande Valley will create Katrina, with brown skin. I take my friend's words as a challenge. I pray.

I still see them at night sometimes: pushing their babies through the flood in buckets, begging the television crews for help; spilling from buses into the Austin shelter, carrying plastic grocery bags filled with whatever is left of their lives. Unbidden, my imagination carries me into desperate attics where the horror is too great even for nightmare; so I rise and go through the dark to breathe into the hair of my sleeping child. What life will she have in a world where this can happen? What do I teach her? And how?

Hurricane Katrina and the Floodwaters of New Orleans: A Reflection

Sister Jamie T. Phelps

The fifth year of the twenty-first century was marked by a series of natural disasters that claimed the lives of thousands of innocent victims of many ages, cultures, and nations.

That hurricane season in the United States has been determined to have been one of the most disastrous in our nation's history. As a scholar who had accepted an academic appointment at Xavier University two years ago, I was not prepared for the challenge that would evolve on the Gulf Coast. The following are some of my reflections as I engaged in individual and collective thought in my search to find meaning for Hurricane Katrina for our life in light of the gospel and the social justice teachings of the Catholic Church.

Initial Response

What a difference a day makes! For those whose lives have been directly touched by the events of Hurricane Katrina and its aftermath, life will never be the same. For some, this crisis is an opportunity to build a new life grounded in a profound sense of the meaning of life. How easily all that we take for granted can be altered! What really matters is life in relationship with God, with family, and with all humanity and all creatures because of God. "I have come that [you] may have life, and have it to the full!" (John 10:10 NIV).

Realization that a Category 5 hurricane was headed toward New Orleans struck fear in the hearts of some, defiance in the hearts of others. The poor, who had no choice, embraced resignation. Those of us from New Orleans who by some coincidence were not at home, looked on with amazement and outrage as we watched the slow response to the cry of the poor. On a personal level we searched the faces of the poor, disabled, elderly, and people who refused to leave. Where do the poor go? How can they leave without their families—extended families and the church communities who are the anchors of their lives?

In the first days and weeks of the tragedy we called and searched for friends, students, and colleagues wondering, Did they get out or are they among the dead? Through the past months we have contacted many of those members of our Xavier University and Institute faculty, staff, and student body, and hear daily of their struggle to begin anew while they battle FEMA, insurance companies, and landlords who seem to be either overwhelmed by the magnitude of the disaster or opportunistic scavengers of those suffering economic and personal loss. Confronted by such a disaster, one immediately searches for meaning. While my first impressions still linger, as more and more data is reported in the media my thought and analysis continue to deepen.

I firmly believe that every situation in life contains good and evil aspects at the same time. After identifying these elements it is important to identify and challenge the individual or social immorality of the evil aspect, uncover the source of hope, and articulate the hope for the future as rooted in the good aspects understood in the light of our life of faith. This essay is an exercise in faith, seeking to understand how God's unconditional love is being revealed in and through the Katrina-flood disaster and how people of faith should act in response to that love by doing right, loving goodness, and walking humbly with God (paraphrase of Micah 6:8).

Unmasking the Mask

I was horrified, saddened, and angered as the television images unmasked the shrouded systemic patterns of social injustice that characterize much of our current social, political, economic, and ecclesial relationships. Sadly these dynamics have operated so long within the social systems of our society that too many of us, regardless of our ethnic-racial identity, think that racial and class segregation and alienation is natural. One need not harbor a specific negative thought about blacks or the poor; such thoughts are anchored within our collective cultural unconscious. The poor, disabled, elderly, and black people, who are generally invisible on a day-to-day basis in the South and all over our country, became visible as the floodwaters made us see poor black and white people and other people of color who are poor.[1]

Ordinarily we see and do not see; we hear and do not hear; because our self-absorption, materialism, individualism, and economic greed blind us to the reality of the poor. Ordinarily the poor, who are at the heart of the mission of Jesus Christ (Luke 4:14), live in the invisible margins of church and society. Ordinarily the poor of the gospel are the despised who are viewed as the disposable of our society. We forget that New Orleans embodies a distinct blend of the rich and diverse traditions of Native American, African, and French cultures augmented by an array of European cultures. We forget that under the Napoleonic Codes all peoples of Louisiana were Catholics, and thus the Creole and black cultures of New Orleans were traditionally diverse expressions of Catholic culture. Although many come to party in the "Big Easy," others have not forgotten the rich history and the legacy of faith and fortitude of African slaves, Native Americans, and French, which gave birth to a new culture (Creole) and new classical music (jazz, blues), poetry, and southern soul. Today, New Orleans and Louisiana are indeed a diverse society both ethnically and religiously. This pocket of society embodies a microcosm of the best and worst of our nation and world. The hurricanes and their aftermath unmasked the good and the social immorality of our sociopolitical thought and structures that characterize not only New Orleans and the southern Gulf Port region, but also our entire nation and the world.

The Good

My two-year experience living in New Orleans deepened my appreciation of the centrality of family values that dominate this part of our country. Sociologists warn us of the decline of family and family values; yet these despised, marginalized, poor, black, brown, yellow, and white folk of the South refused to leave their elderly grandparents, fathers, and mothers. They refused to abandon those children and adults who were hospitalized or challenged by mental or physical illnesses.

As I watched the television montage of those stranded in New Orleans in the aftermath of Hurricane Katrina, I did not see criminals or animals but black and Creole people of faith, Catholic and Protestant, clutching their children protectively. Thrown into random assemblies, they had formed small groups and communities of love and protective power mediating God's care for people in the midst of suffering. Individual human beings became the mediating, comforting arms of the God of Jesus Christ. A nameless white nurse called for insulin and it appeared from the crowd. Black men stood around making an effort to revive a fallen companion. Others creatively organized a soup kitchen, taking supplies from abandoned stores to feed the multitudes, as it became apparent that help was not coming soon. Black women and men cradled their children, holding them close, protecting them from the natural disaster and the storm of those who were unhinged by chaos.

Later we would learn that the gunshots reported first as attacks on the rescuing forces of the army and coast guard were in fact attempts to call attention to those still needing help. Later we would hear of the young black men who had been labeled "street thugs" organizing the waiting throngs so women and children were able to board the buses first. They had become a protective guard rather than a menace. Later we would hear of people seeking refuge in their churches, temples, and synagogues as places of safe harbor. In one instance, a group of twenty-five, including eleven children and a disabled person, gathered with their minister to seek safety in their church. Once the church was flooded, they had to depend on God and the resourceful skills and social networking of church members to wade through the water and find peace in the midst of the chaos of the convention center. They began their post-Katrina life in the warm and hospitable Red Cross shelter in Houston.[2] Seemingly, those who relied on faith and community survived as they worked collectively to assist family members and neighbors escape the dangerous waters. These men and women of faith knew well the wisdom of the gospel. "If one part of the body suffers, all the other parts suffer with it; if one part is praised, all the others parts share its happiness" (1 Cor. 12:26 GNT).

When we observe and listen with eyes and ears of faith, we see the fortitude, resourcefulness, creativeness, wisdom, and holiness of large numbers of poor and middle-class black people and those of every culture, who empowered by the Spirit remain determined and hope-filled in the midst of hopelessness. United States Coast Guard personnel, Catholic charity workers, Red Cross volunteers and other rescue teams, and police officers of all religious persuasions risked their own lives and left their own families in order to respond immediately to the needs of the hurricane victims. Those individuals and nations who observed and listened with eyes and ears of faith and humanity at those displaced by the storm responded generously with offers to aid other human beings in extraordinary need. Homes and hearts opened. Food, medical help, money, and clothes flowed to the places where the evacuees had traveled for safety.

Social Immorality of Our Sociopolitical Thought and Structures

The storm unmasked our collective social immorality. To many, the dark and brown skin of many of the evacuees who assembled in the Superdome and convention center marked them stereotypically as poor, subhuman criminals—looters and thugs—who lacked intelligence and morals. The party politics of Louisiana, a Republican state with Democratic local and state leadership, complicated the federal government's ability to hear the cries of the marginalized and displaced evacuees and their state representatives. Regional devaluation, race, class, and political factors produced the delayed indifference we first witnessed with horror. The U.S. government was found woefully neglectful or ill prepared as reflected in a statement by the U.S. chapter of the Ecumenical Association of Third World Theologians (EATWOT). EATWOT described the multifaceted aspect of the inadequacy and failure of the early response to Hurricane Katrina in their statement drafted collectively at their 2005 fall meeting held in Chicago, Illinois.

> The United States government and citizenry failed in responding to the devastation of the hurricane. The failures included:
>
> 1. A squandering of resources for an illegal war in Iraq and the repressive "war on terror." As a consequence, we did not fund infrastructure and environmental protection in poor communities and communities of color, a failure that made much worse the devastation the hurricane caused. This same war diverted National Guard and other resources that could have helped provide a timely and adequate emergency response.

2. An assumption that the U.S. could not be affected by catastrophe. Government officials did not prepare for Hurricane Katrina despite adequate advanced warning. Our government ignored information available from science about Global Scorching in favor of an ideology that placed corporate profits above facts, and it disregarded the clear information from scientists about the impending hurricane.

3. A sustained dismantling of social safety networks, which have resulted in increasing poverty, exacerbated by racism and neglect of immigrant populations, all of which aggravated the effects of this natural disaster.

4. A failure to provide prompt, humane assistance to poor people and people of color. Moreover, the most oppressed people were blamed for their predicaments by suggesting that they should have left earlier (with the assumption that everyone had the same financial ability to leave).

5. Contempt for the poor and people of color who were not treated equally when rescue efforts began, a contempt which suggests that they will not be treated equitably in recovery. Assistance to rich people before providing for the people who needed it the most—poor people— showed a failure to understand or acknowledge the interrelationship between racism and economic justice.

6. Ongoing government claims that racism and economic justice had nothing to do with the inadequate response to Katrina. These denials mean government officials continue to be unaccountable for their actions.[3]

In the long run, however, when we ask who was responsible for the inadequate response and follow-up, the most honest answer must be all of us—individuals; local, state, and federal governments and their agencies; those who did not heed the warnings for hurricane Categories 4 and 5. After years of avoiding serious damage and devastation, Gulf Port natives adopted a false sense of invincibility. Years of masking the reality of the economic poverty that characterizes the majority of those who live in New Orleans made us insensitive to the special needs for relocation posed by the economic poverty of the area. The poor people in the Big Easy— the cooks, janitors, laborers, staff workers, and others—are largely invisible to those who benefit from their talents and services.

Though local New Orleans officials had an evacuation plan that had been implemented three times before, only when Katrina struck and the levee broke was the inadequacy of the Counter-flow Plan made evident to all of us. I, and many people like me, never once thought about people who did not have cars. Nor did most natives of the Gulf Coast and I think of the reality that a real disaster would bring, although many native New Orleaneans told me that if "the big one comes and hits the lake and river at the same time, New Orleans will be under water." No one anticipated what the reality would harbor. No one really expected "the big one" to come.

The state government was understandably reluctant to abdicate all its power and decision making to federal authorities, but later we would discover that such relinquishment was not necessary and federal agencies already had the authority and responsibility to collaborate and intervene in the event of such catastrophic devastation.[4] The party politics and power plays blinded the decision makers and delayed some rescues that added to the death toll of the region.

Stereotypical thinking blinded many in their reporting and assessing the character of the victims and the self-reliant resources available within the native peoples of the region. Despite the fact that the Gulf region is one of the major native sources of oil for the United States and a major port for the importation of goods needed for the country, most U.S. citizens are not mindful of this reality. Too often northerners think of the South in terms of great vacation spots (e.g., Florida, New Orleans, Houston, and so forth), ignoring the economic and cultural gifts of the region. Too often the lives and contributions of people of color who hold service positions in these areas and throughout the country are invisible backdrops to the material and cultural assets sought on Gulf Port beaches, casinos, and restaurants. In the South and throughout the United States, many remain unaware of the gifts of hospitality, generosity, family, and God-centered spirit that characterize the culture of the black poor and other poor people of faith.

Devaluing and disrespecting the humanity and needs of the poor, we close the churches and schools and special programs in cities across the nation, citing economic limitations. In many other areas of U.S. public life, those who have money have access to privilege and service, and those who are poor remain marginalized and/or invisible objects to be of use solely for the benefits of the middle and upper classes. Forgetful of our rich religious history and mission, some churches of all denominational and cultural identities cultivate and placate the rich at the expense of the poor. We forget the evangelizing and social justice mission of Jesus and the Christian churches that compels followers of the way of Jesus to serve all people because of God's call to universal communion and mission of salvation (*Lumen Gentium*, no. 1, and *Gaudium Et Spes*, no. 1).[5]

The Future

Looking through the lens of the gospel toward the future of the Gulf region in general and New Orleans in particular, we must actively urge our church and civic leaders to embrace the fundamental option for the poor and encourage the redevelopment of New Orleans and the other Gulf Port cities of the South in such a way that they remain culturally and class diverse. The Gulf region, which has experienced "death" from the destructive forces of water and political bungling, must experience a new birth that transforms the old systems of racial, cultural, and class exclusion from power and decision making into a region that welcomes all God's children as fully human subjects and colaborers who are called to be midwives for God's will and way "on earth as it is in heaven." In this new life the divisions between rich and poor, racial-ethnic groups, and gender privileging will cease.

EATWOT members expressed their collective dream of the future in the conclusion of the EATWOT statement.

> The aftermath of Hurricane Katrina revealed ruptures—deep divisions and deep inconsistencies—in our society. Appropriately addressing these ruptures means looking for moral resources to guide our movement forward. The tragedy of Hurricane Katrina requires that we must first be motivated by love and compassion for all those affected. Through generosity and kindness, we must tend to those most in need first. However, our vision and work cannot stop with simply meeting immediate needs. We must address the power structures in our society that allowed this situation to happen in the first place. The lack of adequate hurricane and flood protection laid bare the country's injustices toward and devaluation of people of color and the poor. At the same time that we meet the needs of those affected by Katrina, we must move forward with a transformative and integrated mind-body-spirit framework so that this kind of travesty of justice does not happen again.
>
> We must restore a sense of the common good, an understanding that we share life together and that when we are all whole and strong separately, we are stronger collectively. We must also determine ways to give agency to those who are most affected by this disaster and determine

ways to act in concert with them. In the immediate and long term, this means that we must develop structures to empower persons at all levels of society to speak for themselves about the things that they need, thereby shifting the center of authority and voice in ways that lessen the control of persons with the most access, the most expertise, and the most resources. We must strive for justice by holding accountable those who are responsible for developing state systems and policies, calling on them to build systems that empower all, and that especially attend to removing structures that destroy the lives of people of color and poor people.

We must respond to the failures of our government with a call to all citizens to prophetically speak truth to power, justice to discrimination, and life to the pursuit of death.[6]

As Christians, we are always called to walk in the light of Jesus, who is "the way, and the truth, and the life" (John 14:6). "We may be sure that we know Jesus" if we "keep his commandments. . . .Whoever keeps his word, the love of God is truly perfected in [them] the way that we know we are in union with him: whoever claims to abide in him [Jesus] ought to walk just as he walked" (1 John 2:3-6, author's translation).

Walking in the way of Jesus is to walk in the way of the Paschal Mystery. In our individual and collective lives we will experience the joys and sorrows of daily life, and suffering death and rising again empowered by the Holy Spirit. Those of us challenged by the aftermath of the hurricane season must live in the spirit of fortitude, wisdom, and hope that characterizes the Resurrection. We are suffering the pangs of uncertainty, anxiety, and death today, but we live in the hope and blessed assurance of a new life and joy of resurrection in the mornings of tomorrow!

Notes

1. The shock of realizing the depth of poverty in New Orleans made the author research more deeply the reality of poverty in America. Though a frequent visitor to the Catholic Campaign for Human Development website documenting U.S. poverty, http://www.usccb.org/cchd/povertyusa/povfacts.shtml, I suddenly found this not enough and searched for more documentation. See Mark Robert Rank, *One Nation, Underprivileged: Why American Poverty Affects Us All* (New York: Oxford University Press, 2005), for an interesting argument for policy addressing the need to eliminate U.S. poverty.

2. I was fortunate to be able to communicate with my program assistant, who was a part of this church group, and she gave me a first-person account of her and her family's ordeal in the convention center in New Orleans and the Red Cross shelter in Houston. She experienced both bad and good treatment in the evacuation process.

3. "A Response to Hurricane Katrina from the Ecumenical Association of Third World Theologians, U.S. Minorities Group," http://www.faithvoices.org/programs/eatwotkatrina.html. The statement was written by a team of eleven members of the U.S. Minorities Group of EATWOT, who used an online technology, Synanim, provided by Faith Voices for the Common Good (www.faithvoices.org).

4. See Homeland Security Act of 2002 #505, http://www.whitehouse.gov/depofhomeland/bill/title5.html#505.

CONDUCT OF CERTAIN PUBLIC HEALTH-RELATED ACTIVITIES. (a) Except as the President may otherwise direct, the Secretary shall carry out the following responsibilities through the Department of Health and Human Services (including the Public Health Service), under agreements with the Secretary of Health and Human Services, and may transfer funds to him in connection with such agreements: (1) all biological, chemical, radiological, and nuclear preparedness-related construction, renovation, and enhancement of security for research and development or other facilities owned or occupied by the Department of Health and Human Services; and (2) all public health-related activities being carried out by the Department of Health and Human Services on the effective date of this Act (other than activities under functions transferred by this Act to the Department) to assist State and local government personnel, agencies, or authorities, non-Federal public and private health care facilities and providers, and public and non-profit health and educational facilities, to plan, prepare for, prevent, identify, and respond to biological, chemical, radiological, and nuclear events and public health emergencies, by means including direct services, technical assistance, communications and surveillance, education and training activities, and grants. (b) With respect to any responsibilities carried out through the Department of Health and Human Services under this section, the Secretary, in consultation with the Secretary of Health and Human Services, shall have the authority to establish the preparedness and response program, including the setting of priorities.

5. See "Dogmatic Constitution on the Church *Lumen Gentium* Solemnly Promulgated by His Holiness Pope Paul VI on November 21, 1964," http://www.vatican.va/archive/hist_councils/ii_vatican_council/documents/vat-ii_const_19641121_lumen-gentium_en.html.

Since the Church is in Christ like a sacrament or as a sign and instrument both of a very closely knit union with God and of the unity of the whole human race, it desires now to unfold more fully to the faithful of the Church and to the whole world its own inner nature and universal mission.

See also "Pastoral Constitution on the Church in the Modern World *Gaudium Et Spes* Promulgated by His Holiness Pope Paul VI on December 7, 1965," http://www.vatican.va/archive/hist_councils/ii_vatican_council/documents/vat-ii_cons_19651207_gaudium-et-spes_en.html.

The joys and the hopes, the griefs and the anxieties of the men of this age, especially those who are poor or in any way afflicted, these are the joys and hopes, the griefs and anxieties of the followers of Christ. Indeed, nothing genuinely human fails to raise an echo in their hearts. For theirs is a community composed of men. United in Christ, they are led by the Holy Spirit in their journey to the Kingdom of their Father and they have welcomed the news of salvation which is meant for every [one]. That is why this community realizes that it is truly linked with mankind and its history by the deepest of bonds.

6. "A Response to Hurricane Katrina."

Pastoral Reflections on Hurricanes Katrina and Rita

J. Alfred Smith Sr.

My wife JoAnna and I, along with two of our spiritual armor bearers and JoAnna's caregiver, were completing a Mexican cruise when Hurricane Katrina moved closer to New Orleans and other Gulf Coast areas of devastation. My eyes were glued to the television set in our cabin for disabled travelers. Others were caught up in the ecstasy of the activities on the ship. But my heart was troubled because Louisiana was the home of my father; and, two-thirds of the membership of Allen Temple Baptist Church, where I serve as pastor, have family members in New Orleans, Baton Rouge, and Biloxi, Mississippi. These persons were directly in harm's way. How could I, as pastor, be effective in meeting the pastoral care needs of the members and their relatives who would be victims of the hurricane? I had no answers for the haunting questions. Plus, I am sad to admit, the theological questions that people ask when natural tragedy strikes could not be given easy answers by a simplistic theology or by the sophisticated arguments of scholars who embrace the diverse viewpoints of thinkers regarding theodicies.

Upon arriving in Oakland, I called a meeting at Allen Temple to bring clergy and community leaders together to plan a citywide fund-raising effort at the Oakland Coliseum to develop strategies for hurricane relief, and to coordinate organizational and institutional efforts for receiving persons evacuated from the hurricane centers of devastation. Allen Temple leaders organized the infrastructure of the church to aid the hurting families of Allen Temple members and others who were in need of assistance. A minister and a medical doctor, who is a valued and esteemed

Allen Temple member and friend, went to Houston, Texas, with two nurses who study with her at the American Baptist Seminary of the West in Berkeley, California. Allen Temple laypersons provided them with resources to foster their ministry to evacuees inside of the Houston Astrodome. Prayer services and Sunday worship services were designed to help heal the emotionally wounded and the collective grieving of the membership. My own struggle with theodicy was lessened when a bishop of the Full Gospel Baptist Fellowship spoke at the September 2, 2005, 8:00 a.m. Allen Temple worship service. His church of twenty thousand members had three worship locations prior to Hurricane Katrina; he informed us that his church members had been scattered to cities as far away as Atlanta. The bishop's opening words answered the "Why, Lord?" question of Professor Anthony Pinn.[1] However, in fairness to Professor Pinn, he does not blame God for Hurricane Katrina, nor does he embrace a theology of redemptive suffering. Dr. Pinn embraces a humanistic position that challenges the suffering community to unite to turn chaos into cosmos.

Dr. Pinn justifies his embracing black humanism as a religious system by quoting Dr. Charles Long's definition of religion in *Significations*, where he says both theism and humanism are religious to the extent that they provide ultimate orientation and the framework for values, morality, and ethical patterns of conduct and activity.[2] Relieving God of any blame, the bishop answered the "Why, Lord?" question when he simply opened his remarks to us by saying: "Hurricane Katrina is a tragedy that could have been averted." These words placed the blame squarely on human irresponsibility: human sin or human greed that manifested itself in the politics of government spending that cut the amount of money needed to maintain the levees while rejecting requests to increase the spending needed to make the levees safe. Professor Dwight Hopkins tells how such action can take place in writing about "a theological anthropology that maintains a demonic and toxic status quo."[3] Dorothy Sayers's modern version of the Faustus legend, "The Devil to Pay," clarifies the senselessness of blaming God for natural and human evil. She says: "All things God can do, but this thing [God] will not: unbind the chain of cause and consequence, or speed time's arrow backward. When [people] chose to know like God, [they] also chose to be judged by God's values."[4] However, when I think of the fundamentalism of American Christianity that expresses itself in prosperity gospel preaching, I long for an open-minded theology that will motivate us to think beyond the narrow legacy of Christian right fundamentalism. Such thinking is represented in the writings of Gustavo Gutiérrez.[5] Gutiérrez says that first, sin is the social, economic, and political oppression that exploits the oppressed, particularly the poor. Second, sin is the historical determinism that discourages the oppressors from determining their own destiny in history. Third, sin is a breach of communion with God and neighbor.[6]

America is in denial of her economic, social, and political oppression. One thing Hurricane Katrina did was unveil the masses of black, white, and brown poor victims who had no transportation to leave the city of New Orleans. It is tragic that both political parties have maligned the poor. They have painted all poor people as being lazy, unethical, and parasitical. It is even more tragic that black and white prosperity gospel preachers have fortified the greed and the self-righteousness of the greedy. Little or no attention has been given to government public policy that imprisons persons in the caste of poverty. *Caste* differs from *class*, because caste, unlike class, freezes upward social mobility. In the central city where I serve as pastor, I have seen jobs flee from the city not only to suburbia, but also overseas where labor is cheap. I have seen the supermarkets, banks, and businesses leave the central city. I have seen the transportation system decay so that the central-city poor have no way of traveling to where the jobs are located. The declining tax base, the failed educational system, the lack of jobs that pay living wages, and the shortage of affordable housing force upcoming and aspiring young adults to leave the central cities to seek opportunities in the cities of the Sun Belt of Arizona, Nevada, and New Mexico, or in the new southern cities of economic opportunity such as Atlanta, Dallas, Houston, and Fort Lauderdale. How incorrect was the September 15, 2005, speech of President George W. Bush when he stated that poverty in America is restricted to the nation's southern states?[7] Has the president visited Harlem or the Bronx? Has he visited the projects in Philadelphia, or the South Side of Chicago, or Hunters Point in San Francisco, or the 'hood in East Oakland? America has the highest level of poverty in the industrialized world. Thirty-seven million Americans are living below the poverty line.[8] This is the fourth consecutive year that the poverty rate has risen. The poverty rate in New Orleans at the time of Hurricane Katrina was double the national rate. Forty percent of the children of New Orleans were living in poverty when Hurricane Katrina hit.[9]

A little less than two months after Hurricane Katrina, Congress and the White House indicated that they will not initiate new measures to aid the poor. Instead, they will strive to reduce the cost of existing programs that help the poor, such as Medicaid and food stamps. Possibly Iraq War deficits are causing the proposed budget cuts. Congress is being pressured to cut thirty-five billion dollars over the next five years to reduce the budget. The cuts, if the House has its way, will be increased to fifty billion dollars to help pay for hurricane cleanups.[10] A coalition of 750 social welfare groups urged Congress not to cut programs because of the thousands of evacuees from Louisiana, Mississippi, and Alabama.

The number of people without health insurance in the United States also increased by eight hundred thousand last year, reaching 45.8 million.[11] The picture is even worse among poorer Gulf Coast states that were hurt by Hurricanes Katrina and Rita. Senate Finance Chairman Chuck Grassley, a Republican, is promoting a bipartisan aid bill that would allow Medicaid to pay the health care expenses of all evacuees who have relocated to other states. This bill would also expand unemployment benefits in the affected states. Treasury Secretary John Snow warned Congressman Grassley that the administration is afraid of spending more money for these services since these services will contribute to increasing the national deficit. To make matters worse, more than thirty-two thousand persons at the time of this writing are forced to live in shelters.[12] Will the churches move beyond providing charitable assistance to becoming united verbal advocates of the poor?

Long after the visual images of hurting hurricane victims are no longer shown over television and in newspapers, the physical, emotional, and economic pain of the wounded will exist. The aftermath of this American tragedy cannot be calculated. The long-term effects of Hurricanes Katrina and Rita cannot be measured. But immediate energy costs can be determined. The cost of natural gas, which is used to heat 52 percent of American homes, is expected to cost 50 percent more than last year and 70 percent more in midwestern states. These increased costs are blamed on Hurricanes Katrina and Rita. The federal Low Income Home Energy Assistance Program (LIHEAP) provides an average energy assistance grant of about three hundred dollars, which is far less than the fifteen hundred dollars predicted cost of heating a home.[13] Where will the poor obtain help? What can the poor do to alleviate this crisis? Can churches afford to provide housing for the homeless at the risk of producing fuel bills they cannot pay? How does a servant church model the model of Jesus, the Servant Lord? Jesus said:

The Spirit of the LORD is upon Me,
Because He has anointed Me to preach
  the gospel to the poor.
He has sent Me to heal the
  brokenhearted,
To preach deliverance to the captives
And recovery of sight to the blind,
To set at liberty those who are
  oppressed,
To preach the acceptable year of the LORD. (Luke 4:18-19 NKJV)

Poverty is a failure of national will, political courage, and Christian conscience, and not the moral failure of poor people. Yet many Christians in America behave as if racism is a thing of the past. They have great difficulty accepting the reality of racism as it manifests itself in institutionalized forms and in the way power is shared or diffused in colleges, seminaries, and churches, as well as in business, corporate, political, and secular structures of society. Sociologist Michael Emerson and Christian Smith speak honestly and directly about the sin of an unreconciled fellowship masquerading as a reconciled church. They say:

> With few exceptions, evangelicals lack serious thinking [on race relations in America]. Rather than integrate their faith with knowledge of race relations, inequality, and American society, they generally allow their cultural constructions to shape one-dimensional assessments and solutions to multidimensional problems. This will not do. The first step evangelicals might consider, therefore, is engaging in more serious reflection on race-relations issues in dialogue with educated others.[14]

Unconscious racial bias and feelings of unconscious superiority are so deeply imbedded in the psyche of some Christians that they unconsciously relate to poor people with an "I know it" attitude that prevents them from listening to what disaffected minorities have to say. However, the oppressed cannot capitulate to the arrogance of privileged piety. Unfortunately, too many educated blacks, in an effort to earn white acceptance, fail to confront the racism of white liberal self-righteousness. The morality of white America is often based on public opinion polls and not on the truth. This is why many whites could not agree with blacks that the slowness of the government's response to the Katrina crisis was because the majority of the victims were black and poor. The majority of white Christian Americans were unable to inform America that black life

54

in America has always been cheap. Dr. Homer U. Ashby Jr., Pastoral Care Professor at McCormick Theological Seminary in Chicago, Illinois, reminds us:

> Where once there was sympathy for the plight of African Americans, there now is resentment about the perceived cost to whites of the black struggle for empowerment. Recent changes in the welfare system, attacks on affirmative action, and judicial decisions on voting rights that discount the tyranny of the majority all have at their core a retreat from a previous era's commitment to full freedom, justice, and equality for blacks.[15]

Where are liberal white Christians who are needed to support the survival of the poor and marginalized? In order for black Christians to have survived and maintained rapport with many in the white community, they have had to mask their authentic motives and message.

> We wear the mask that grins and lies,
> It hides our cheeks and shades our eyes,—
> This debt we pay to human guile;
> With torn and bleeding hearts we smile,
> And mouth with myriad subtleties.[16]

Our fragile relationship with white American Christians is so thin that black Christians who seek to preserve the relationship in the interest of reconciliation have no other choice than that of wearing the mask. In America, white is right. Whenever white is questioned, critical-thinking black Christians hear the privileged who control the power ask: "How could you question us? Have you forgotten all that we have done to help you?" This is the response that I received from some in the larger dominant community when I endeavored to share with them the cheapness with which black life was treated in New Orleans during the crisis of Hurricane Katrina.

This reality was difficult for me to live with until I read *A Troubling in My Soul*, edited by Professor Emilie M. Townes. In her provocative and prophetic book, Townes writes in her essay "Living in the New Jerusalem" about Professor Audre Lorde's clear distinction between pain and suffering.

> For Lorde, suffering is unscrutinized and unmetabolized pain. Suffering is the inescapable cycle of reliving pain over and over again when it is triggered by events or people. It is a static process which usually ends in

oppression. Pain is an experience that is recognized, named, and used for transformation. It is a dynamic process pointing toward transformation.[17]

Both Professors Townes and Lorde put my mind at ease. I know that I cannot afford to worry or be distressed about those who would question my response to the injustices that I encountered, but that I should move from suffering to the transforming power of pain. Pain motivates us to get up from suffering and act creatively to give birth to health, wholeness, positive change, and victorious living. In her chapter "Wading through Many Sorrows," M. Shawn Copeland provides resources for womanist resistance to the disturbing dimensions of death.[18] Rosita deAnn Mathews wisely counsels those on the periphery on the art of using power for survival in systems of injustice.[19] The principles advocated by womanist theologians are gifts to be used by all who live as marginalized, irrespective of gender. A practical application of these ideas will guide hurricane victims in struggling for the renewal of their neighborhoods so that gentrification will not rob people from the land and the neighborhoods that they sacrificed to purchase and build.

As I reflected on the tyranny of Hurricanes Katrina and Rita, my mind turned to *Exorcizing Evil: A Womanist Perspective on the Spirituals* by Professor Cheryl A. Kirk-Duggan. In this voluminous work, she gives an extensive commentary on a spiritual that has relevance for the survivors of Katrina and Rita. The lyrics talk about hope in the midst of evil. They speak of disruption, disturbance, destruction, disappointment, and despair. They speak of storms that you and I cannot escape; but they uphold the power of prayer as humans unite with God for safety, security, and salvation.

> I been in the storm, so long.
> I been in the storm, so long children.
> I been in the storm, so long.
> Lord, give me a little time to pray.[20]

African American spirituality is not only a spirituality of survival; it is also a spirituality that is deeply rooted in the soul of a people whose victorious faith was rooted in the soil of a legacy that survived the middle passage, the dehumanizing of slavery, and the demonizing of separate but equal, all of which proved to be centuries of inequality. Black spirituality will enable and empower the victims of Hurricanes Katrina and Rita to actualize the statement of Professor Marcia Riggs to "awake, arise, and act."[21] According to Professor Teresa L. Fry Brown, their throats may be weary, but they will arise with new songs.[22]

Hurricanes Katrina and Rita have done their damage. They have destroyed the lives and earthly possessions of many persons. They have eliminated jobs and they have caused what pastor-scholar Matthew V. Johnson calls "psychic fragmentation." But the richness of black spirituality will bless the hurricane victims to "transform the absurd in their existence into something beautiful and meaningful and into the power to 'go on.' "[23] Professor Edward Wimberly speaks of how black suffering participates in "the eschatological plot." Professor Homer U. Ashby defines the eschatological plot of Professor Wimberly to mean:

> The biblical narrative is one in which the story of God's people is always in the process of unfolding. No single defeat or downturn marks the end in the eschatological plot. Rather, difficult times or seeming defeat point to a twist in the plot. The divine plan and outcome are still in place, but the way there has been altered.[24]

What roads we will travel in recovering from the devastation of Katrina and Rita are unknown to me; but I am confident that we will emerge a stronger people. Across the years the richness of black spirituality has sustained the courage, faith, and strength of the African American community. Perhaps the gift of black spirituality enables all of us to embrace the quest for the beloved community, which was the theme of the ministry of Dr. Martin Luther King, Jr.

Notes

1. See Anthony B. Pinn, *Why, Lord? Suffering and Evil in Black Theology* (New York: Continuum, 1995).

2. Ibid., 19.

3. Dwight N. Hopkins, *Being Human: Race, Culture and Religion* (Minneapolis: Fortress Press, 2005), 4-8.

4. Dorothy L. Sayers, *The Devil to Pay* (London: Victor Gollancz, 1939), 100.

5. Gustavo Gutiérrez, *A Theology of Liberation* (Maryknoll, NY: Orbis Books, 1973), 25-37.

6. Ibid., 175-76.

7. "President Bush Addresses the Nation," September 15, 2005, http://www.thepoliticalseen.net2005/09/15/bush_nation.

8. Ceci Connolly and Griff Witte, "Poverty Rate Up Third Year in a Row," *Washington Post*, August 27, 2004.

9. *Wikipedia*, http://en.wikipedia.org/wiki/New Orleans.

10. Patrick O'Connor, "K Street on Budget Sidelines," *The Hill: The Newspaper for U.S. Congress*, October 26, 2005.

11. The Institute for Policy Studies and Cities for Progress, http://www.ips-dc.org/citiesforpeace/healthnational2004.pdf.

12. *Pravda.RU*, http://english.pravda.ru/, October 27, 2005.

13. Energy Information Administration, http://www.eia.doe.gov/oiaf/aeo/index.html, October 12, 2005.

14. Michael Emerson and Christian Smith, *Divided by Faith* (New York: Oxford University Press, 2000), 171.

15. Homer U. Ashby Jr., *Our Home Is Over Jordan: A Black Pastoral Theology* (St. Louis: Chalice Press, 2003), 3.

16. Paul Laurence Dunbar, "We Wear the Mask," in *Black Voices: An Anthology of Afro-American Literature*, ed. Abraham Chapman (New York: New American Library, 1968), 355.

17. Emilie M. Townes, *A Troubling in My Soul* (Maryknoll, NY: Orbis Books, 1996), 84.

18. M. Shawn Copeland, "Wading through Many Sorrows," in Ibid., 109.

19. Rosita deAnn Mathews, "Power from the Periphery," in Ibid., 92.

20. "I Been in the Storm" in Cheryl A. Kirk-Duggan, *Exorcizing Evil: A Womanist Perspective on the Spirituals* (Maryknoll, NY: Orbis Books, 1997), 67.

21. See Marcia Y. Riggs, *Awake, Arise, and Act* (Cleveland: Pilgrim Press, 1994).

22. Teresa L. Fry Brown, *Weary Throats and New Songs* (Nashville: Abingdon Press, 2003), 25. For additional information, see Riggs, *Awake, Arise, and Act*.

23. James A. Noel and Matthew V. Johnson, eds., *The Passion of the Lord: African American Reflections* (Minneapolis: Fortress Press, 2005), 12.

24. Ashby, *Our Home Is Over Jordan*, 11.

NEW ORLEANS IS AMERICA

DWIGHT N. HOPKINS

Hurricane Katrina showed the United States what it should have seen before. Under monopoly capitalism, fewer and fewer people amass wealth, and more and more people become poor. In the midst of all of this, black folk receive their disproportionate negative share. The defining crisis in the United States is not terrorism but poverty. In fact, this country is witnessing the largest redistribution of wealth and disposable income upward than at any time in human history. The very definition and purpose of "capital-ism" is to accumulate capital privately in fewer and fewer hands. The structure of capitalism, in contrast to the good intentions of different monopoly corporate individuals, is to use resources in such a way that the owner of these resources can make a profit at the expense of someone else. The goal is not helping society's citizens to live healthy spiritual and material lives. The purpose is not to build community. The immediate and long-term end is to increase the privatization of wealth among a small group of white American families headed by men. At the same time, for the elite barons, Christianity is only useful as long as Jesus does not threaten monopoly capitalism. In this sense, the "prosperity gospel" movement in Christian churches is receiving increased visibility because they are aligned with the current political and economic climate.

Katrina just pulled the covers off the reality of poverty—a poverty that is disproportionately racialized and disproportionately feminized. For example, the majority of American citizens on welfare are poor and working-class white women.[1] Prior to the August 29, 2005, Katrina disaster, more than one-third of New Orleans residents hovered at or below the official poverty line. They literally lived in the bottom—areas below sea level; areas guaranteed to yield death and destruction if the city ever flooded. Then we add on the working-class poor. And if you were black or brown and had a college education and a professional job, you would fall back into the poverty or working-class status of your parents' generation if you missed two paychecks. No question; the face of poverty in that city was black. These faces also included, to a lesser extent, Vietnamese, Latino, and white faces.[2] The horror photos and eyewitness reports told the world of black, dead, floating bodies. Why were so many African American people left behind? Sixty-eight percent of blacks were overwhelmingly poor. The rich white (and the fortunate professional and middle-income blacks) could afford to leave because they owned cars; had money for airline, train, or bus tickets; or had inside connections to big businesses or government that rescued them.[3]

New Orleans is not an aberration or exception: it represents America. In 2004, there were 1.1 million more North American citizens in poverty than in 2003. Since the current president of the United States came to power, there has been a 17 percent poverty rate increase. The infant mortality rate in Washington DC is twice that of Beijing, People's Republic of China, whereas Cuba is moving to eliminate infant deaths. A black American baby has less chance of survival than a baby during its first year of birth in Kerala, India. The United States ranks forty-third in world infant mortality rate categories. Though it is the richest country in the world and the undisputed global superpower, the United States has worse poverty than other industrialized nations—twice as much as Canada and Britain and three times as much as many European countries. Thirty-seven million or 12.7 percent of American citizens are officially poor. But the figures are more like 48 million or 18 percent. Why? These statistics are so heinous because the federal government's definition of poverty for a household is obsolete and irrelevant to the reality of those in structural poverty or the working-class poor. For instance, the official federal poverty policy states that a family of four is in poverty when their household income falls to $18,850. In other words, all families of four with incomes of $18,851 and up are not in poverty![4] And if the poverty criterion were raised above barely surviving but equated with homes that are thriving and experiencing human dignity, the numbers of poor would swell and really show the true face of American poverty. In other words, millions and millions of U.S. citizens survive daily in poverty while federal politicians pass policies in favor of capital accumulation and not in favor of people.

To add insult to injury, the federal government (the executive, judicial, and legislative branches, excluding the Congressional Black Caucus) waited five days before responding to these black bodies (some frightened and alive; some decaying and dying). Eventually, African Americans were plucked out of Katrina's deadly remainders. But what kind of massive removal has taken place? Figures abound—was it 1.4 million African Americans displaced or several hundred thousand? At any rate, a whole lot of poor black people are out of New Orleans. Plans for rebuilding this city suggest that ongoing urban renewal could indeed be called "black folk urban removal." Or is it "racial cleansing"? It is hoped that thousands of poor African Americans can afford to return to their own city; but the rebuilding plans give us ominous signs. Immediately after Katrina hit and up to the current moment, giant real estate corporations began land speculating and forcing New Orleans housing prices up. These potential and real buyers of African American residential and small business properties are not little mom-and-pop operations or regular working-class citizens trying to get a piece of the "American dream" where they can raise their children.

The reality is quite the contrary. Major corporate elite players and wealthy individuals bought individual homes and groups of homes at one time. For instance, one capitalist company purchased one hundred fifty homes.[5] Their plan is to sell real estate as commodities with inflated prices for capital and income accumulation. Under capitalist logic and ethics, this is merely making good and sound business decisions. There is no law preventing such transactions in America. Actually, the U.S. Constitution and public fiscal policies encourage such actions. Here is precisely the point. Capitalism legally displaces and hurts the marginalized majority of society. Its lifestyle is for a small group of citizens to monopolize the resources of the earth. Inevitably, others get hurt; and the added racial factor means most blacks get hurt even more. Under U.S. culture, to have a law stating that people's spiritual and material health, coupled with the basic necessities of survival and thriving, are the nation's number one priority contradicts the legal right and moral practice of capital's existence to exploit people for the benefit of a few families. Capital rules, not people. If the opposite were the case, we would not have capitalism.

New Orleans represents the United States. The Crescent City exposes increasing poverty of black, brown, red, yellow, and white citizens throughout the fifty states. It exposes the hyper redistribution of wealth upward into fewer and fewer hands. The way of living in America is not primarily defined by the good intentions and wholesome nature of individual powerful people. Rather, a system or structure provides the context for how citizens interact (that is, live and die) on a daily basis.

The parallels and connections between New Orleans and Iraq underscore this point. Katrina and shortly thereafter Rita hit the poor, and, in a disproportionate racialized fashion, the black poor. The young men and women sent to Iraq are overwhelmingly poor and working class; again with a disproportionate racialized element. Few wealthy New Orleans individuals or families have been reported as killed or devastated by Katrina. So too, few wealthy Americas are fighting in Iraq (and Afghanistan). Remember the part of Michael Moore's movie *Fahrenheit 911* where he asks U.S. congressmen if they would send their children to fight in Iraq? The response of one white congressman was symbolic. He looked at Moore as if Moore had escaped from an insane asylum for even asking the question. In America, most people do not even imagine wealthy people fighting and dying for their country. Normative U.S. ethics assume that the poor will shed blood—but for what?

The cleanup of New Orleans and the natural resources in that region and the cleanup and reconstruction of Iraq offer some clues. In September, a month after Katrina, some estimates put the trashing and rebuilding of the Gulf region at two billion dollars a day, or sixty billion dollars a month. The U.S. occupation and colonizing of Iraq costs more than eight billion dollars a month, or more than ninety-six billion dollars a year.[6] An obvious series of questions comes to the surface immediately. Who is paying this money? Where is it coming from? And who is getting this money? Where is it going? The financial resources originate from several sources.

One source is the budget surplus inherited from the previous White House. In October 2000, the federal budget enjoyed a surplus of two hundred thirty billion dollars. With the January 2001 inauguration of a new presidential regime, that surplus began to move in a negative direction. Specifically, increased tax cuts for the wealthy eased into federal policy along with increased spending on pet projects (i.e., so-called pork-barrel kickbacks) for financial and political supporters of the new administration. When the top 10 percent of wealthiest citizens no longer had to pay any taxes or token taxes, the federal government could chew on its surplus and still appear afloat.

But then things changed. Foreign nationals became angry at U.S. global policy and used American commercial planes as suicide payback on September 11, 2001. In response, the federal government (i.e., executive and legislative branches, with no opposition from the judicial branch) and its monopoly corporate sponsors decided to go to war in Iraq. Quickly, a national surplus evaporated. What was once a black balance sheet became red. So, to pay for a contrived war, the second avenue of federal income is borrowing from China and Japan. At first glance, it seems as if the People's Republic of China and Japan are covering American expenses in Afghanistan and Iraq. In reality, the billions owed on the principal and the billions owed on the interest fall to our children and our children's children. If history and today's reality hold for the future, those children will disproportionately be the working poor and people of color communities writing the checks by way of federal taxes in payroll deductions and downsizing.

A third source to pay for Iraq and Katrina comes from increased taxes on small businesses and middle- and lower-income Americans and their households. The majority of Americans are struggling to survive by leveraging whatever resources they have and by digging their lives and their futures deeper in loans and debt.

A fourth source is robbing some of the sacred cows that citizens hold dear. The federal government has been borrowing and continues to borrow money from the Social Security trust fund and employee pension funds. The government simply deposits IOUs in the vaults of these lenders.[7] This way of behaving mortgages the future of our elderly, our children, and the people who have and continue to build this country— working people.

A fifth source to cover the expenses of Katrina and Iraq is the "cost saving" measure of eliminating social programs for the most vulnerable citizens of this country—the elderly; the sick and medically dependent; the unemployed, underemployed, and underpaid; the widows; the homeless; the retirees; the veterans without benefits; the incarcerated; those lacking adequate shelter, food, and clothing; the emotionally and mentally abused; people needing education; and those people who lack hope in a better future.

Where did the October 2000 surplus go and who is receiving the Gulf Coast two billion dollars a day and Iraq's seven billion dollars a month outflow of monies? The answer is simple: a small cohort of superwealthy families are reaping the whirlwind of billions of dollars. The dollar figure (let alone the redistribution upward through acquisitions and mergers of concrete, material wealth) is astounding. Again, the October 2000 federal budget surplus was two hundred thirty billion dollars. The current federal budget deficit is eight trillion plus. The federal government has given away more than eight trillion plus two hundred thirty billion dollars to somebody. Post-Katrina cleanup and reconstruction and post-Iraq invasion and reconstruction provide pointers.[8]

Many of the same monopoly capitalist corporations are receiving no-bid contracts in both instances. For example, Halliburton and others now operate in Iraq and the Gulf region. A small group of U.S. private firms decide the fate of the oil and gas natural resources of Iraq. Money is taken from the majority of the people of the United States—and our children's pockets and futures—and given in a no-bid process to a handful of wealthy families. The taxes of everyday citizens pay for the military support of these wealthy firms who make money in the reconstruction of Iraq while these same firms take over the ownership and profits of the Iraqi people's oil reserves. Poor and working-class U.S. citizens, disproportionately black and brown, die and receive wounds in battle to help the megarich. Likewise, poor (particularly black folk) suffered the most from Katrina and Rita. Borrowed money (i.e., debt that our children will inherit) and resources from cut social programs go to similar monopoly barons who are in charge of Katrina removal and rebuilding; and, the beneficiaries of the new New Orleans reconstructed will not be mainly poor and black people.

The elite banks, too, reap rewards. Anyone in the United States who has a credit card knows that credit-lending institutions and banks are rapidly eating each other up through mergers. This means bank ownership consolidation lands in fewer and fewer hands. Therefore, the role of banks in financing the future of the Gulf Coast region and the Iraq occupation indicates a further dynamic of wealth redistribution upward. For that tight inner circle of banks, financing organizations, private reconstruction businesses, and military suppliers, it is a glorious day in the good old U. S. of A. For most U.S. citizens, however, the financial, political, employment, medical, housing, household debt repayment, and spiritual uncertainties and pressures persist. Malaise, not capital accumulation, is the order of the day. Given this scenario for "mainstream" America, need we say anything about black folk's precarious status?

In reviewing a healthy way forward for the post-Katrina/Rita Gulf Region—a symbol for an alternative future for the United States—there are at least two mistakes we need to avoid. First, we need not focus all or most of the attention on the personal attributes of the president and his wealthy friends and political allies. Painting individuals as evil and demonic does not allow the possibility (or "miracle") of change for any human being.

Second, satanizing these individuals actually can blur the real culprit in the Katrina/Rita tragedy and subsequent reconstruction. The real demon exists in the structure of monopoly capitalism—a transgenerational (thus transcendent) beast whose ethics is a prosperity gospel. That is, according to the prosperity gospel, the essence of Jesus Christ is the accumulation of private wealth and redistribution upward of a country's natural and human-made resources. This spiritual, economic, and political structure underlies the rationale why the current federal administration refuses to sign the Kyoto Accord banning human-made toxic waste. Monopoly corporate interests, who instruct the U.S. presidential office, fear a loss in profits if they have to care about the destruction of the environment. Human-made lethal waste emissions influence global warming, which increases the intensity and levels of a hurricane's force. Hurricanes and extreme storms do occur during the cyclical flow of nature. The difference, however, is that global warming ratchets up the strength from, say, a Category 2 or 3 to the more devastating movement of Category 4 or 5.

Likewise, independent studies, available to national government, had already mapped the life-threatening scenario of Hurricane Katrina.[9] But nothing happened because it would have cost money to secure New Orleans from catastrophic flooding. In addition, because black folk constituted the highest fatality and injury rates in these predictable case studies, national government was reluctant to reorient priorities to forestall the inevitable and known consequences of a Katrina-like occurrence.

The system of elite hoarding and its prosperity gospel contradict the fundamental path of Jesus the Christ. The majority of the recorded words of Jesus in the Christian gospel indicate a God whose primary purpose is to share resources with all people, especially the poor. The literal words in the biblical Gospels and the overwhelming metaphorical parables attributed to the mouth of Jesus focus on poor folk and working people. The reason the rich man has a difficult and unlikely possibility of entering heaven, Jesus teaches, is because this man puts faith and trust in mammon—the personal accumulation of capital and income. He cannot sell all that he has hoarded and follow the path. Yet, Jesus offers clear and decisive criteria for entering heaven. And that belief and witness exclude and argue directly against a prosperity gospel. Rather, the necessary way of the path of Jesus is following Jesus where Jesus is already present; that is, among the elderly; the sick and medically dependent; the unemployed, underemployed, and underpaid; the widows; the homeless; the retirees; the veterans whose benefits are under attack; the incarcerated; those lacking adequate shelter, food, and clothing; the emotionally and mentally abused; people needing education; and those people who lack hope in a better future (see Luke 4:18 and Matthew 25:31-46).

From Jesus' birth narratives to his life in opposition to official state endorsed religious leaders (i.e., the superpower president and national television prosperity gospel preachers of his time) to his recorded words in Luke (i.e., where he proclaims that the Spirit of the Lord is upon him and commands his personal mission to be with and for the poor) to his own definition of the Great Commission for those who follow his path (i.e., the sheep and the goat instructions are the direct content for what his disciples are to be and do), the gospel is for the poor and working people and against superelite individuals and families and their national clergy representatives. Following a prosperity gospel of capital and income monopolization, the latter created a false war in Iraq not to follow the gospel of Jesus but to control the oil wells, oil lines, and oil distribution and sales. Similarly, the false Iraq war was made up so these robber barons could make profit off of no-bid contracts. Pursuing the same demonic gospel, similar elite forces are reaping a whirlwind of profit and wealth in Katrina's deadly aftermath.

If the prosperity gospel preachers separated U.S. Christian capitalism from Jesus' gospel, their theology would likewise change toward the lower sectors devastated by Katrina and Rita. First, we all need to affirm creation as belonging to a power greater than human productive capabilities. In other words, we two-legged creatures are stewards. Stewards are called to share with others the resources that God has allowed humans to share in. If God created and owns air, fire, land, and water, then a small cohort of families owning the majority of wealth goes against God's ownership. Second, Jesus' own mission and his mission for his followers focus on those U.S. communities signifying the least segments in society. Thus, the health and sanity of the United States would consist of free health care; free education; free or subsidized transportation; free or subsidized housing; free medicines; free vacation and recreation for poor and working-class people; guaranteed employment for all; affirmation of different languages; welcoming strangers; and special consideration for the Native Americans, the original dwellers of this time and space that some call the United States.

In this midst of following the Jesus gospel, we have to attend also to the political and cultural requirements of God's positive relation with oppressed racial and ethnic communities. The African American folk in New Orleans are a case in point. Freely sharing all resources that belong only to God applies to the entire poor and working people in the rebuilding of the Gulf region. Simultaneously, we have to safeguard the rich and historic cultural contributions, particularly African-derived music and religions. New Orleans jazz and blues; the unique flavors of food; the more direct connections to African legacies of burial, specific African Christian forms; black English; folktales; vodun; sensuality of the black body—all bring vibrant life to the African American neighborhoods and parishes and to the United States in general. Politically, the racial dimension cautions us against reconstructing a new New Orleans that erases or dilutes poor black folk's voting and grassroots organizational infrastructures. Rebuilt price-inflated residential and commercial real estate, therefore, pressures against the grain of maintaining political cohesion for culturally unified racial, ethnic parishes. The fear of antiblack racial dispersion among returning evacuees or, worst-case scenario, the prevention of black poor and working people from returning home, thins out a potential voting block for progressive change.

The handling of New Orleans and the wider Gulf region can set the pace for the rest of the United States. Will the gospel of prosperity of U.S. Christian, monopoly capitalism prevail, or a gospel whose normative gauge hinges on the well-being of the bottom of society? The nation called the United States clearly has access to material resources, some of which are questionable because of historical and current removal from so-called Third World countries. The eight trillion plus two hundred thirty billion dollars given to the elite by the federal government clarifies the reality of wealth access. The persisting problematic consists of the overall country's will, determined by all classes and racial and ethnic groups. A will linked to justice, compassion, and a business ethic of common wealth sharing fundamentally derives from a view of a divinity whose very being and works ooze with a vision of a new tomorrow that begins today.

Actually, Katrina and New Orleans and Rita ask us, What kind of "now" will we leave our children and our children's children? One religion offers a seemingly endless, postponed debt along with a depletion of natural and technological resources for the private coffers of roughly 10 percent of the top of society. Another way of life belief points to healing of individual spirit, equal collective economic stewardship of God's total creation, and respect for creative African American culture. One way walks down the norm of the "Wall Streets" of the country while ever prompt to craft black folk as racial scapegoats; the other always normalizes public conversation around the path of Jesus' presence with the joyful and suffering realities of people dwelling in the low-lying lands of our urban and rural areas. The latter good news dares to go beyond the accepted perimeters of established debates around Katrina and Rita.

Katrina, Rita, and a new New Orleans present an opportunity to rethink, redo, and rebe a new America. The old New Orleans is the old profit-driven spirituality. There is nothing sacred or permanent about such a society. Human beings created the status quo and human beings can alter it. We have to envision that a better world is possible.

Notes

1. See Frank D. Gilliam, "The 'Welfare Queen' Experiment: How Viewers React to Images of African-American Mothers on Welfare," http://repositories.cdlib.org/ccc/media/007.

2. See *Atlanta Journal-Constitution*, September 14, 2005, B3.

3. See Cornel West, "Exiles from a City and from a Nation," *The Observer* (United Kingdom), September 11, 2005, 1; and Peter D. Bell, "Poverty Requires More Than a Quick Fix," *Atlanta-Journal Constitution*, September 19, 2005, A13.

4. See "Facts about Poverty That Every American Should Know," http://www.osjspm.org/101_poverty.htm; Nicholas Kristof, "A Nation Lets Down Its Most Vulnerable," *Atlanta Journal-Constitution*, September 7, 2005, A15; and David Brady, "Poor More with Us Than We Know," *Atlanta Journal-Constitution*, August 29, 2005, A9.

5. See *Chicago Tribune*, October 5, 2005, section 1, p. 7.

6. See the June 16, 2006, transcript of Rep. John Murtha's House speech on Iraq withdrawal, http://www.alternet.org/blogs/themix/37707/.

7. See *Newsweek* CXLVI, no. 13 (September 26, 2005): 32.

8. Ibid., 28-29.

9. See *Washington Post*, March 3, 2006, A01; "Army Corps: *Washington Post's* Grunwald Criticizes Congress' Relationship with Army Corps," E&E TV, June 12, 2006, http://www.eande.tv/transcripts/?date=061206; and Robert Caldwell Jr. and Joanna Dubinsky, "New Orleans: The Making of a Social Catastrophe," http://www.fflic.org/node/10, the website of Families and Friends of Louisiana's Incarcerated Children.

WE, TOO, ARE AMERICA: BLACK WOMEN'S BURDEN OF RACE AND CLASS

DIANA L. HAYES

Z ora Neale Hurston, in a memorable statement now more than fifty years old, had her fictional character Nanny state: "The [Black] woman is de mule uh de world. . . . Ah been prayin' fuh it tuh be different wid you. Lawd, Lawd, Lawd!"[1] And so, black mothers and grand-mothers have been praying for the sake of their daughters for more than four hundred years as they have attempted to deal with the beauty but also the burden of being black and female in the United States. To be black was seen, historically, as the antithesis of being female, of being beautiful, as African women brought to the Americas in chains quickly learned. They were everything a white woman was not, and were con-demned—and still are—and often severely punished for any efforts on their part to see themselves in ways that contradicted the images white society had molded for them.

> The social and legal institution of slavery which assigned ownership of slave women's bodies to their owners, officially denied slave women the right to reject any sexual overtures and, by extension, also denied the presumption of virtue to [black women, free or slave] who often had to deal with the sexual advances of white men.[2]

In this article, I discuss and analyze the impact of Hurricane Katrina on black people on the southern Gulf Coast of the United States, especially African American women. Employing a womanist historical-critical methodology, rooted in the particular historical experience of African American women, I explore how black women, as depicted on the cover of every major U.S. and foreign newsmagazine, were the true face of this tragedy. Such recognition reveals the ongoing disgrace of U.S. unwillingness to confront and systematically deal with the overlapping issues of race, class, and gender in the United States. Throughout the weeks after the devastation, many questioned the impact of race, class, and gender as factors in the poor preplanning, the failure to ensure that all could safely evacuate, the scapegoating of black Americans as thugs and predators, and the slow response of the federal government. As we reflect on the treatment of blacks in the United States historically, the only answer is a shameful and denunciatory yes!

Sociocultural, Historical Context: Creating Black Savagery

Today, some four centuries later, black women, their children, and their men are still too often seen as the antithesis of humanity. Their blackness, their strength, their coping skills, their ability to survive all that was inflicted upon them led Euro-Americans to see blacks as quintessentially "other." During slavery, that otherness was the basis for their enslavement, for blacks were viewed as savage but tamable children who needed guidance and care if they were to survive in the New World, to which they had been forcibly and involuntarily brought. Slavery's aftermath, and the freeing of blacks in the South, lead to a redrawing of their otherness, one that casts a dark and evil gaze upon black men and women, rendering them as savages, incapable of being civilized, a danger to those who had sought to keep them under control. In either case, dominant culture saw them as less than human, barely civilized savages, incapable of self-control. Thus, it is not surprising that once blacks were herded like beasts into a dark, dank arena, the Superdome, and left without resources of any kind, the rumors (most of which have since been disproved) of a people running wild, raping, killing, fighting one another for the little food and water that existed, began to spread, accompanied by other stories, avidly fed on by the media and too easily believed by many, of a city overrun by gangsters who were indiscriminately looting, killing, and attacking everyone in sight.[3] Logistically, this was impossible, of course, but it led to the halting of search and rescue missions so that the city could be "recaptured" from the comparatively small number of thugs while starving family members were arrested for taking diapers, infant formula, water, milk, and other items from stores that were themselves destroyed by the storm and its aftermath. This is how people are demonized, are rendered inhuman, and are therefore left open to scapegoating and further neglect.

Images of the black savage, usually male but also female, are still a part of the cultural history of the United States as generation after generation is exposed to the dangerous black man and the lazy welfare queen. Stereotyped and stigmatized, black men and women and their children, who in cartoons that entertained millions were depicted as idiotic and animalistic,[4] are still seen in the United States as less than others simply because of the color of their skin. If anyone doubts this statement or sees it as overly broad, they need simply to read the media and governmental depictions that proliferated in the aftermath of Hurricane Katrina.

Katrina was not an act of God but a powerful manifestation of nature's wrath. Its horrific impact was a result of humanity's indifference and greed. Those who suffered were of every race and ethnicity, but it cannot and should not be denied that those who felt the brunt of the hurricane and especially its aftermath were the poor who, in New Orleans and throughout the Gulf region, were predominately black and female. Hispanics and Native Americans were also severely affected but because of this nation's historical and often hysterical fascination with all things black,[5] they were the ones seen, heard, and ignored, as well as demonized, on national television.

Some Facts: Mapping the Poverty; Naming the Oppression and the Disregard

New Orleans was almost 65 percent black before Katrina hit. The unemployment rate in New Orleans was almost double that of the nation, and for blacks it was even higher; 35 percent were unemployed. More than 20 percent of residents of New Orleans live under the U.S. poverty line, most of them women with children. More than one hundred thousand or 20 percent of the population had no access to any form of motorized transportation because they did not own cars and learned too late that bus and train service had shut their doors.[6] The only way out of New Orleans was by car, if you were able to find enough gas, or by foot. Yet even that mode was not open to the many who were physically or mentally disabled, sick in hospitals or at home, elderly, or too young. Those who tried found out quickly, as the waters rose, that the outlying suburbs accessible by the Crescent City Bridge were not open to their efforts to flee; instead, rows of police with weapons in hand greeted them with a cruelty that was breathtaking. They wanted nothing to do with those fleeing for their lives, fearing they would overrun their towns.

> If anyone doubted that there were two Americas, this disaster has made those divisions clear. The victims have been largely poor and Black. The devastation from Hurricane Katrina only underscores the disastrous consequences of the Administration's failure to take even the most basic steps to alleviate poverty in the U.S. The Administration cannot ignore this reality.[7]

Yet that is initially what happened. As the waters rose and people frantically took shelter in the Superdome and the convention center in New Orleans or scrambled up into their hot and sealed attics, the nation watched as its president went to a birthday party, played a gift guitar, and only after four days of flooding, and with reluctance, ended his five-week vacation two days early and deigned to do a flyover of the now drowned city.

The events that transpired in New Orleans should not have come as a surprise to anyone; it had long been predicted but at the same time ignored. Efforts by parishes (counties) and the Corps of Engineers to rebuild, shore up, or in other ways strengthen and stabilize the levee system protecting the city had been underfunded for years, coincidentally the years of the Bush administration and the wars in Iraq and Afghanistan. Local politicians even admitted, as did the New Orleans *Times-Picayune*, that over several years, from 2001 to 2005, funds intended for the city's protection had been cut and redirected to these wars as well as to supporting the tax cuts and other gifts to the wealthy that the heavily Republican Congress supported.[8] Yet this story of neglect is even older. Senator Barack Obama was quoted as saying: "I hope we realize that the people of New Orleans were not just abandoned during the hurricane. They were abandoned long ago—to murder and mayhem on the streets, to substandard schools, to dilapidated housing, to inadequate health care, to a pervasive sense of hopelessness."[9]

The poor and black in New Orleans experienced neglect in all of its forms as the city flourished as a sought-after site for conventions and conferences. They were the ones who enabled these events to run smoothly—especially the women who made sure the beds and rooms of hotel guests were clean and properly made, who cooked behind the scenes while the chefs took the credit, who worked long hours as servers in restaurants and fast-food establishments, yet who often had not enough to feed their children and clothe them properly; but somehow they did. One of the comments made by a black woman who once knew what it was like to be poor and neglected struck me as I watched the unfolding horror of that long week. Oprah Winfrey, who toured the Houston Astrodome where thousands had been relocated, wondered at and admired the hair of little black girls whose mothers, in order to keep themselves sane as best they could, made sure their sons and daughters were clean; their hair neatly braided and pinned up with bows, braids, ribbons, even string—whatever they could put their hands on—to help their children and the children of those they collected on the way maintain their dignity and self-respect. Yet, Barbara Bush, mother of the president, likened their experience of near death from drowning, starvation, and dehydration, and their current life in the Astrodome without privacy or proper facilities for eating and sleeping, as a step up for the underprivileged.[10]

Loretta Ross made a powerful statement on the Z-Net (Z *Magazine*) online, on October 10, 2005.

> Poverty in America is not only racialized but it is also gendered. The aftermath of Katrina must be examined through a gender lens that identifies the myriad of violations experienced by women. A disaster like Katrina is a violation against the entire community, but when threats to women's lives are not recognized, and steps are not taken to ensure that they are, women become doubly victimized—by the disaster and by the response to it.
>
> The hurricane and the subsequent flooding exposed the specific vulnerability of women, children, the elderly, and the disabled by revealing the harsh intersections of race, class, gender, ability, and life expectancy. Many people could not escape not only because of poverty, but because they were not physically able to punch through rooftops, perch on top of buildings, or climb trees to survive.[11]

Initially, the media and government at every level sought to place blame on those who died for making incorrect or poor choices. The truth is that many who died in their attics and living rooms, who found themselves abandoned in the Superdome without food, water, and medicines, or dumped and left stranded on Interstate 10 in blazing heat for more than four days, had no choices. They found themselves at the mercy of others who should have taken the responsibility to ensure their safety but who, like Pontius Pilate (Matt. 27:15-26), washed their hands and thereby washed away the lives of thousands, asserting that they had to use their own initiative to escape the rising waters. Some even sought to blame single black mothers for their plight, admonishing them that if they had married the father of their children, they would be at a higher economic status and would therefore not have suffered as they did. This notion, of course, ignores the fact that white and Hispanic women are also increasingly having children without marrying; for some it is a matter of choice, for others a matter of immigration, but for none is it a willful decision to choose poverty for themselves and their children rather than marry. In actuality, however, there has been a significant decline in teenage pregnancies since the early 1960s, especially among African American girls, signifying greater rather than less responsibility on their parts.[12]

Again, this is not new but the same sad and horrific story played out now in the twenty-first century. Alisa Bierria, writing in the September 11, 2005, newsletter of Incite! Women of Color Against Violence, spoke painfully of "memories of hurricanes and floods past in New Orleans [that] help put Katrina in a historical perspective."[13] Her mother lived through Hurricane Camille, which hit New Orleans in 1969. As the waters rose in their home, her father and other men hurriedly smashed wooden barrels to build emergency makeshift rafts to save families from drowning. In 1927, the Great Mississippi Flood poured down into New Orleans, provoking white people to round up black people and force them into work camps held by armed guards. Black people were prevented from leaving, though the flooding had already begun. Some black people were used as human sandbags at gunpoint to keep the levees from breaking. New Orleans has a history of black bravery and ingenuity, as well as violent racism, in the face of environmental disaster.[14]

Bierria concludes:

> And as I am searching for ways to deal with this current disaster, I am also feeling a familiar rage that I felt after September 11, 2001. A terrible knowledge in my gut that this devastation could have been avoided if it had not been for actions of my government.
>
> But I am seeking out hope and I am turning my rage into organizing because I refuse to give up on my people.[15]

The Women: Like Hagar, Working for a Quality of Life in Community

Bierria's words are ones that echo down through the generations of black women who, forced to live lives seemingly bereft of all hope, still managed to reach down within themselves and bring forth not just hope but the courage to "keep on keepin' on" despite all that they had to deal with. Shorn of their right to the respect and dignity promised by God to all of God's creation (Gen. 1), black women, often at risk of their own lives, somehow made a path that those coming after them could walk. They fought against the diminution and degradation of not just slavery, but also Jim Crow segregation and all other efforts by their fellow Christians and others in the United States to deny them their rightful place in the human race and as U.S. citizens. Many were lynched; even more were raped and forced to bear children for the profit of their owners; but they resisted as best they could and, most important, they lived to pass on the knowledge and wisdom needed for black people to survive. Theirs was not and is not today an easy path to walk. Black women have truly, as Hurston noted, borne the burdens that others refused to bear, but they did so in order to ensure the survival of black humanity in the United States.

Delores Williams asserts in her discussion of Hagar, the concubine of Abram and the slave of Sarai, that black women had to work out their liberation in ways that were different from that of their men. Liberation was the final goal, but in order to achieve it black women had to first deal with issues of survival and quality of life.[16] What is the point of freedom if it is only for oneself and is at the cost of others? What kind of life is it if it is lived in barrackslike stadiums, in cities and states far from one's home, and without the barest of life's necessities to enable one to at least have some hope of a better day?

> The term quality of life . . . refers to persons, families, and/or communities attempting to arrive at well-being through the use of, search for and/or creation of supportive spiritual, economic, political, legal or educational resources. . . . In the context of much black American religious faith, survival struggle and quality of life struggle are inseparable and are associated with God's presence in the community.[17]

This mind-set obviously flies in the face of today's overemphasis on individualism and "I gotta get mine" ideologies that are systematically destroying all forms of community life in the United States. Black women have historically sacrificed themselves for their men and their children. Although today that is no longer necessary—nor was it ever fully legitimate or healthy—as black men and women have been able to climb out of the ghetto through education and other means, the emphasis on communal rather than individual success is still a critical aspect of black women's lives.

Alice Walker recognized this when she coined the word *womanist* in the early 1980s, which provided a framework that gave birth to a spiritual and theological movement that continues to develop to this day.[18] Cheryl Townsend Gilkes describes Walker's efforts:

> Alice Walker introduced the word womanist in 1982 when she sought an alternative word for organizing our thinking about black women's self-definitions, relationships, activities, and history and their meaning for the black experience. To my mind, her dictionary style definition offered a grounded theory of black women's culture that was constructed out of the dialogues within the fundamental female-female relationship of any culture, mothers and daughters, and the distinctive values ("loves") that she observed in the world of black women. Walker's definition asserts the existence of a black women's culture that values not only women and women's relationships but the men and the "entire community male and female." Walker identifies a fundamental commitment to the "survival and wholeness" of this community as a hallmark of this womanist idea.[19]

And the Beat Goes On: Black Women, Too, Sing America

There are many questions that still need answering after Hurricane Katrina. In the largest involuntary dispersal of humanity quite possibly in U.S. history, we must ask what will happen to those who were snatched from their daily lives, lost all that they had including proof of their identity, and were unceremoniously evacuated and dispersed throughout the country. The scenes brought back memories of slave auctions where men, women, and children were separated from one another and thrown into the back of wagons or led away on foot while the screams and despairing cries of their loved ones echoed in their ears. Just as, in the aftermath of the Civil War, thousands of African Americans took to dusty roads in the

South seeking to find a beloved mother, a lost child, a missing husband or wife, so today, many are still struggling to reconnect, attempting to find out who lived or died, where their children are, and what is to become of them. Some fear that it is the hope of many that they will settle where they were dispersed, becoming a problem for other states. But how do you rebuild a life without friends, lovers, and family in areas where no one looks, acts, or speaks like you or fully understands your plight? African Americans were forced to do this over and over again during and after slavery; must they walk this road again? The fear is that their homes, flooded and now polluted with mold and death, will be destroyed and, unable to make a claim without papers, they will lose even the property they owned as gentrification takes place, replacing poor blacks with higher-income whites. Can this really be happening in the twenty-first century?

Yet somehow, I believe, those who have been dispersed will return, perhaps not in the same numbers, but in sufficient numbers to demand that they are included in the decisions being made about the rebuilding of New Orleans; for New Orleans without African Americans will not be the same city. They built this city with their blood, sweat, and tears during slavery; they created tapestries in wrought iron; they flavored it with their gumbos and red beans and rice; they spiced it with jazz and the second line. African Americans are the roux that makes the city of New Orleans. Without them it will be flat and tasteless and the tourists will not return.

But most important, the women must come back. As Cheryl Townsend Gilkes notes, "if it wasn't for the women"[20] there would be no black community, in New Orleans or anywhere else in the United States.

> I have concluded that black women are fundamentally correct in their self-assessment: "If it wasn't for the women," the black community would not have the churches and other organizations that have fostered the psychic and material survival of individuals and that have mobilized the constituencies that have produced change and progress. At every level of social interaction and cultural production women are present, and at the same time they are conscious of the way the dominant white society disrespects and rejects their presence. Furthermore, white society historically has communicated that disrespect and rejection through a wide variety of stereotypes that have invited shame and exhortations that black women change their behavior.[21]

Loretta Ross asserts therefore:

> To counter this, women must seize our power and make our concerns known in the media, to government agencies, and to the humanitarian organizations. . . . Women must ask critical questions during this crisis. Who are the groups benefiting from this crisis and who are the groups hurting or excluded . . . ? We need to demand economic re-development strategies that center our needs, not those of casino owners, in the picture. . . . We have to claim our human right to sustainable development and insist on the enforcement of economic and social strategies. We have the right to quality schools for our children, jobs that pay living wages, communities free of environmental toxins, and opportunities to develop our full human potential. We have the right to reclaim our land, rebuild our homes, and restore our communities.[22]

Sadly, many of the Gulf Coast historical records of the efforts of black women to sustain life and promote community have now been lost for the most part as a result of Katrina. The archives of the second oldest religious order of black Catholic women, the Holy Family Sisters (1851), was flooded along with their motherhouse, their nursing home, and their schools. Their very existence was almost washed away, as were the records of the only black Catholic university in this country, Xavier University, most of whose buildings suffered serious damage. Dillard, Southern, and so many other black universities that thrived in New Orleans have been seriously damaged, but I have no doubt they will all over time recover. We are a resilient people, steeped in faith in a God who is a "wonder-working" God who will "make a way out of no way." We recognize and affirm that we are and have been a critical part of this country since its earliest beginnings and can, therefore, affirm with Langston Hughes that we not only can "sing America,"[23] but that we also are America in its fullest sense.

Notes

1. Zora Neale Hurston, *Their Eyes Were Watching God* (New York: Harper & Row Perennial Library Edition, 1990), 14.

2. Darlene Clark Hine, ed., *Black Women in America: An Historical Encyclopedia* (Bloomington: Indiana University Press, 1994), 457.

3. See September 12, 2005, issues of *Newsweek*, *Time*, and *U.S. News and World Report*.

4. See, for example, the film *Ethnic Notions*, directed by Marlon Riggs and narrated by Esther Rolle (California Newsreel, 1986).

5. See Robert E. Hood, *Begrimed and Black: Christian Traditions on Blacks and Blackness* (Minneapolis: Fortress Press, 1994).

6. "A Special Report: After Katrina," *Newsweek* CXLVI, no. 11 (September 12, 2005): 30.

7. A statement issued by the office of Congresswoman Barbara Lee, September 2, 2005; quoted on the same day in *Time Out*, an online news and politics journal, http://www.timeout.com/.

8. "A Special Report: After Katrina," 46.

9. John Alter, "The Other America," *Newsweek* CXLVI, no. 12 (September 19, 2005): 43.

10. Ibid., 44.

11. Loretta Ross, "A Feminist Perspective on Katrina," http://www.zmag.org (October 10, 2005).

12. Ruth Rosen, "Get Hitched, Young Woman," TomPaine.com (Common Dreams Newscenter), Sept. 26, 2005, http://www.commondreams.org/view05/0926-32.htm.

13. Alisa Bierria in the newsletter of Incite! Women of Color Against Violence, http://www.incite-national.org/issues/katrina.html.

14. Ibid. This disaster, like Katrina, displaced thousands of African Americans, many of whom stayed in the north, which resulted in a massive redistribution of blacks and later led to the shifting of many blacks from the Republican to the Democrat political party because of the former party's failure to live up to its promises. For more, see John Barry, *Rising Tide: The Great Mississippi Flood of 1927 and How It Changed America* (NY: Simon & Schuster, 1998).

15. Ibid.

16. Delores Williams, *Sisters in the Wilderness* (Maryknoll, NY: Orbis Books, 1993).

17. Ibid., 246.

18. Alice Walker, *In Search of Our Mother's Gardens: Womanist Prose* (San Francisco: Harcourt Brace Jovanovich, 1983).

19. Cheryl Townsend Gilkes, *If It Wasn't for the Women* (Maryknoll, NY: Orbis Books, 2001), 10.

20. Ibid.

21. Ibid., 7.

22. Ross, "A Feminist Perspective on Katrina."

23. See Langston Hughes, "I, Too," in Arnold Rampersad, ed., *The Collected Poems of Langston Hughes* (New York: Alfred A. Knopf, 1994), 46. In the title of my essay, "We, Too, Are America: Black Women's Burden of Race and Class," I have used *American* in keeping with its usage in Hughes's poem, while recognizing that *America* denotes both North and South America.

Myths and Media: A Socioethical Reflection on Hurricane Katrina

Doll Kennedy

My communities of accountability call me, as an ordained minister, ethicist, and black feminist, to expose the fatal collision of the many layers of oppression, particularly when the response exacerbates the problem and causes more harm. My essay explores the interplay of racism, classism, and sexism that turned a natural disaster into a nightmare of "epic proportions." This disaster could have been prevented had historical myths that portrayed blacks as "savages," "immoral brutes," and "overbearing strong black women" not dehumanized and overshadowed their victim status. After analyzing the nature of myth and the stereotypical, poisonous impact of these myths on the black impoverished in New Orleans, I examine the use of the media in the further objectifying, oppressive mythologized portrayal of blacks; the complicity of local, state, and federal government in creating more disaster after the fact; and the blatant disregard and the denial of the real status of black victims in the United States.

Myths Unveiled, Uncovered, Revealed

In the days following Hurricane Katrina it became clear to me that the media was portraying "the black image in the white mind" as well as providing the world with a close-up view of the plight of black people in

America. The images that [dis]graced the covers of newspapers and magazines, and headlined seemingly every radio and television show, reflected this nation's long history of oppression as it portrayed the helpless, poor black people of New Orleans, Louisiana, as thieves, malcontents, and irresponsible bums. These images reiterated stereotypical myths about Africans, myths that originated in America as early as 1492 when Christopher Columbus "sailed the deep-sea blue."[1]

These images, as appalling as they were, reflected the nation's long history of racism, classism, and sexism. However, to understand the significance of these images we need to understand the myths that made them possible.

Myth, according to Charles H. Long, is both true and fictive. "It is true as a structure with which one must deal in a day by day manner if one is to persevere, but it is fictive as far as any ontological significance is concerned."[2] This points to the power of myth because it creates a world and a way of seeing that world that in turn becomes the vehicle through which realities are understood and engaged. Noted scholar Lawrence Sullivan explains, "Myth not only shapes and explains social and economic political orders . . . it reveals the imagination itself, the human ability to draw together disparate experiences into one imagic reality."[3]

During the formation of the Western world, myths were used to exploit and conquer groups of people. By perpetuating the myth of the threatening other, the West was able to justify the murder of Native Americans and the enslavement of Africans. These acts eventually paved the way for Buchenwald, Hiroshima, Nagasaki, Auschwitz, lynching, and the post-hurricane Katrina disaster. These disasters happened because the myths that were perpetuated began to function as history, causing the lie of the myth to become the truth of history. In other words, entire races of people have been marginalized in the United States and the world because the dominant culture relates to them based on these myths: the myth of the savage who is animalistic in behavior and incapable of civilization explains why blacks are portrayed as sexual deviants as well as the increasingly high poverty levels among blacks; the myth of the immoral one who is carnal and is unfit to participate in civil society explains the disproportionate incarceration rate of black men; and the myth of the "strong black woman" explains why black women are depicted as being masculine, domineering, and amazonic creatures who possess an animalistic, subhuman strength.[4] These myths were created to dehumanize and objectify blacks.

The manifestations of these myths were not derived from observation, experience, or perceptible realities, but from a psychological urge.[5] This psychological urge creates an image that is ahistorical and creates an alternative reality—mythical reality. The myths created by this urge were so powerful that oftentimes when the people who created the myth came in contact with the actual people, they made no effort to adjust their previous understandings of the people. These myths got in the way and jaded the truth about the injustices that were wrought upon vulnerable victims. This is why the media images of blacks as "savages," "immoral," and "strong black women" seemed to saturate the television and print media's covers.

Media Madness: Demonizing the Victims

The portrayal of black people as "savages" was evident by the numerous images of blacks with scarves on their heads, rollers in their hair, matted braids, bloodshot eyes, and sweat pouring down their faces. They showed dusty children in filthy clothes playing around dead bodies, drug addicts shaking and displaying withdrawal symptoms, as well as angry men shouting at news crews. The media, while covering the tragedy, portrayed these victims as "savages." There was a white couple, stranded near the Superdome, who told a news reporter: "This is especially hard for us because we are not use to sleeping outdoors." Their comment suggested that the thousands of black folk in New Orleans were accustomed to doing so. Another reporter thought it was necessary to note that one black man was not wearing any shoes.

The portrayal of blacks as "immoral" gained national attention when two pictures surfaced: one of a young black male in chest-deep water that stated that he had just finished "looting" a local grocery store, and the other picture of a white couple in chest-deep water that said they had "found" food at a local grocery store. These pictures were examples of the double standard that exists when it comes to the analysis of black and white behavior. Black people, more often than not, are depicted in the worst possible light, whereas white peoples' behaviors are seemingly innocent and justified.

My outrage continued to grow as I witnessed the endless streams of attacks on the moral character of the victims of the disaster. They were said to have resorted to anarchy and lawless behavior that led Mayor Ray

Nagin, a black man, to order military and law enforcement officials to stop search and rescue missions and focus on restoring order and containing the packs of "looters" that were growing violent. Meanwhile, inflated reports were surfacing about women and children being raped and murdered inside and in the area surrounding the Superdome. One rumor that surfaced stated that women and children needed male escorts if they wanted to get to and from the restrooms without being attacked. These reports turned black men into sexual predators, lurking in dark places, waiting for the opportunity to fulfill some deviant desire.[6]

When it came to the myth of the "strong black woman," there was no shortage of footage of large black women taking care of the needs of others while their own needs were going unmet. Images of black women carrying heavy loads on their backs while pushing strollers or holding the hands of crying babies signified to the myth of the "strong black woman" because these women were portrayed as possessing an unnatural strength and as not seeming to have any real needs.

Many of the black women's selfless acts seemed to be promoted as newsworthy. During one interview, a news reporter gave a woman a bottle of water; the woman immediately turned around and rationed the water among her children without saving any for herself. The reporter classified the woman's actions as "strong" and "courageous" because she seemed more concerned with the welfare of her children than with that of herself. Another woman was seen assisting an elderly person when she herself was clearly in need of assistance, for she was eight months pregnant. To the media, the fact that these women seldom complained and continued to assist the needy suggested that they possessed an unnatural strength that was to be applauded. However, black feminist-cultural critic bell hooks contends that "when people talk about the 'strength' of black women they are referring to the way in which they perceive black women coping with oppression. They ignore the reality that to be strong in the face of oppression is not the same as overcoming oppression."[7]

This is why W. E. B. Du Bois argued that blacks must contend with the black image in the white mind as well as the white image of the black in the black mind in his book *The Souls of Black Folk*.[8] He pointed this out in his metaphor of the veil, which revealed two competing realities—that which is mythical and that which is historical.[9] The tensions created by myths serve to devalue black people and excuse white people from acknowledging the former's humanity and acting justly. This tension also requires blacks to lift the veil to see beyond the images that their oppressors unjustly project upon them. Therefore, any ethical reflection on Hurricane Katrina that desires to rescue the victims from the imaginations of their oppressors and stereotypical images requires a hermeneutical excursus from the myth of the "savage," the "immoral," and the "strong black woman" into a lived reality where truth is discovered and their victimization is revealed.

Hurricane Katrina uncovered the history of oppression as well as poverty within the United States, which is the manifestation of years of racism, classism, and sexism that resulted from the myths that depicted blacks as savages and immoral, as well as the myth of the strong black woman. These images displayed to the world the plight of blacks in America.

The victims' appearances bore testament to the fact that they were being forced to live under dire, inhumane conditions in the richest country in the world. Poor blacks and blacks who were now poor as a result of having lost everything resembled residents of a war-torn country, rather than taxpaying U.S. citizens, as they wandered aimlessly through the streets. Some of the people photographed in filthy-looking clothes swam from their homes through the toxic waters to the Superdome, whereas others had evacuated prior to the storm with just the clothes on their backs. The images of children playing near corpses, and relatives keeping watch over the bodies of dead loved ones, proved that some of the people who made it to higher ground still died as a result of the neglectful governmental system that conveniently broke down when it was called upon to respond to the plight of the black victims of Hurricane Katrina— a system that had a forty-eight-hour turnaround nine months earlier when the tsunami hit Sri Lanka. That the victims of the tsunami received greater empathy and support from the U.S. government than its own taxpaying citizens during what has been called one of the worst natural disasters in U.S. history is an indisputable fact.

Governmental Grifters: Defrauding and Swindling through Absence

After waiting for the government to send supplies for several days, people became desperate. Abraham Maslow's "hierarchy of needs" lists food, water, and shelter as basic human needs; when these needs are not met people become frustrated and desperate, eventually resorting to *basic sur-*

vival skills.[10] Therefore, the people cannot be classified as "looters" simply because they were trying to survive. Black people had trusted a system that by virtue of being citizens had "swindled them" into trusting that the government would live up to the constitution in "insur[ing] domestic tranquility, [and] promot[ing their] general welfare."[11]

As desperate as the situation was, Mayor Nagin ordered military and law officials to abandon their search for survivors and concentrate on "looters" and restoring order, instead of using all available resources to help bring supplies and food to the victims. Order could have been restored and "looting" would have ceased had more effort been placed on getting the victims' basic needs met. These needs seemed to have gone unnoticed by government officials for days. These heartless actions bring us back to the dehumanization of blacks in the United States, which serves to prevent them from being viewed as victims.

In the United States, blacks are rarely viewed as "victims," because of factors that I illustrated earlier—blacks have been dehumanized because of historical myths that characterized them as "savages," "immoral," and "strong black women." A victim is "one who has been subjected to cruelty, oppression, or other harsh or unfair treatment, or suffering death, injury, or ruin, as a result of an event, circumstance, or oppressive or adverse impersonal agency, whether or not the person might have contributed wholly or partly to the adversity experienced."[12] According to this definition, blacks could be classified as perpetual victims because of the intersectionality of race, class, and gender. However, Western society rarely acknowledges their victim status because to do so would expose the role that the governments play in the revictimization of blacks. To acknowledge black victimization would also be an admission that the United States is a society shaped around the interest of white people. But most important, the acknowledgement of blacks as victims would validate their humanity and require that something be done to alleviate their victimization and suffering.

The fact that the media dehumanized blacks in New Orleans explains why it took the government so long to acknowledge blacks' victim status actively and to respond to their needs. When a person's humanity is denied it allows for those who have dehumanized them to justify their oppressive behavior toward them. This is why, three days after the catastrophe, Mike Brown, the former director of the Federal Emergency Management Agency (FEMA), was able to deny knowing about the victims at the Superdome during an interview with CNN's Paula Zahn:

Brown: And so, this—this catastrophic disaster continues to grow. I will tell you this, though. *Every person in that Convention Center, we just learned about that today.* And so, I have directed that we have all available resources to get to that Convention Center to make certain that they have the food and water, the medical care that they need.

Zahn: Sir, you aren't telling me . . .

Brown: . . . and that we take care of those bodies that are there.

Zahn: *Sir, you aren't just telling me you just learned that the folks at the Convention Center didn't have food and water until today, are you?* You had no idea they were completely cut off?

Brown: *Paula, the federal government did not even know about the Convention Center people until today.*[13]

This is also why the National Guard and Louisiana's Governor Kathleen Blanco were able to deny the Red Cross entrance into the city by maintaining that if they entered the city, it would hinder the evacuation effort.[14] Red Cross officials defended their agency by noting that they had adequate supplies, people, and vehicles, but were prevented from entering Louisiana by governmental officials who claimed they needed twenty-four hours to provide an escort and prepare for the Red Cross's arrival. However, twenty-four hours later, a large-scale evacuation was underway and the Red Cross relief effort *never* reached New Orleans. In the meantime people were allowed to die on sidewalks.

This dehumanization and devaluing of black life is most apparent in the actions of President George W. Bush. In the days prior to the hurricane, Bush seemed to mention Katrina as a footnote during his congratulation speech to the Iraqis on their new constitution.[15] On the day of the hurricane, Bush dedicated one hundred fifty-six words to the hurricane during his forty-four-minute Medicare promotional speech. Fifty-one of the words are found in this quote:

> I want the folks there on the Gulf Coast to know that the federal government is prepared to help you when the storm passes. I want to thank the governors of the affected regions for mobilizing assets prior to the arrival of the storm to help citizens avoid this devastating storm.[16]

The day after the hurricane his concern for the people of New Orleans continued to dwindle, because during his speech celebrating the sixtieth anniversary of the end of World War II he acknowledged the victims with this statement: "We're beginning to move in the help that people need."[17] Two days after the hurricane Bush flew over New Orleans and released this statement: "It's devastating; it's got to be doubly devastating on the ground."[18] After seeing the devastation he decided to hold a cabinet meeting on the hurricane and delivered a nine-minute speech outlining the federal relief efforts.[19] Four days after the hurricane Bush finally made his way to New Orleans and said: "I know the people of this part of the world are suffering, and I want them to know that there's a flow of progress. We're making progress."[20]

As outraged as I was about the entire situation and the blatant disregard for the lives and welfare of the black people in New Orleans, I was seething at the actions of George W. Bush. His inability to understand or comprehend the fact that there were real people down there at the Superdome with children and needs of their own revealed his character to the world. George Bush's lackluster leadership allowed a systematic breakdown in relief efforts during one of the worst natural disasters in U.S. history and caused the unnecessary deaths of many black people.

Although Bush has apologized profusely, it does not absolve him from the role that he played in the victimization of the black citizens of New Orleans by not having capable, experienced leadership of FEMA and by not mandating FEMA officials to move in and provide food and supplies to the victims the day after the hurricane. The injustices that the people of New Orleans were forced to endure require more than a lifeless apology. Such blatant disregard requires a serious investigation into the intersectionality of race, class, and gender and the role that the government and media plays in perpetuating the myths that dehumanize black people in the United States. Instead of Bush requiring members of the Executive Office of the President to attend an ethics refresher course because of a CIA leak, he should personally take an ethics course that will teach him how to act on behalf of those who have been marginalized because of racism, classism, and sexism, as well as a black history course to illustrate the systemic oppression that blacks continue to endure because of the history of slavery and oppression in the United States.

Notes

1. Jean Marzollo, *In 1492* (New York: Scholastic, 1991).

2. Charles Long, *Significations: Signs, Symbols, and Images in the Interpretation of Religion* (Aurora, CO: The Davis Group, 1995), 183.

3. Lawrence Sullivan, *Icanchu's Drum: Orientation to Meaning in South American Religions* (New York: Macmillan, 1988), 18.

4. bell hooks, *Ain't I a Woman: Black Women and Feminism* (Boston: South End Press, 1981), 82.

5. Long, *Significations*, 96.

6. As a women's rights activist I am not saying that people were not raped during the days following the hurricane. I am saying that the media overexaggerated the issue in order to perpetuate the myth of blacks as being sexually deviant.

7. hooks, *Ain't I a Woman*, 6.

8. W. E. B. Du Bois, *The Souls of Black Folk* (New York: Fawcett, 1965).

9. Ibid., 5.

10. See Abraham Maslow, *Motivation and Personality* (New York: Harper, 1954).

11. See The Preamble to the Constitution of the United States of America. http://www.law.cornell.edu/constitution/constitution.preamble.html.

12. Ian Kruppa, "Perpetrators Suffer Trauma Too," *Psychologist* 4 (1991); 401-3.

13. Paula Zahn, "Desperation in New Orleans: Interview with FEMA Director Mike Brown," Transcript, September 1, 2005, http://www.transcripts.cnn.com/TRAN-SCRIPTS/0509/01/pzn.01.html. (Emphasis mine.)

14. "Red Cross: State Rebuffed Relief Efforts: Aid Organization Never Got into New Orleans, Officials Say," CNN.com, September 9, 2005, http://www.cnn.com/2005/US/09/08/Katrina.redcross/index.html.

15. "President Discusses Hurricane Katrina, Congratulates Iraqis on Draft Constitution," August 28, 2005, http://www.whitehouse.gov/news/releases/2005/08/20050828-1.html.

16. "President Participates in Conversation on Medicare," August 29, 2005, http://www.whitehouse.gov/news/releases/2005/08/20050829-5.html.

17. "President Commemorates 60th Anniversary of V-J Day," August 30, 2005, http://www.whitehouse.gov/news/releases/2005/08/20050830-1.html.

18. "Press Gaggle with Scott McClellan," August 31, 2005, http://www.whitehouse.gov/news/releases/2005/08/20050831-2.html.

19. "President Outlines Hurricane Katrina Relief Efforts," August 31, 2005, http://www.whitehouse.gov/news/releases/2005/08/20050831-3.html.

20. "President Remarks on Hurricane Recovery Efforts," September 2, 2005, http://www.whitehouse.gov/news/releases/2005/09/20050902-8.html.

Questions of Calamity and Justice in Luke 13:1-5

Eung Chun Park

Suffering is an issue that every major religion has struggled to understand or explain. Oftentimes, the ultimate desideratum in religion is expressed in the language of overcoming suffering. Disasters that befall a large number of people do not necessarily cause deeper suffering than individual calamities do, but they tend to raise questions that go beyond the scope of the individual victims. Those who had to evacuate from the Gulf Coast after Hurricanes Katrina and Rita have raised many questions. Certainly during these catastrophic events and since, hurricane victims, especially the poor, have known great suffering and have raised many questions. These questions often have more to do with concrete sociopolitical issues than with abstract theological ideas. The latter, if disproportionately emphasized, tend to obfuscate rather than clarify the former.

Luke 13:1-5 is a representative passage in the New Testament that addresses the issue of the meaning of disaster, humanly induced or caused by accident. This text contains two otherwise unknown sayings of Jesus about two recent incidents in which a group of people perished. Right on the surface of the text there is the question of the relation between suffering and sin. More remotely there is the issue of theodicy only covertly implied in the text. Perhaps not intended by the author of the Gospel of Luke, the text also raises the question of who is/are ultimately responsible for these disasters. What complicates the textual world of this passage is that there are multiple layers of traditions embedded in it. First, there is the perspective of the historical Jesus, who may or may not have said these sayings.[1] This position would have represented, among others, a viewpoint of a Galilean Jew from the peasant class who lived under the powerful presence of the Roman Empire at the hands of such colonial officers as Pontius Pilate. This perspective depicts a colonized people and as such all the Jewish characters of the story in our pericope would have shared it. Second, there is the invisible but dominant presence of the narrator of the Gospel of Luke. The narrator's presence would represent a perspective of the unknown author of the Gospel, who would have been highly educated (relatively speaking) and probably belonged to a higher socioeconomic class than Galilean peasants. Then finally there are the unidentified, unlimitedly diverse perspectives of intended and unintended readers of this Gospel.

This essay is an interpretation of these two sayings of Jesus in Luke 13:1-5 on the basis of historical critical analysis as well as reader response criticism. The historical criticism regards the authorial intent and the historical circumstances of the author, which it tries to reconstruct as objectively as possible, as determinative for the meaning of the text, while it disregards the subjectivity of the reader as irrelevant to the textual meaning. Conversely, reader response criticism recognizes the impossibility of "pure" objectivity and the unavoidability of the reader's subjective input in interpretation and invites the reader's self-conscious contribution in construing the meaning of the text. For this reason these two hermeneutical models are often regarded as mutually incompatible. They may or may not be so. Without giving a verdict beforehand, I will employ these two seemingly incompatible hermeneutical perspectives in this article as an experimental exercise to see if the two can inform each other. To avoid arbitrary distinction, I will do so not in a linear manner but in a more integrated way.

In the larger literary structure of the gospel this pericope belongs to the section of the great journey of Jesus from Galilee to Jerusalem (Luke 9:51–19:48). This journey is one of an innocent itinerary preacher of the kingdom of God toward a place of suffering and death. Even though it may not have been part of the authorial intent of Luke,[2] whose identity is hidden, a Galilean Jewish reader, who lived under the oppressive rule of the Roman colonial regime, would have immediately recognized it as a journey of his or her compatriot from one place of suffering to another and would have brought that aspect into his or her interpretive horizon of this pericope.[3] In other words, for the intended audience and even more so for the unintended Galilean Jewish readers, the theme of *suffer-*

ing looms large throughout the entire travel narrative in Luke 9:51–19:48, to which our pericope belongs.

More immediately, our pericope (13:1-5) is directly linked to what precedes it (12:54-59) through the adverbial phrase "at that very time" (*en auto to kairo*, v. 1), even though the current chapter division obscures it. The theme of the preceding passage (12:54-59) is the meaning of the present time (*ho kairos houtos*, v. 56). Jesus laments that people know how to interpret the appearance of earth and sky but they do not know how to interpret the present time. The present time is a time of magisterial cruelty (12:57-59) as well as a time of murder by a foreign ruler (13:1). Present time is a time of violence and death.[4] The call to discern and understand this aspect of the present time is part of the backdrop against which our pericope should be interpreted.

Our pericope can be classified as a dominical saying with a minimal narrative framework.[5] The only narrative element provided is some unidentified individuals (*tines*) who reported to Jesus about the Galileans whose blood Pilate had mingled with their sacrifices. Obviously Pilate murdered a number of Galilean pilgrims while they were offering sacrifices at the Temple of Jerusalem and mingled the blood of these murdered Galileans with that of the ritually slaughtered animals. This incident is not attested anywhere else. This event could just be a rumor without historical basis, or it could be something that really happened but escaped other historians' notice. Either way, such violent behavior would be well in accordance with other similar cruelties that Josephus reports about Pilate.[6]

To this report Jesus responds by saying, "Do you think that because these Galileans suffered in this way they were worse sinners than all other Galileans?" At least, in the text provided by the narrator of the Gospel of Luke, Jesus seems to be making an assumption that these individuals in Luke 13:1 or the crowd he was originally addressing in 12:54 believed that those murdered Galileans suffered the inhuman calamity because they were worse sinners than others. Even within the present context it is an unwarranted assumption. Whether fictitious or real, those who reported it or the crowd, who were most likely Jewish commoners from the peasant class, would have believed (as they should have) the murdered Galileans first and foremost to be innocent victims of Pilate's violent act. But such a natural reaction from the subjugated people finds no place in the current text that is dominated by the voice of the narrator that Luke has created in the literary world of the Gospel. Instead, it is implied that they blame the victims for their allegedly greater sins, and by doing so they implicitly regard Pilate as an agent of God's righteous pun-ishment. Such would have been an outrageous idea, at least for the colo-nized Jewish people, but that is what the text wants to communicate to unsuspecting readers.

Clearly in the Hebrew Scriptures there is a belief that God rewards the faithful and punishes the wicked;[7] hence the idea that calamities happen as a result of divine punishment for sins.[8] However, biblical writers also struggle with the reality that sometimes disasters just happen to innocent people without explainable cause. One way to deal with such a problem is to somehow find faults with those who suffer and preserve the justice of God. That will be a typical case of blaming the victims.[9] Another way is to raise the issue of theodicy by challenging the justice of God. Theodicy may be a difficult theological question but at least it gives the victims the benefit of the doubt.

Jesus, in Luke 13:2, apparently challenges the conventional idea of the direct connection between sin and calamity.[10] But, if he does so, he does to people who probably never invoked such a conventional idea for this case at all. Then the Lukan Jesus adds, "No, I tell you; unless you repent, you will all perish likewise (*homoios*)" (author's translation). In other words, Jesus universalizes the meaning of this particular murder incident by Pilate and warns his audience against the prospect of suffering the same kind of calamities. One striking aspect of this saying of Jesus is that Pilate, with all the imperial power that he represents, is completely out of the picture, even though he is solely responsible for the calamity.

Then it becomes clear at this point that only *apparently* does Jesus deny the conventional idea of the direct connection between sin and judgment in this passage. Jesus challenges only the degree of sin, not sin *per se*, as the cause of this particular incident.[11] In other words, he seems to be say-ing, "Those murdered Galileans were no greater sinners than you are. If they perished because of their sins, which are not necessarily greater than yours, you may also perish because of your sins, probably in a similar man-ner (*homoios*) unless you repent." In this statement, the actual victims are implicitly blamed and the equally helpless potential victims are warned and charged to repent while the real villain, who still possesses the power and will to kill innocent people, is not even mentioned, as if he had no reason to repent at all.[12] According to this statement, the potential calamities that the audience of Jesus might suffer at the hands of such a person as Pilate in the future will all be part of the divine punishment for not repenting whatever sins they have allegedly committed.

A popular way of dealing with this disturbing saying of Jesus is a spiritual interpretation. Jesus intentionally turns their attention from sociopolitical issues to spiritual self-reflections. In such an interpretation, Jesus is not unaware of the political dimension of the murder case, but he intentionally avoids discussing it because drawing spiritual lessons from it is far more important for him.[13] This line of interpretation is based on the unwarranted though popular assumption that spiritual matters and sociopolitical ones could be separated. Therefore, this interpretation is unrealistic at best and dangerous at worst. Such a spiritualizing interpretation will never adequately explain the glaring silence of the text on the imperial violence Pilate did to the subjugated Galileans, whatever the immediate cause was to trigger it. Moreover, by failing to address the issue of injustice, which is potently present in the text, it may even have an effect of condoning the imperial violence in the name of the presumed divine punishment.

The saying of Jesus in Luke 13:2-3 has a doublet in the following two verses. That is, Jesus volunteers a piece of information about eighteen people who were killed in an accident at Siloam. Then, in the same manner as the first saying in this pericope, he says, "Do you think that they were worse debtors/offenders (*opheiletai*) than all the others living in Jerusalem? No, I tell you; unless you repent, you will all perish likewise" (author's translation). The most significant thing about this pairing is that the two incidents are not of the same kind. One is a state crime of murder and the other a disaster probably caused by a natural cause such as earthquake or by mechanical failure. The latter does not involve human intentionality; the former certainly does. By combining these two as if they were of a same kind, the Lukan Jesus effectively brushes aside the difficult question of injustice in the case of humanly induced violence and finds as a common denominator between the two what he believes to be the divine punishment for sins. In other words, as Jesus puts together the two very different cases of disaster, as if they were the same at a higher level of abstraction, all the historical particularities are removed and what amounts to a generic statement of sin, repentance, and punishment remains.

Having thus judged spiritual interpretation as inadequate and misleading, we are left with only one option: to declare the sayings of Jesus in our pericope as disturbing and even scandalous. This is a result of reading the passage against the grain, that is, reading in resistance to the dominant voice of the narrator of the text. Our next step will be to identify and discuss the perspective of this narrator that seems to have colored the perspectives of the original characters in the narrative, including that of Jesus, which have now permanently been lost, if they existed (as I believe they did), independently of the narrator's viewpoint.

As was mentioned earlier in this essay, it is not an unreasonable conjecture, judging from the internal evidence, that the author of the Gospel of Luke is a highly educated person who belongs to a rather privileged class in the socioeconomic stratum. Also, this unknown author of Luke-Acts seems to be the only gentile person among the writers of the New Testament.[14] More important, the author of the Gospel of Luke and the book of Acts seems to have an apologetic concern as one of the main purposes of writing the combined volume; that is, to present the gospel of Jesus to the Greco-Roman world as a harmless, intellectually sound, and socially acceptable form of faith, and at the same time present the Greco-Roman world to the followers of the gospel of Jesus Christ as a positive field and fertile soil for mission.[15] That is why Pilate appears at the trial of Jesus as a "good guy" who finds Jesus not guilty of any charge brought against him and who even tries to release him (Luke 23:13-16). The same idea is operative in Acts 21–26, in which it is the Roman colonial officers who "rescue" Paul from the deadly plot of the "Jews," who are against him, and put him in protective custody. In other words, the author of Luke-Acts is pro-Roman.

These three aspects combined would have a significant impact on the hermeneutical stance of the narrator created by the author of the Gospel of Luke. As a gentile person, Luke does not share with first-century Palestinian Jews the existential plight of a subjugated people under a repressive foreign ruler. Therefore, he just does not understand at the visceral level the gut feelings that Galilean Jews have when they hear or talk about some of their compatriots whom Pilate murdered and ritually insulted. Instead, as a cultured Greco-Roman intellectual who honors law and order, he may want to give Pilate the benefit of the doubt, assuming that Pilate must have had good reason to do what he did.

So, between the characters and the narrator of the narrative there seems to be a huge hermeneutical or interpretative chasm with regard to the meaning of the calamities that befell some Galileans and Jerusalemites. In the current canonical context, the perspective of Luke's narrator is the sole dominant voice that has effectively suppressed or distorted the voice of the colonized, oppressed people. However, some readers of the Gospel of Luke, whether contemporary with Luke or later, whether intended or unintended, could intuitively understand what the lost perspectives of the colonized people must have been like. Others could not have. Most likely those who could are the ones who have experienced the humility of subjugation of some kind, directly in their own lives or indirectly through their collective historical memory. These particular kinds of readers are existentially disposed to read against the grain whenever they encounter such passages as Luke 13:1-5. With the hermeneutics of suspicion, their reading detects and exposes a perspective that overtly or covertly condones colonial injustice. By doing so, they may sometimes, if not always, be able to resurrect what was once a permanently lost voice of powerless people, however partial and vague it may turn out to be. I hope that is what has happened in this essay even on a small scale.

A benign form of deconstructive reading strategy is to find in a text something that reveals a crack in the system upheld by the text—be it a philosophical, ideological, or theological one—so that the whole system may disintegrate and collapse onto itself.[16] This reading strategy is not necessarily destructive, because by exposing the "less-than-perfect" nature of whatever system the text represents, this kind of reading creates a new meaning that invites a contribution of the reader(s) and therefore goes beyond the scope of the text. How, then, does this text inform our "reading" of the recent disasters on the Gulf Coast and its catastrophic aftermath?

The Gospel of Luke is known to be *the* social Gospel *par excellence* in the New Testament, for good reason. Luke indeed pronounces salvation as reversal (*katastrophe*) of social status and release (*aphesis*) of captives. This Gospel proclaims good news for the poor and the marginalized in a radically unqualified manner.[17] But in our pericope, in which both Jesus and his audience are part of the defenseless colonized people, an implicitly but potently colonial perspective prevails, which is a telling irony. I regard it as a small crack in the so-called Gospel of liberation. This crack may not necessarily cause the entire Gospel system to disintegrate, but it certainly alerts unsuspecting readers of the Gospel of Luke against reading too much with the grain. Also it may function as an antidote for any harm done by the passage with its complete silence about the unspeakable injustice inflicted by an unjust colonial ruler, who represented the dominion of the Roman Empire, which was the sole superpower of the then known world. That may be a new meaning that was never intended by the author of the Gospel of Luke but is nevertheless forcefully called forth by an unintended reader who tries to reconstruct by deconstruction.

When a catastrophe of such magnitude as Katrina or Rita happens, Christians raise a question about the role of God in it with a theological assumption that nothing happens without God's intention, and they immediately turn to the Bible for an answer. Then, if they read Luke 13:1-5 uncritically, their conclusion will be as follows. Those who suffered Katrina or Rita did so because they deserved it. They may not necessarily have been worse sinners than the rest of the world, but nevertheless they were sinners and therefore God duly punished them for their sins. The rest of the world should not rest relieved, because, unless they repent, they will perish likewise.

Such an interpretation and application of the Bible, although looking "truthful" to the text, leaves untouched the question of justice in terms of the race, gender, and class of the victims and the way they were treated. And, with a seemingly benign religious rhetoric devoid of any awareness of concrete sociopolitical dimensions of what is happening to real people in the real world, such an interpretation puts the blame on the innocent people, who have been doubly victimized by natural disaster and subsequently by unjust human treatment. What good is there in a religious rhetoric if it successfully preserves theodicy only by *not* addressing the question of unjust human systems and by doubly victimizing the most helpless people who had already been victimized? If such a destructive religious rhetoric is a result of reading the Bible with the grain, the other way of reading, that is, reading against the grain, might be able to provide an antidote.

A deconstructive reading of a biblical passage with a hermeneutics of suspicion, such as the one I employed in this essay, can be a painful exercise; but it is far less painful than seeing the Bible misused as a tool for victimizing the people whom God gives "preferential treatment," because of their being poor and marginalized. For, after all, biblical interpretation does not exist for its own sake; it should be done to restore, preserve, and enhance the justice and shalom of all God's people, especially those who have been deprived of the God-given justice and shalom in their lives.

Notes

1. In the color-coded edition of the Gospels by the Jesus Seminar, these sayings in Luke 13:2-5 are in black, which means that according to the collective judgment of the Jesus Seminar scholars they are not spoken by Jesus. See Robert Funk et al., *The Five Gospels: What Did Jesus Really Say?* (Santa Rosa, CA: Polebridge Press, 1993), 344-45.

2. By "Luke" I mean in this essay the anonymous author of the Gospel of Luke, without making a connection to any historical figure with that name.

3. The Travel Narrative (Luke 9:51–19:48) comes after the Transfiguration (Luke 9:28-36), in which Moses and Elijah discuss with Jesus his departure (*exodos*), which he

was going to fulfill in Jerusalem (v. 31). Because of the Greek word *exodos*, it has been sug-gested that there is an allusion to the exodus event in the Hebrew Scriptures. This allu-sion makes sense only when it is recognized that Galilee was indeed a place of subjugation for the Galilean Jews, just as Egypt was one for the Hebrew slaves. Then, with this allu-sion, the ultimate departure (*exodos*) mentioned in Luke 9:31 would have concrete polit-ical implications in addition to whatever spiritual meanings it entails.

4. Franklin W. Young, "Luke 13:1-19," *Interpretation* 31, no. 1 (1977). See especially page 62.

5. Bultmann classifies it under *Apophthegmata* and calls it a scholastic dialogue. See Rudolf Bultmann, *History of the Synoptic Tradition* (New York: Harper & Row, 1963), 54-55. *Dominical* pertains to Jesus Christ as the Lord; or relates to Sunday as the day of the Lord.

6. Joel B. Green, *The Gospel of Luke* (Grand Rapids: Eerdmans, 1997), 514. Here Green provides the following list of passages: Josephus, *J.W.* 2.9.4. §§175-177; *Ant.* 18.3.2. §§60-62.

7. Frederick W. Danker, *Jesus and the New Age: A Commentary on St. Luke's Gospel* (Minneapolis: Fortress Press, 1998), 259.

8. John Nolland, *Luke 9:21–18:34*, vol. 35B, *Word Biblical Commentary* (Waco: Word Books, 1993), 718. Here he has a list of passages for the connection between sin and calamity in Jewish literature.

9. Robert L. Cohn, "Biblical Response to Catastrophe," *Judaism* 35 (1986): 263-76. See especially page 268.

10. Cf. John 9:1-3.

11. Luke Timothy Johnson, *The Gospel of Luke*, Sacra Pagina Series (Collegeville, MN: Liturgical Press, 1991), 211.

12. Johnson, *Luke*, p. 213. Here Johnson correctly says, "The repentance called for by the prophet Jesus, of course, is not simply a turning from sin but an acceptance of the vis-itation of God in the proclamation of God's kingdom." Even so, in the immediate context of this pericope, the offence of blaming the victims is hardly alleviated.

13. Darrell L. Bock, *Luke*, vol. 2, *Baker Exegetical Commentary* (Dartmouth, MA: Baker Books, 1994). "Perhaps the crowd is curious to know if Jesus plans to do anything in defense of his compatriots. Jesus does not enter into the social, racial or natural issues, but instead turns the incident into an opportunity to issue a warning" (p. 1205); "But the oppor-tunity for political commentary becomes an occasion for spiritual reflection" (p. 1206).

14. Joseph A. Fitzmyer, *The Gospel According to Luke (I-IX)*, vol. 28, *The Anchor Bible* (New York: Doubleday, 1981), 41-47.

15. For a similar view, see Ben Witherington III, *The Acts of the Apostles: A Socio-Rhetorical Commentary* (Grand Rapids: Eerdmans, 1998), 68-76; and Ernst Haenchen, *The Acts of the Apostles: A Commentary* (Philadelphia: Westminster Press, 1971), 106-8.

16. An example of deconstructive reading by Derrida himself is the concept of *khora* in the *Timaeus* by Plato. The *khora*, which is a liminal space where human souls temporar-ily stay during their transmigration, belongs neither to the realm of *to on* nor the realm of *to phaenomenon* and therefore it destablizes the seemingly perfect dualistic ontology of Plato so that it eventually disintegrates and collapses onto itself. See Jacques Derrida, "*Khora*," in *On the Name*, ed. Thomas Dutoit (Stanford, CA: Stanford University Press, 1995), 87-127.

17. Joel B. Green, *The Theology of the Gospel of Luke* (Cambridge: Cambridge University Press, 1995), 76-91.

Shouting at an Angry Sky: Thoughts on Natural Disaster as Theological Challenge

Anthony B. Pinn

In this essay, I argue that natural disasters such as Hurricane Katrina pose a theological problem in that traditional modalities of theodicy do not prove useful, for they do not highlight human fault, such as original sin, but rather challenge traditional notions of theological anthropology. This challenge involves an inability to concentrate on what humans cannot accomplish because of ontological flaws, forcing instead a confrontation with limits on praxis resulting from evil within as a hermeneutic for assessing proper response to radical human need. Language is often nuanced in contemporary conversation by an unclear framework of wrongdoing. Finally, I suggest a useful response to natural disasters might: (1) entail a shift away from traditional theodical formulations that seek a rationale for trouble in intrinsic human flaws; and (2) an appreciation for humanism with a less explicitly theologically contrived retelling of the metanarrative.

The United States still tends to think of itself as privileged based on a divine economy of attention that marks "Americans" as a special group, one upon which God smiles and grants socioeconomic and political arrangements and a reach not granted to others. From the Puritans on, this perspective has guided the shaping of physical and intellectual geography, and it has framed a national epistemology, or way of knowing.

Substantial damage to this U.S. mythology of privilege has typically resulted only from large-scale wars such as the Civil War and both World Wars, massive economic decline such as the Great Depression, and more recent events such as 9/11 (but in a surprisingly superficial way, at least on the level of theological discourse and political rhetoric). Of course, one cannot forget the impact of natural disasters on this mythology.[1] Natural disasters of Hurricane Katrina's magnitude point out the fragile and in some ways illusionary strength of the United States, and punch holes in the dominant paradigm of national identity and self-understanding as a secure and unshakable power.

The metanarrative of uncontestable U.S. progress and security was shaken; and religious and political leadership has been unable to provide an adequate response—one that patches the holes in the mythology of U.S. resiliency. This is because natural disasters call into question theological aesthetics related to the geography of divine manifestation in that the earth, subdued and rendered beautiful through an economy of utility and productivity, is made "ugly" and unproductive. The "face" of God is hard for most to locate in the aftermath of such events—in the sewage, the destroyed human lives and bodies, the crippled industries, and so on. In short, the aftermath of natural disaster lacks the aesthetic qualities many find necessary when "mapping" religious life and its ramifications.

For the theologically minded, the first effort to address environmental trauma often involves theodicy, that is, an attempt to address massive, and what appears to be indiscriminate, destruction in terms of divine righteousness and moral justice. In its most crude and troubling form, this theodical response seeks to project the problem as one of sin, of theological anthropology, of human shortcomings. Such a stance often results in the religiously narrow-minded arguing that those who suffered the effects of the hurricane that destroyed much of New Orleans did so because of failure to follow the dictates of God. For New Orleans, this assumes, no doubt, that Voodoo offends the Christian God and that this God views with moral outrage celebration of the human body. In this regard, consider the religious rhetoric of Michael Marcavage, who runs Repent America, the evangelical organization committed to the transformation of American life through adherence to a rather strict and conservative reading of scripture. He argues that whereas we should pray for those affected by Hurricane Katrina, we should recognize the destruction of New Orleans as divine punishment for a permissive social ethos that embraces and celebrates what Repent America understands as problematic lifestyles. He says: "Although the loss of lives is deeply saddening, this act of God destroyed a wicked city. From 'Girls Gone Wild' to 'Southern Decadence,' New Orleans was a city that had its doors wide open to the public celebration of sin. From the devastation may a city full of righteousness emerge."[2] Marcavage's theodicy is marked by theological distortion, manipulation through which the challenge of ambiguity in scripture is forgotten, and the dilemma of interpretation ignored: God makes it rain on the just and unjust, or so scripture says.[3]

Others view natural disaster through the lens of theodicy and seek to provide comforting responses revolving around an individualized need for proper perspective on the arena of God's love and compassion. For example, according to internationally known evangelist Billy Graham, the spiritually sensitive should appeal ultimately to mystery with respect to the nature and meaning of natural disaster.

> I can recall walking through the aftermath of hurricanes in Florida and South Carolina, and a typhoon in India that killed tens of thousands, and earthquakes in California and Guatemala, and every time I have asked "Why?" Job in the Bible asked the same question thousands of years ago, and his only answer was that God's ways are often beyond our understanding, and yet He is sovereign and He can still be trusted. The Bible says evil is a mystery. Someday we will understand, but not now.[4]

Yet, for Graham this situation does no permanent damage to God's integrity because

> God knows what we are going through, and He still loves us and cares about us. In the midst of suffering and tragedy we can turn to Him for the comfort and help we need. Times like this will make us react in one of two ways: Either we will become bitter and angry—or we will realize our need of God and turn to Him in faith and trust, even if we don't understand.[5]

Although comforting on some level in that the basic attributes of God are undamaged and humanity's relationship to the universe remains intact, such a response is not enough.

I am not trying to remove the legitimacy of wondering why disaster occurs; such questions are natural. In fact, my initial response to Hurricane Katrina involved an attempt to view it using a hermeneutic framed by theodical considerations. Yet with further reflection it occurred to me that natural disasters are not addressed best as theodical matters.

Such analysis, particularly when combined with conservative political leanings as in the case of Repent America, masks (whether consciously or unconsciously matters little) what I would consider the more relevant and productive questions. Even those who propose theodicy-formulated responses that seek to point out the good humans accomplish in light of such misery—a redemptive suffering–type approach—seldom highlight the large structural issues that would benefit from religio-theological analysis.

Natural disasters expose an uneven "playing field" and lay bare the structures of injustice and discrimination that define the formation of life options. In this respect, ecological and social ethics trump theodicy as a tool of analysis. Furthermore, natural disasters such as Hurricane Katrina are an issue of theo-religious cartography in two respects: (1) the human construction of boundaries to mark space is disrupted if not destroyed; (2) in the wake of such disaster another mapping is exposed—the layout of human life options and the restrictions of more productive modes of citizenship and public existence are shown with all their inconsistencies and long-established inequalities.

Proper theologizing in such cases is a matter of justice-based responses to trauma, rather than attempts to theologize changes to the natural environment in ways that circumscribe conversation to traditional notions of theological anthropology and doctrine of God. I am not suggesting the "we can't know the mind of God" response so common in many modalities of the "prosperity gospel" advocated by figures such as Joel Osteen of Lakewood Church in Houston, Texas.[6] Confrontation with such trauma based on the prosperity gospel tends to be theologically weak in that its concern is based on an individualization of the American dream that seeks advancement, without questioning the structures that define and shape our very understanding of success.

A hermeneutic of environmental racism/classism and ecological/social ethics might provide a useful mode of analysis for natural disasters. And, the posture for this type of critical analysis—one that opens us to liberative processes and modalities of transformation—can be premised on strands of humanism that appreciate the integrity of human life within the context of a larger concern for the natural environment. With this in mind, several of the principles of humanism I have noted on numerous occasions prove helpful here:[7]

- humanity is fully and solely accountable for the human condition and is responsible for bettering life options for all humans;

101

- there is a strong commitment to both individual and social transformation;
- there is a controlled optimism that recognizes both human potential and human destructive tendencies.

By means of these principles, the "religious" are encouraged to concentrate on the application of theological and religious principles to the healing of the consequences of natural disasters while giving consideration to the forms of inequality that shape levels and rates of recovery. One of the benefits of these principles is the manner in which they give high regard, theo-religious primacy, to the physical body and the manner in which it is placed in time and space.

Humanists such as Alice Walker take this further and argue that such regard for the texture of life must include recognition of humanity as a part of the natural environment, resulting in an epistemological and ontological link between all that is. Yet, one need not be a humanist to embrace such a perspective. Christian womanist (and process-thought influenced) scholar Karen Baker-Fletcher speaks in theological terms about this ontological synergy. "It is necessary," she writes, "to move beyond the notion that 'man' is supposed to 'dominate' the earth rather than love it as we love our own bodies."[8] Furthermore, Baker-Fletcher continues, "This vital step toward liberation is interlocked with steps that resist the interlocking oppressions of patriarchy, classism, racism, and homophobia."[9] Disruption of the natural environment—disasters increased and strengthened by means of human deeds and misdeeds—raises questions concerning human failure to love deeply creation.

What Walker and Baker-Fletcher suggest points to a rejection of traditional notions of stewardship that allow humans to dominate the environment and that prevent modes of conduct in the face of disaster, fostering health and wholeness through a recognition of human need and the integrity of nature. The connections between human life and the health of the larger environment are vital but fragile when notions of human progress and development go unchecked.

Whereas Baker-Fletcher frames the ethical dimensions of this mutuality within the context of the Christ event, humanists avoid notions of transcendence—seeking instead to continuously concentrate on the "natural" dimension of the natural environment. Both Christians and humanists operate out of an ethic of belonging, but for the humanist this is grounded in human obligations and appreciations for complex and nurturing relationships. By grounding its work within the realm of human endeavor, humanism avoids the theodical considerations that ultimately arise in Christ-based approaches to world health and harmony. Take Baker-Fletcher's words as a case in point: "A wildness, a free, natural growth, is therefore part of all that lives. Like the waters, the wind, and the groaning of the earth when it quakes, it frightens us with its fury, its ability to turn and stir into storminess and seeming chaos. Such freedom is necessary for life. New life can emerge from the wreckage of nature's storms."[10] Life becomes recognized for its fluidity; hence, disaster is understood as a part of life, and dilemmas mount.

In all fairness, liberal theologians such as Karen Baker-Fletcher argue that natural disasters should be considered "wild" as opposed to being framed in the traditional dichotomy of "good" versus "evil." Yet the way in which the effects of this wildness are described with respect to human life suggests a more charged understanding. That is to say, framing this "wildness" in the context of human life as destructive certainly places it within the context of the dichotomy Baker-Fletcher seeks to avoid: "It [wildness] provides life and sustenance but can also bring destruction to human life and civilization in the form of tornadoes, hurricanes, mad dogs, floods. Ultimately, it is necessary for our survival."[11] In short, destruction by natural forces is a vital reality because, "Sometimes the force of nature creates natural disasters and suffering. But God is still present in the midst of it all."[12] It is, for Baker-Fletcher, a part of God's work in the world, pointing to the power of God—divine force that revives and reveals. In the hurricane, according to this perspective, is manifest a modality of *mysterium tremendum*. How can such an understanding of disaster, couched in the Christ event, not generate theodical anxiety?

When faced with natural disaster, the humanist response as exemplified by figures such as Walker offers insightful lessons—a hermeneutic and system of ethics, both premised on a deep desire for wellness and wholeness. Accordingly, proper and responsible living entails a synergy between the various components of the natural world, an ethic of "green" whereby the preservation and celebration of the earth becomes essential conduct. Not only is oppression structurally weblike in nature, life is also intimately intertwined and mutually dependent.

For Walker and like-minded humanists, relationship between humans and the rest of the earth is the equivalent of the theist's relationship to God. Intimate connections between various layers of life remain vital, complex, "thick," evolving, and serving as the operating paradigm of existence. And, behavior in relationship to the earth is judged not by the activity of individuals, but rather by the collective movement of humanity against the integrity of the environment.

Mindful of this economy of life, disaster should raise a set of questions first and foremost—questions premised on a modality of anthropodicy: Has this event resulted from a failure on the part of humans to remember and act in accordance with a deep connection to all life? That is, has an imbalance because of human manipulation of the earth (e.g., global warming), premised on a disregard for mutuality, contributed to this devastation of life? And then, what can be done to correct this imbalance, to address the immediate concerns but to do so in ways that allow for a fullness of human life and the integrity of life in more general terms?

The challenge is to respond to the immediate demands of disaster, but in ways that hold in creative tension sensitivity to the larger issues of justice exposed by the disruptive force of the earth's elements.

Amen. . . . Ashé.

Notes

1. Some of this information is drawn from my response to Hurricane Katrina provided in abbreviated form in "Promote Healthy Options: A Response to Hurricane Katrina," *Vital Theology* 2, no. 7 (September 25, 2005): 10.

2. "Hurricane Katrina Destroys New Orleans Days Before 'Southern Decadence,'" August 31, 2005, http://www.repentamerica.com/pr_hurricanekatrina.html.

3. See Matthew 5:44-46, KJV. Other versions use the terms *righteous and unrighteous*.

4. "Deep Waters: A Spiritual Response to Hurricane Katrina," http://www.beliefnet.com/story/174/story_17418_1.html.

5. Ibid.

6. See Osteen's website at http://www.joelosteen.com.

7. See for example, Anthony B. Pinn, ed. *By These Hands: A Documentary History of African American Humanism* (NY: New York University Press, 2001); Anthony B. Pinn, *African American Humanist Principles: Living and Thinking Like the Children of Nimrod* (NY: Macmillan, 2004).

8. Karen Baker-Fletcher, *Sisters of Dust, Sisters of Spirit: Womanist Wordings on God and Creation* (Minneapolis: Fortress Press, 1998), 6.

9. Ibid.

10. Ibid., 25.

11. Ibid., 26.

12. Ibid., 30.

CROSSING MANY WATERS

TONI DUNBAR

Mwezi and the Storm

In "Mwezi's Journey," a biography of mythic self-discovery,[1] the little-boy spirit of Mwezi is conveyed and transmuted across land, time, experience, gender, and faith. Mwezi was an adventurous little boy of the forest who believed he was destined for great things. Too early in life he left home, before knowing the sufferings of the wider world and before he had developed a concept of evil. Mwezi believed in the righteousness of his life and his destiny, and in his gods, and was startled to discover beings who did not value him so highly. He was also startled to find that he was incomplete in himself, and that he had never truly known pain and tears. In time a new Mwezi emerged, now Woman as well, and at an unexpected crossroad in life:

After many days Mwezi came to a crossroad, one of many, like patterns on her cloth. A man lay in the crossroad. He seemed to be pointing but Mwezi could not clearly see because a great wind was blowing her up, out of the forest and into the sea. The loas were waving to her in the air, on the wind and in the sea.[2] They were singing. "Shall my journey come to an end here?" Mwezi asked. But no, the man at the crossroad whose light was all golden and the beautiful Yemanja were waiting for her when the new Mwezi washed up upon the shore.[3] She still had her bag for all the treasures she would find, and her flute. The buffalo horn was gone, for there was no trading with the sea, but Yemanja and the man from the crossroad welcomed her. She ate with them, and slept. In the morning Yemanja said, "If you eat with me, you must serve me." And she gave Mwezi to the man at the crossroad and said, "He is my friend." The new Mwezi cried.

She obtained a cookpot, prepared one last meal for the loas, *and then left with the stranger for his land. All of Mwezi's meals were seasoned with the salt from her tears, and like magic all who ate them lived. Those who did not eat were carried away. The land grew and the stranger became Mwezi's friend as well. Yemanja still visited in dreams and sometimes flowed as blood in Mwezi's veins. The new Mwezi grew old.*

As a people we have never ceased to reinvent ourselves; we never cease to be tried by water. We have dug our own wells; washed our own dead; and baptized one another in the same waters that tell our tale—the Mississippi, that river of black folks' bones, and the Atlantic, where our ancestors rest in Yemanja's arms, at the foot of the cross, doused in the water and blood of the crucified Christ. We never cease to be tried by water, stealing away to Jesus, climbing on board that old ship of Zion, rolling in leviathan's belly, headed for the Bahamas, Nova Scotia, freedom, "de Norf."[4]

Like the spirit of the Child-Now-Woman-and-Man Mwezi, our crucible is the sea, reflected in our composition, our cellular memory, and our saltwater tears. The Maafa was our trial by water, our inquisition, proof of innocence by death—at least innocence to a form of evil unimaginable to the fifteenth-century African mind, the mind that had never conceived of permanent chattel slavery or the seductive, demigod-like power of rum and guns.

My essay begins with an allegory of recovery through the never-ending trauma of the African American experience. I briefly compare the Maafa, the African holocaust, to the ongoing political and social disenfranchisement of African Americans as depicted by the mood and federal response to Hurricane Katrina, and cite specific examples of African American complicity. I end with reflecting on gospel imperatives, and call to unified prophetic action. I refer throughout to various water-crossings motifs, for the black diaspora has unfailingly found herself in the same waters where she was lost.

Maafa

"So tragically, so many of these people, almost all of them that we see, are so poor and they are so black, and this is going to raise lots of questions for people who are watching this story unfold."
—Wolf Blitzer, CNN, September 1, 2005[5]

Maafa is a Kiswahili word used to describe real calamity, catastrophe, tragedy, or disaster. Maafa is the African holocaust—the European trade across the Atlantic and the earlier Arab trade across the Indian Ocean. Between the seventh and twentieth centuries, about eighteen million[6] children, men, and especially women marched across the north, from the interior, and up the African east coast into a markedly antiblack sentiment. Females were bound into harems; boys were castrated and became "*aghas*," servant eunuchs; black African men were exploited for their labor throughout the Muslim Mediterranean. Between the sixteenth and nineteenth centuries, about eleven to twelve million other captives embarked in chains from West Africa, about two million dying in the diabolical Middle Passage.[7]

As much as the Portuguese were at the root of the Maafa, so were the Ashanti; as much as the Catholics were involved, so were Ife, Protestants, and Muslims. As much as was Maafa the spawn of mercantile greed, it was the rotten fruit of political expedience and religious zeal. Politics, greed, and religion, then as now, formed an unholy trinity. Ignatius Sancho,[8] survivor of the Middle Passage and by the grace of God and conscious allies critic of the social order that controlled yet disputed its ability to dismantle chattel slavery, wrote against charges that Africans were a "canting, deceitful people."

> You should remember from whom they learnt those vices: - the first Christian visitors found them a simple, harmless people - but the cursed avidity for wealth urged these first visitors (and all the succeeding ones) to such acts of deception - and even wanton cruelty - that the poor ignorant Natives soon learnt to turn the knavish - and diabolical arts which they too soon imbibed - upon their teachers. . . . Commerce attended with strict honesty - and with Religion for its companion - would be a blessing to every shore it touched at. - In Africa, the poor wretched natives - blessed with the most fertile and luxuriant soil - are rendered so much the more miserable for what Providence meant as a blessing: - the Christians' abominable traffic for slaves - and the horrid cruelty and treachery of the petty Kings - encouraged by their Christian customers - who carry them strong liquors - to enflame their national madness - and powder - and bad fire-arms - to furnish them with the hellish means of killing and kidnapping. - But enough - it is a subject that sours my blood.[9]

The spirits, if not progeny, of the "petty Kings and their Christian customers" inhabited Greenville, Mississippi, in 1927, during an eerie precursor to the devastation of 2005. It began with a catastrophic but anticipated and well-documented flood of the Mississippi River. Whites were evacuated as the levees burst; the poorest people were made homeless. A high-ranking federal official paid a perfunctory visit to the area. The left-behind blacks were conscripted into service; the National Guard was deployed, with rifles trained on black folk. Aid was distributed preferentially to whites, with blacks and the poor herded into "refugee" camps without food or clean water. Anarchy arose; in some cases the scofflaws were troops and local police. Those who were once allies of beleaguered black folk turned back toward profiteering and maintaining King Cotton; blacks were accused of being indolent, ungrateful, and the source of their own problems. When the muddy waters receded, a living river of disillusioned and disenfranchised blacks flowed from the Delta to the urban centers in the north. The waters and levee breaks of 1927 left a thousand dead, a million homeless, and twenty-seven thousand square miles from Cairo, Illinois, through New Orleans to the Gulf of Mexico in ruins. The U.S. Army Corps of Engineers said it had thought that the levees would hold.[10]

With the welfare of the poor and servant class always in question, and in keeping with the United States' unbroken history of exploiting class distinctions, the service economy and the Gulf Coast underclass bore the brunt in 1927 as in 2005.

So Poor and So Black

Myriad analyses flooded media and the blogosphere following Hurricanes Katrina and Rita,[11] with prurient emphasis on Louisiana, though storm damage in Mississippi was just as catastrophic. The international *bon temps* destination was revealed to the world as surprisingly overrun by poverty and neglect; New Orleans's Mayor Ray Nagin was excoriated as inexperienced and overwhelmed at best, incompetent at worst. Louisiana Governor Kathleen Blanco was depicted as indecisive, lacking in credibility, and motivated by political self-preservation. President George W. Bush and FEMA director Michael Brown were again unmasked as pretenders to their thrones.[12] If the mood prior to Katrina was understated and preoccupied, the post-Katrina response was ramshackle and laden with political expediency. Katrina presented a study in denial and hedged bets.

At safe distance is a black intelligentsia who through their fortuitous circumstances cannot or will not identify with the desperate, unkempt poor—a flotsam "so poor and so black"[13] as to astonish an international community.[14]

Seeing No Evil

It takes a special kind of blindness to not see the creation and perpetuation of an underclass that serves the foibles and interests of the well heeled, and the simultaneous manipulation of its key constituents. Imagine: beachside Pascagoula, Mississippi; George W. Bush and Mississippi Senator Trent Lott sitting on Lott's porch,[15] watching Mexican day laborers[16] and token African Americans lay finishing touches while Bush and Lott discuss the merits of yet another multimillion-dollar contract for Halliburton.[17]

Indeed, black conservatives lament the black and poor of the Gulf Coast's inattention to their own waterlogged bootstraps. Shelby Steele, confessing to "a consuming empathy but also another, more atavistic impulse,"[18] converts the hurricane's mayhem into an occasion for black elitist "shame" and a paean to the extinction of white racism.

> White responsibility cannot overcome black inferiority. This is a truth so obvious as to be mundane. Yet whites won't say it in the interest of their redemption and blacks won't say it in the interest of historical justice. It is left to hurricanes to make such statements.

Although Steele differentiates between inferiority that is "the result of oppression, not genetics," he asserts that "poor blacks have not held up their end of the bargain" and "in the '60s whites finally took open responsibility for their racism despite the shame this exposed them to."[19]

Ward Connerly reprises his assimilationist arguments post-Katrina, turning a blind eye to his own and our common circumstances. Connerly, chairman of the conservative think tank American Civil Rights Institute, in Sacramento, said it was simply coincidence that most of the hurricane victims on television were black. He said, "The hurricane happened to hit New Orleans, which happens to be predominantly black and poor. To seek out deeper, more insidious reasons for the crisis in New Orleans is to focus on the wrong thing. I wish we were not talking about race at all. It's a needless distraction. . . . For the black leaders who are blaming racism, shame on them."[20]

The Bishop T. D. Jakes, beloved among many black religious and anointed "The Best Preacher in America" by *Time* magazine in 2001,[21] lent legitimacy to George W. Bush with a shallow appearance scant days after Bush was warned of the polls and public opinion threatening the GOP outreach to African Americans—a campaign opposed, ironically, by Bush supporter Ward Connerly.[22] The *New York Times* reported that Bush was advised by a black supporter to "grab some black people who look like they might be preachers."[23] On the same day, Michael A. Fletcher of the *Washington Post* wrote:

> Overcoming mistrust of blacks compounded by Katrina is an important hurdle in one of Bush's political goals—making the GOP more competitive with traditionally Democratic African Americans. . . . To underscore his outreach efforts, when the president toured a hurricane evacuee shelter near Baton Rouge last week, he was accompanied by the Rev. T. D. Jakes, a prominent black evangelist who has known Bush for years. He also went to New Orleans yesterday. Those trips came after Bush was criticized for having little contact with poor, black victims during an earlier visit.[24]

Bush and Jakes toured the homeless shelter of the conservative megachurch Bethany World Prayer Center in Baton Rouge; Jakes later delivered the sermon during the National Day of Prayer and Remembrance service at the Washington National Cathedral in Washington DC.[25] Ingenuously, perhaps, Bishop Jakes aided Bush's effort to mine black public opinion, but for unrealized reward: six months later the Bush administration had yet failed to deliver the twenty million dollars in aid for faith organizations along the Gulf Coast, dollars that were slated for distribution through Jakes' hand, leaving Jakes humiliated and perturbed.

> "I am annoyed. I am frustrated. I am angry," said Jakes, who is co-chairman of an advisory panel set up to help the Bush-Clinton Katrina Fund distribute the $20 million to churches. "We need to focus more on rebuilding our country."
>
> "It is really embarrassing," said Bishop Paul Morton, pastor of the 20,000-member Greater St. Stephen Full Gospel Baptist Church. "We had all of these preachers coming together, about 2,000 filled out applications and there is still no money. They are all blaming Bishop Jakes, but he doesn't have the authority over the money. It is not his fault."[26]

U.S. Secretary of State Condoleezza Rice, the highest-ranking African American in the Bush administration, and with Colin Powell the high-est-ranking known African American in U.S. government history, said in the aftermath of Hurricane Katrina, "I don't believe for one minute that anybody allowed people to suffer because they were African American. I just don't believe it."[27]

Rice's summary protestation could be a motto for Maafa. Faced with the ruthlessness of the conditions defining the new slavery ("Surely," wrote Olaudah Equiano—victim, firsthand observer, and averse partici-pant in the trade—"this is a new refinement in cruelty"[28]), did the Dahomey amid their legendary raidings say, *I don't believe it?* Black ances-tors wrested uncertain futures from the waters of despair and are role models for our contemporaries along the Gulf Coast. When confronted by our own vestigial fears and evidence of self-directed racism do we say, *I don't believe it?* Or worse, accept as a perverted gospel: "So many of the people in the arena here, you know, were underprivileged anyway—this, this is working very well for them"?[29] Might Steele's and Connerly's ver-sions of shame be better reserved for black leaders who fail to acknowl-edge the confluence of race and poverty and its consequences in the public sphere?[30]

Small Things

No matter how deep the shame of our own complicity it pales beside the relentless devaluation of the black contribution to life and society, such as CNN anchor Daryn Kagan's characterization of the Congressional Black Caucus's response to Hurricane Katrina as "the emo-tional" aspect of the news day versus "the technical" cover of the U.S. Army Corps of Engineers.[31] Is it a small thing, worthy of no mention? Or another of the tiny little wounds by which a people bleeds to death?

A Catalog of Voices

Too many to catalog are the comments linking Katrina to sin and the moral failings of poor people. Just as that task is too large, it is also too sad to undertake. Conversely, too few to catalog are the liberal and progres-sive voices.

Progressive hip-hoppers offer acerbic commentary through underground luminaries such as e-zine journalist Radio Raheem and Houston-based rap group The Legendary K. O. Raheem, who styles himself "Mr. [Shelby] Steele's Official Nemesis," deconstructs Steele's arguments "from the street," and entreats his readers: "Just look at the facts of the situations we have argued. Which one of us sounds more like what you see, with your own eyes, every day of your life?"[32]

The Legendary K. O. penned a notable protest remix of Kanye West's "Gold Digger" entitled "George Bush Doesn't Care about Black People."[33] K. O.'s original audio, produced and distributed by Kanye West, is embellished by successive hip-hop filmmakers whose creative video mashups erase any ambiguity about the progressive or radical hip-hop stance on the Bush administration's response to Katrina[34] (while a growing constituency of conservative hip-hoppers actively defend the same response).[35] West captured both headlines and imaginations when he, like a hurricane, ripped the roof from the media, FEMA, powerlessness and despair, hurricane relief, black extended family, classism, racism, volunteerism, war, oppression, and the cover from the elephant in the room—President Bush's cavalier attitude toward the death of a city and its people—with his closing remark at NBC's fundraiser for Hurricane Katrina victims: "George Bush doesn't care about black people!"[36]

Though the young rapper offered no remedies, Dan Froomkin of the *Washington Post* was moved to ask, "Was Kanye West right?" First noting the contrast in the opinions of black and white Americans, Froomkin then moved the question from President Bush's weak and peripheral refutation of racial preference to the central issues of abandonment and poverty.[37]

Cornel West writes in *The Observer* newspaper:

> What we saw unfold in the days after the hurricane was the most naked manifestation of conservative social policy towards the poor, where the message for decades has been: "You are on your own." Well, they really were on their own for five days in that Superdome, and it was Darwinism in action—the survival of the fittest. People said: "It looks like something out of the Third World." Well, New Orleans was Third World long before the hurricane.[38]

West recommends "a Marshall Plan for the South." On examination, the Marshall Plan is a time-tested, viable template for reconstruction, yet still compatible with states' rights and "compassionate conservatism."

Paradoxically, near the core of the Reverend Jesse Peterson's vitriolic rants against black civil rights leaders, Democrats, liberals, and the "moral poverty" of blacks in New Orleans is a single laudable nugget,[39] his ideal of a strong black man acting out of self-sufficiency to protect and maintain his community. Peterson's polar opposite, the Reverend Louis Farrakhan, built the original Million Man March and its successor Millions More Movement on a virtually identical principle. Parenthetically, against all other criticism Farrakhan is both a careful and an honest man: on April 29, 1927, the U.S. Army Corps of Engineers did, as Farrakhan asserts, blow up the levee at Caernarvon, Louisiana.[40] Phantasmagoric conspiracy theory it may be, but history lends Farrakhan immense credibility—renders him a sleeping giant—among young urban African Americans whose hip-hop has an unwittingly socialist bent. Farrakhan's ten-point plan, unveiled at the Millions More Movement event,[41] is a Marshall Plan in reverse—challenging but achievable, by degree and to scale.

Jim Wallis, founder of Sojourners: Christians for Justice and Peace and editor of *Sojourners* magazine, offers a compassionate yet precise prescription for amelioration and change in his article "What the Waters Revealed." Wallis's analysis is thoughtful and elegant, interspersed with a commonsense platform of social and political activism.

> [The] waters of Hurricane Katrina also washed away our national denial of the shockingly high number of Americans living in poverty and our reluctance to admit the still-persistent connection of race and poverty in America, and perhaps even eroded the political power of a conservative anti-social services ideology that, for decades now, has weakened the idea of the common good. There are two obstacles to making real progress against poverty: the lack of *priority* and the lack of agreement on *strategy*. . . . We must be disciplined by results.[42]

To its campaign of public education and faith community activism,[43] Sojourners offers the simple but eloquent Katrina Pledge:

> As a person of faith, I believe that the poverty we have witnessed on the rooftops of New Orleans and the devastated communities of the Gulf Coast is morally unacceptable. Therefore, I join my fellow Americans across the barriers of race, religion, class, and politics in the following commitments:
>
> 1. I pledge to be personally involved in helping those whose lives have been affected by this natural disaster—by praying for the victims and

their families and by offering my time, talents, and resources to relief and recovery ministries that are meeting their needs.

2. I pledge to work for sweeping change of our nation's priorities. I will press my elected representatives to protect the common good—especially the needs of our poorest families and children—rather than supporting the twin social disasters of tax cuts for the rich and budget cuts that hurt the poor.[44]

Too few as well are women's voices in public discourse. Maya Angelou's apologetically flavored inspirational reflection broadcast on CNN's *Larry King Live*[45] stands in stark contrast to her candid interview with George Arney, host of *World Today*, BBC World Service.

Arney: Was there anything in the aftermath of the hurricane that . . . did shock and disappoint you?
Angelou: I was amazed that the media showed the African American only. There are whites who suffered as much, need as much. I wonder at that propensity or that decision among media to look at the exotica. I see that all over the world. What is that? What kind of sickness is that?
Arney: Do you think there was a racist element as has been alleged in the way the administration handled the aftermath of the hurricane?
Angelou: Oh, I'm sure. Racism is in everything. Absolutely. Absolutely.[46]

Nevertheless, Angelou's voice was welcome, immediate, and public, rushing in to fill an unutterably painful void.

Feminist Lucinda Marshall, founder of the Feminist Peace Network,[47] and Women's E-News correspondent Nancy Cook Lauer[48] examined the issue of rape and the phenomenon of women's (and children's) increased risks of sexual assault during times of social destabilization. The international womanist community collected books, clothing, food, supplies, prayers, tuition, and housing—tangible provisos in the "traditionally capable . . . 'Mama, I'm walking to Canada and taking you and a bunch of other slaves with me'" way[49]—and offered outrage and scholarly critique.

Diana L. Hayes, Associate Professor of Theology, Georgetown University, framed the event as apocalyptic,[50] likening our anesthetization to the looming potential of destruction along the Gulf Coast to the inurement of the villagers in "The Boy Who Cried Wolf."[51] In a superbly incisive essay entitled "When Race Matters and Nobody Mentions It," Cheryl Townsend Gilkes, professor of Sociology and African American

Studies at Colby College, exposed the delegitimization of black social criticism via accusations that blacks are "playing the race card, or 'politicizing' the problem." She reminds us of "cancer alley" in Louisiana, and the potential abandonment of that ecologically damaged area to the profit of the polluter litigants. She shows again the media's fascination with, and refusal to differentiate between, violence and the *appearance* of violence because of one's desperate circumstances. She samples the increasingly sociologically sophisticated disenfranchisement visited upon those who are not the neoconservative Republican "base." Gilkes ends with an austere warning and with what may be an explanation of the location of those intentionally naive and Pollyannaish who ignore the confluence of race, color, and class: "See no race, see no racism!"[52] Yet still, women's voices in the public sphere are too few.

A Divergence of Gospels

"When Bush moved to Washington in 1987 to help run his father's campaign, he seized the main chance: to take over the job of being the 'liaison' to the religious right...Bush and [Karl] Rove built their joint careers on that new base."
—Howard Fineman, Newsweek, March 10, 2003

"New Orleans now is abortion free. New Orleans now is Mardi Gras free. New Orleans now is free of Southern Decadence and the sodomites, the witchcraft workers, false religion—it's free of all of those things now."
—Rev. Bill Shanks, New Covenant Fellowship of New Orleans, quoted on Agapepress.org, September 2, 2005

"Katrina gave us a preview of what America would look like if we fail to fight the war on terror. 'Did God have anything to do with Katrina?' people ask. My answer is, he allowed it and perhaps he allowed it to get our attention."
—Author and ex-politico Charles Colson, quoted on BreakPoint.org, September 12, 2005

On the first Sunday following Hurricane Katrina, Christians across the country were invited to remember the broken body of Jesus Christ, to discern through self-examination the worthiness of our particular embrace of the faith. We were transported in our imaginations to a fateful day of decision, a day of either hubris or melancholy based upon one's location in the maelstrom of politics, economics, and religion. We were invited to treat first betrayal—to give it heft and substance—and remembrance.[53] We conjured, though briefly, Judas Iscariot, prototype of the betrayer, and then joined with Christ in thanks. Perhaps some thought of the morality of this Christian country where the wealthy and the middle-class were evacuated to safety while the poor, infirm, and ignorant stayed or were left behind. Perhaps others reflected upon the astounding duplicity of this Christian administration, with leaders who dithered and obfuscated at every turn[54] and offered one another rousing congratulations while people lay dehydrating and dying in full view of the world.[55] Still others may have offered silent repentance for the inhumane squandering of emergency personnel and resources,[56] and against the "Christian" sentiment that the Superdome was an improvement in living conditions for evacuees because they were "underprivileged anyway."[57]

As some of us crushed the symbol of the body of our Lord between our teeth and washed it away with a symbol of the blood of the new covenant, perhaps we contemplated the blood that cries out from the ground of this great Christian nation; and we certainly pondered the lawlessness of people who, if one had asked, would probably have said that they believe in God.

And perhaps we realized that according to canon Judas was the most religious of Christ's disciples, the one who believed he understood the workings of the kingdom of God better than Christ himself. Judas held to a proprietary gospel—the Gospel with a capital G, commodified and commercialized, tied to the purse and to power.

Whether shared by key figures in the administration or not—whether sincerely or superficially adopted, as were flannel shirts and down-homey straight talk early in Bush's first term—Bush's provincial, self-absorbed religiosity sets the tone for discourse on empire and manifest destiny. Simplistic, dualistic, uncritical; accommodating, subsumed, assimilated; Bushian theo-politics make easy work of the inclusive, egalitarian gospel of Christ, in favor of the proprietary, monopolistic Gospel-with-a-capital-G, theo-political trademark of hegemony domestic and worldwide.

The Prophetic Task

The bombed-out-looking churches in the wake of Hurricane Katrina and the irresponsible commentary of persons out of touch with the redemptive gospel of Jesus Christ issue a mournfully prophetic challenge. In the words of an old children's rhyme, "Here is the church, here is the steeple. Open the door . . . but where are the people?" Religious extremists breathing calumny on the excesses of New Orleans are neither exclusively the church nor "the people," no more so than if they eisegeted the destruction of the home and headquarters of white nationalist Representative David Duke (R-LA) or the middle-class suburb where Duke "resuscitated the Ku Klux Klan."[58] Curiously, the riotous French Quarter was spared, a suggestion that the catastrophe followed geographical contours, not moral ones.

The instinct to fear and hate runs counter to the imperatives of the gospel. It renders us primitive and superstitious, inured to the suffering of others. It corresponds more closely to the reasons—and mechanisms—of Jesus' crucifixion, than a *Weltanschauung* colored by the power of resurrection. Conversely, there is no sanguine righteousness due the religious and political left that is not accompanied by a unified and sacrificial effort to provoke change, with an energy that bespeaks "in our lifetimes." This is the prophetic task. Says Jim Wallis, "A new moral logic must reshape our political habits."[59]

What is happening on the Gulf Coast is a wrong of biblical proportion. Morally and spiritually, it is inextricable from the exploitation of the poor in the Middle East; by the World Bank; in the U.S. penal system; by the Wall Street windfall in the proposed restructure of Social Security; and in policies formed in the upper echelons of corporate America that balkanize America's inner cities and rural areas.

Katrina was not just a "natural" disaster; it was a technology-enhanced catastrophe because of shoddy levees and floodwalls built to enhance commerce, not to protect people. Although officials parse words about "overtopping," almost daily the New Orleans *Times-Picayune* publishes irrefutable evidence of poor levee design and construction.[60] And of course, the storms were stronger, more destructive, and plentiful because of climate change.[61] The earth itself is raped so that a few men and women might make more money.

In the chairs and pews of a million little churches each day lies the corrective. Media bristles with scenes of blown-out churches, with nothing left standing but doors, struts, and steeple. Are they analysis, or metaphor? Clarion call, or indictment? Is the church post-Katrina and post-Rita yet purposeful and prophetic, a survivor and sustainer? Or, like the battered frames of once-vibrant houses of worship, is it vulnerable and empty wreckage?

The second verse of the children's rhyme concludes joyfully, "Open the door, and here are the people!" The prophetic mandate for prayer, recovery, and justice permeate the elegantly simple Katrina Pledge, and the mission philosophy of secular and faith organizations worldwide.[62] Did we see Christ in the fetid waters of New Orleans? Is there enough common ground between progressive and conservative, between black, white, and multiracial, that we might cross over together as if on dry land?[63]

The Young-Mwezi-Now-Old traversed and found salvation in many waters. So must this generation be baptized into its unique commitment to social change and ask, *What if?* Jesus said, "You always have the poor with you" (John 12:8). What if . . . from the destruction of Katrina and Rita could arise a new determination to end the invisibility of the poor and to reshape an infrastructure that maintains—and benefits from—an underclass? What if . . . we hold accountable those people and organizations who consider the elderly, voiceless, infirm, and the poor expendable? What if . . . we work together, and yet still on many fronts? And what if . . . we do not quit?

Notes

1. Toni Dunbar, "Mwezi's Journey," 1999. Although "Mwezi's Journey" is a personal mythos, I find in it concurrence with the reintegrative journey of "my people." Ref. Clyde W. Ford, *The Hero with an African Face: Mythic Wisdom of Traditional Africa* (New York: Bantam, 1999), viii-ix.

> In today's common parlance, the term myth refers to unwarranted falsifications rather than unceasing truths. . . . Myths are in fact the "social stories" that heal. Properly read, myths bring us into accord with the eternal mysteries of being, help us to manage the inevitable passages of our lives, and give us templates for our relationships with the societies in which we live and for the relationship of the earth we share with all life. When trauma confronts us, individually or collectively, myths are a way of reestablishing harmony in the wake of chaos.

2. The *loas* are the general pantheon of spirits in certain West African religions, particularly Vodun.

3. In Vodun, Yemanja is the spirit of the waters.

4. Ship's cook Madison Washington led one hundred thirty-five slaves to the Bahamas and freedom in the Creole slave ship revolt, November 1841; many slaves who fought for the British in the American War of Independence were rewarded with freedom and land in Nova Scotia. The University of San Diego offers an extensive bibliography edited by Steve Shoenherr, University of San Diego, 2000, http://www.history.sandiego.edu/gen/civilwar/03/creole.html.

5. "Aftermath of Hurricane Katrina; New Orleans Mayor Pleads for Help; Race and Class Affecting the Crisis?" *The Situation Room*, CNN, Atlanta, transcript, September 1, 2005, http://www.transcripts.cnn.com/TRANSCRIPTS/0509/01/sitroom.02.html.

6. "Slavery" in *The New Encyclopedia Britannica*, 15th ed., volume 27 (Chicago: Encyclopedia Britannica, 1994).

7. Stephen Behrent, "Transatlantic Slave Trade" in *Africana: The Encyclopedia of the African and African American Experience*, ed. Kwame Anthony Appiah and Henry Louis Gates Jr. (New York: Basic Civitas Books, 1999).

8. Vincent Carretta, ed., *Letters of the Late Ignatius Sancho: An African* (London: Penguin, 1998).

9. Vincent Carretta, ed., "Sancho's Views on Empire and Slavery" in *Letters of the Late Ignatius Sancho: An African*, http://www.brycchancarey.com/sancho/letter4.htm.

10. "Fatal Flood," *American Experience*, WGBH Educational Foundation, 2001. PBS transcript, http://www.pbs.org/wgbh/amex/flood/filmmore/pt.html.

11. *Blogosphere* is a collective term for the world of online journals or diaries, or "weblogs."

12. The blogosphere is reliable primarily as a cross section of public opinion. An Internet search for the words *Nagin* and *incompetent* registers hits on 132,000 websites; the addition of the words *Katrina* with *survivor* yields 34,500 hits, a 73 percent reduction. A similar measurement involving presuppositions about the political character and performance of Governor Kathleen Blanco yields similarly proportioned results. Weblog opinion on the performance of President George W. Bush and FEMA Director Michael Brown splits cleanly between liberal and conservative camps. So unscientific an experiment can suggest only the author's unsubstantiated and somewhat confessional conjecture that the further removed the critic from the actual circumstances of the disaster, the more vitriolic the criticism, without factoring that Katrina survivors may, for example, have reduced access to the Internet and so on. A balanced analysis of the actions of New Orleans Mayor Ray Nagin, Louisiana Governor Kathleen Blanco, FEMA Director Michael Brown, and Secretary of the Department of Homeland Security Michael Chertoff appears in *Time*, "4 Places Where the System Broke Down," by James Carney et al., September 11, 2005, http://www.time-proxy.yaga.com/time/archive/printout/0,23657,1103560,00.html.

13. A flustered Wolf Blitzer, anchor of CNN's *The Situation Room*, struggled for words to describe his firsthand view of the human toll of Hurricane Katrina and uttered the much-lambasted phrase. Later, Blitzer explained to Patricia Sheridan at the *Pittsburgh Post-Gazette*:

> What I was trying to underscore was that most of the people suffering in New Orleans were African American. Some people have tried to distort that or whatever, but it's just a fundamental fact. They were poor and they were black. . . .One of our commentators, Jack Cafferty, was talking about the elephant in the room: this whole issue of race and poverty in America. That is how that whole issue came up.

See Patricia Sheridan, "Patricia Sheridan's Breakfast with . . . Wolf Blitzer," *Pittsburgh Post-Gazette*, October 3, 2005, http://www.post-gazette.com/pg/05276/581641.stm.

14. "Viewpoints: Hurricane Katrina: Comment and Analysis from London, Melbourne, Tel Aviv, Toronto, Edmonton, Auckland and Moscow," Worldpress.org, September 3, 2005, http://www.worldpress.org/Americas/2142.cfm.

15. "President Arrives in Alabama, Briefed on Hurricane Katrina," Presidential News and Releases, Office of the Press Secretary, The White House, September 2, 2005, http://www.whitehouse.gov/news/releases/2005/09/20050902-2.html.

16. "Immigrants Rush to New Orleans as Builders Fight for Workers," Workpermit.com, October 11, 2005, http://www.workpermit.com/news/2005_10_11/us/new_orleans.htm.

17. Rob Kelley, "Rebuilding Post-Katrina—Follow the $$$," Markets & Stocks, CNN/Money, September 21, 2005, http://www.money.cnn.com/2005/09/21/markets/katrina_reconstruction/.

18. Shelby Steele is a research fellow at the Hoover Institution who specializes in the study of race relations, multiculturalism, and affirmative action. Steele holds a PhD in English from the University of Utah, an MA in sociology from Southern Illinois University, and a BA in political science from Coe College, Cedar Rapids, Iowa.

19. Shelby Steele, "The Races: Witness: Blacks, Whites, and the Politics of Shame in America," OpinionJournal, Wall Street Journal, October 26, 2005, http://www.opinion-journal.com/editorial/feature.html?id=110007457.

20. Ward Connerly is a political activist, a businessman, and the founder of the American Civil Rights Institute. Connerly is a former member of the University of California Board of Regents and former chair of the California Civil Rights Initiative (Proposition 209) campaign. He is best known for his controversial opposition to affirmative action.

21. David Van Biema, "America's Best: Spirit Raiser," *Time* archive, September 17, 2001, http://www.time.com/time/archive/preview/0,10987,1000836,00.html.

22. Ward Connerly, "End the Race Party: Identity Politics Will Get the GOP Nothing Good," *National Review Online*, September 30, 2005, http://www.nationalreview.com/comment/connerly200509300813.asp.

23. Elisabeth Bumiller, "White House Letter: Gulf Coast Isn't the Only Thing Left in Tatters; Bush's Status with Blacks Takes Hit." *New York Times*, Washington edition, September 12, 2005, http://www.nytimes.com/2005/09/12/politics/12letter.html?ex=1284177600&en=6c84580d4c59f57b&ei=5090&partner=rssuserland&emc=rss.

24. Michael A. Fletcher, "Katrina Pushes Issues of Race and Poverty at Bush," *Washington Post*, September 12, 2005, http://www.washingtonpost.com/wp-dyn/content/article/2005/09/11/AR2005091101131_pf.html. See also Daniela Relph, *Reporters' Log: Katrina's Aftermath*, BBC News International Version, September 5, 2005, http://www.news.bbc.co.uk/1/hi/world/Americas/4214618.stm. "President Bush was accompanied on this visit by T. D. Jakes, a popular African-American minister and spiritual advisor to the Bush family. They visited the Bethany World Prayer Centre in Baton Rouge, a Baptist church that is now also a shelter for the displaced. The president spoke to evacuees and autographed T-shirts for many of the children at the shelter."

25. "Bishop T. D. Jakes Sermon Delivered at the Washington National Cathedral," PRNewswire, transcript, September 17, 2005, http://www.prnewswire.com/news/index_mail.shtml?ACCT=104&STORY=/www/story/09-17-2005/0004109506&EDATE=.

26. Hamil R. Harris and Jacqueline L. Salmon, "Churches Still Await Katrina Aid: Bush-Clinton Fund Criticized for Delay in Allocating $20 Million." *Washington Post,* March 2, 2006, http://www.washingtonpost.com/wp-dyn/content/article/2006/03/01/AR2006030102379.html.

27. "Secretary of State Condoleezza Rice on International Relief Activities Related to Hurricane Katrina," On-the-Record Briefing, Office of the Spokesman, U.S. Department of State, September 2, 2005, http://www.state.gov/secretary/rm/2005/52478.htm.

28. Vincent Carretta, ed., *The Interesting Narrative of the Life of Olaudah Equiano, or Gustavus Vassa the African* (New York: Penguin, 1995).

29. Barbara Bush in an interview with Bob Moon. "Houston, We May Have a Problem," *Marketplace,* American Public Media, September 5, 2005, http://www.marketplace.publicradio.org/shows/2005/09/05/PM200509051.html. The raw tape may be found at http://publicradio.org/tools/media/player/marketplace/2005/09/feature_barbarabush_sept5.ram. Barbara Bush is the mother of President George W. Bush and the wife of former President George H. W. Bush.

30. See a thoughtful and expanded explanation of Rice's position on Bush and race at "What the Secretary Has Been Saying: Interview with the New York Times Publisher's Group," U.S. Department of State, transcript, September 12, 2005, http://state.gov/secretary/rm/2005/53036.htm.

31. "Congressional Black Caucus Discusses Response to Katrina; New Orleans in Turmoil." *CNN Live Today,* CNN, Atlanta, transcript, September 2, 2005, http://transcripts.cnn.com/TRANSCRIPTS/0509/02/lt.01.html.

32. Radio Raheem, "Radioactive: Shelby Steele Plays the Race Card, Again," *Generator 21, 1996–2006, G21.net—The World's Magazine,* undated, http://www.g21.net/radio38.html.

33. K-Otix, "The Legendary K. O. Delivers Powerful Message against George W. Bush through Song: 'George Bush Doesn't Care About Black People' Receives Widespread Acclaim," http://www.k-otix.com/index.php?option=com_content&task=view&id=43&Itemid=2. See also http://www.k-otix.com/index.php?option=com_content&task=view&id=55&Itemid=2 for links to explicit language and radio versions.

34. A "mashup" is a digital combination and synchronization of two or more sources into a third, new song or video. The first-generation video by the Black Lantern is available at http:www.theblacklantern.com/george.html. A second-generation version by Franklin Lopez appears on the Guerilla News Network website, http://www.gnn.tv/videos/40/NEW_George_Bush_Don_t_Like_Black_People.

35. See for example, writers Dan LeRoy, LaShawn Barber, and others on the weblog Hip Hop Republican, http://www.hiphoprepublican.com.

36. Although the West Coast feed was subsequently time-delayed and censored, the majority of the taping can be viewed at several places on the Internet including *Crooks and Liars: The New Online Virtual Magazine,* http://www.crooksandliars.com/2005/09/02.html. West's constituency, the hip-hop community, entered lively, sometimes contentious, debate following his unscheduled comments. A critical hip-hop video response by rapper/commentator The Legendary K. O. (explicit lyrics) appears at http://www.archive.org/download/TheBlackLanternGeorgeBushDoesntCareAboutBlackPeopleMusicVideo/bdcabp.mov or http://en.wikinews.org/wiki/Rapper_Kanye_West_denounces_Bush_response,_American_media_at_hurricane_relief_telethon.

37. Dan Froomkin, "Was Kanye West Right?" White House Briefing, Washingtonpost.com, September 13, 2005, http://www.washingtonpost.com/wp-dyn/content/blog/2005/09/13/BL2005091300884.html. See also the commentary entitled "Two Writers Explore the Political and Economic Impact of Rap" by Dr. Walton Muyumba, Professor of African American Literature at the University of North Texas, http://www.dallasnews.com/s/dws/ent/stories/DN-kanyeessay_1211gl.ART. State.Bulldog.3d7863c.html.

38. Cornel West, "Exiles from a City and from a Nation," *The Observer* (UK), September 11, 2005, http://observer.guardian.co.uk/comment/story/0,6903,1567247,00.html.

39. For example, Rev. Jesse Lee Peterson, Founder and President, Brotherhood Organization of a New Destiny (http://www.bondinfo.org) declares Jesse Jackson, Maxine Waters, Louis Farrakhan, the NAACP, liberal elite whites, and the Democratic Party "racist," and W. E. B. Du Bois a "communist socialist pig." See "One Jesse Says the Other Jesse is a Racist," March/April 1998, B.O.N.D. Newsletter, *Huntsville Chronicle*, http://www.thehuntsvillechronicle.com/articles/jesssepeterson/other_jesse.htm. Peterson proclaims that liberals and Democrats "hate America," and likens black America's affirmative relationship with Rev. Jesse Jackson to that of a woman serially attracted to rapists. "Responding to the Call: The New Black Vanguard Conference," The Heritage Foundation II, October 11, 2005, http://multimedia.heritage.org/content/Lehrman-101105.ram. Peterson's New Black Vanguard Conferences are sponsored by the Heritage Foundation—a billionaire-supported, conservative, Washington DC think tank, and architect of the Reagan Doctrine and the "Reaganomics" supply-side economic theory. For a detailed commentary see Max Blumenthal, "The Ministry of Minstrelry," *The Nation*, April 11, 2005. Posted March 24, 2005, http://www.thenation.com/doc/20050411/blumenthal/4.

See also Jesse Lee Peterson, "Moral Poverty Cost Blacks in New Orleans," *WorldNetDaily*, September 21, 2005, http://www.worldnetdaily.com/news/article.asp?ARTICLE_ID=46440.

40. Pam Clark, "The 75th Anniversary of the Great Flood of 1927," *Riverside* 13, no. 3 (March 2002): 7-8, http://www.mvn.usace.army.mil/PAO/Riverside/March_2002.pdf. The cover article features a photo of the blast, with a caption reading, "Desperate times, desperate measures: dynamite explodes in the levee at Caernarvon, La."

41. See the official site for the Millions More Movement, http://www.millionsmoremovement.com/index_flash.html. See also "Why a Millions More Movement?" for a discussion of Farrakhan's "Declaration for a Covenant with God, Leadership and our People" and "Issues of the Millions More Movement (e.g., 10-point Plan)," http://www.millionsmoremovement.com/about.htm.

42. Jim Wallis, "What the Waters Revealed," *Sojourners*, November 2005. http://www.sojo.net/index.cfm?action=magazine.article&issue=soj0511&article=051110.

43. For example, from the editors of *Sojourners*, *What the Waters Revealed: Christians and Hurricane Katrina Discussion Guide*, and *Sojourners on the Issues*, an electronic resource for discussion and study about issues of faith and justice. http://www.sojo.net/resources/discussion_guides/DG_katrina_toc.pdf.

44. "The Katrina Pledge: A Commitment to Build a New America," http://www.go.sojo.net/campaign/katrinapledge.

45. Maya Angelou, "Yes, I Am," *Larry King Live*, CNN, Atlanta, transcript, September 9, 2005 (excerpt):

When land became water, and water began to think it was God, consuming lives here, leaving lives there, swallowing buildings, devouring cities, intoxicated with its power, mighty power, and the American people were tested. As a result of our tumultuousness, there abides in the American psyche an idea so powerful it ennoble [sic] us, and lifts us high above the problems which beset us. It can, in fact, evict fear. It can rest [sic] despair from its lodging. Simply put, the idea is, yes, I can. I am an American, and yes, I can. I can overcome.

http://www.transcripts.cnn.com/TRANSCRIPTS/0509/09/lkl.01.html.

46. "Maya Angelou," *The World Today*, BBC World Service, October 5, 2005, http://www.bbc.co.uk/worldservice/ondemand/rams/xin40251___2005.ram.

47. Lucinda Marshall, "Were Women Raped in New Orleans? Addressing the Human Rights of Women in Times of Crisis," *Dissident Voice*, September 14, 2005, http://www.dissidentvoice.org/Sept05/Marshall0914.htm.

48. Nancy Cook Lauer, "Efforts to Track Rape Emerge Between Hurricanes," Feminist.com, September 23, 2005, http://www.feminist.com/news/vaw44.html.

49. Alice Walker, *In Search of Our Mothers' Gardens: Womanist Prose* (San Diego: Harcourt Brace Jovanovich, 1983). In the course of her creation and seminal definitions of the words "womanism" and "womanist" in *In Search of Our Mothers' Gardens*, Walker demystifies the African American woman's culture of strength and perseverance with a reference to the tradition of Harriet Tubman. Tubman, an escaped slave, returned repeatedly to the South and escorted approximately three hundred others to freedom in the northern states and Canada.

50. Diana L. Hayes, "Apocalypse Now" (unpublished essay, 2005).

51. Olivia and Robert Temple, trans., *Aesop: The Complete Fables* (New York: Penguin Books, 1998).

52. Cheryl Townsend Gilkes, "When Race Matters and Nobody Mentions It: Hurricane Katrina, the Superdome, and the Black People No One Mentioned," online posting, Yahoo womanist group, September 2, 2005, http://www.groups.yahoo.com/group/womanist/.

53. See 1 Corinthians 11:23-25.

54. Think Progress, eds., "Katrina Timeline," http://www.thinkprogress.org/katrina-timeline. The Think Progress Katrina Timeline is a documentary trail of daily, sometimes hourly, events involving local, state, and federal response to the disaster.

55. "President Arrives in Alabama."

56. "Katrina Timeline," "President Bush Stages Photo-Op 'Briefing'": "Coast Guard helicopters and crew diverted to act as backdrop for President Bush's photo-op. job" (White House, September 9, 2005).

"Bush Visit Grounds Food Aid": "Three tons of food ready for delivery by air to refugees in St. Bernard Parish and on Algiers Point sat on the Crescent City Connection bridge Friday afternoon as air traffic was halted because of President Bush's visit to New Orleans, officials said" (*Times-Picayune*).

"Levee Repair Work Orchestrated for President's Visit": "Touring this critical site yesterday with the President, I saw what I believed to be a real and significant effort to get a handle on a major cause of this catastrophe. Flying over this critical spot again this morning, less than 24 hours later, it became apparent that yesterday we witnessed a hastily prepared stage set for a Presidential photo opportunity; and the desperately needed resources we saw were this morning reduced to a single, lonely piece of equipment" (Senator Mary Landrieu).

"Bush Uses 50 Firefighters as Props in Disaster Area Photo-Op": A group of 1,000 firefighters convened in Atlanta to volunteer with the Katrina relief efforts. Of those, "a team of 50 Monday morning quickly was ushered onto a flight headed for Louisiana. The crew's first assignment: to stand beside President Bush as he tours devastated areas" (*Salt Lake Tribune*, Reuters).

See also the words of Senator Mary Landrieu (D-LA) in "Landrieu Implores President to 'Relieve Unmitigated Suffering'; End FEMA's 'Abject Failures,'" September 3, 2005, http://www.landrieu.senate.gov/releases/05/2005903E12.html.

> I understand that the U.S. Forest Service had water-tanker aircraft available to help douse the fires raging on our riverfront, but FEMA has yet to accept the aid. When Amtrak offered trains to evacuate significant numbers of victims—far more efficiently than buses—FEMA again dragged its feet. Offers of medicine, communications equipment and other desperately needed items continue to flow in, only to be ignored by the agency. But perhaps the greatest disappointment stands at the breached 17th Street levee. . . . The good and decent people of southeast Louisiana and the Gulf Coast—black and white, rich and poor, young and old—deserve far better from their national government.

57. Barbara Bush, quoted in "Houston, We May Have a Problem."

58. "Lessons from a Historic March: From a Talk Given by Minnie Bruce Pratt at a Workers World Party Meeting on March 24 in New York," *Workers World*, April 1, 2006, http://www.workers.org/2006/us/mobile-new-orleans-0406/.

> In the 1980s, white supremacist David Duke tried to resuscitate the Ku Klux Klan in Slidell, La., as a well-educated, articulate, 20th-century hate group. Duke ran as a Republican for the Louisiana Senate in 1990. But before that, in 1981, Don Black, his right-hand man, put together in Slidell a group of nine other neo-Nazis and Klansmen plotting to invade the Caribbean island of Dominica, overthrow its government, and turn it into a "white state."

59. Wallis, "What the Waters Revealed."

60. "The Katrina Files," *Times-Picayune*, http://www.nola.com/katrina/graphics/.

61. "Study Finds Strong Warming Tie to Hurricanes," *MSNBC*, June 22, 2006, http://www.msnbc.msn.com/id/13477989/.

62. Cf. Micah 6:8. "He has told you, O mortal, what is good; and what does the LORD require of you but to do justice, and to love kindness, and to walk humbly with your God?"

63. Cf. Psalm 66.

Left Behind: Backdrop to a National Crisis

Peniel E. Joseph

The tragic aftermath of Hurricane Katrina is the most recent expression of the deepening crisis of the United States in the age of globalization. This crisis is intimately connected to a series of events and political trends in the post–cold war era. The most notable examples of these recurring circles of crises in recent years were embodied in the 2000 presidential election, the disturbing gap between rich and poor, the growing disaffection of the American electorate, and the domination of information and knowledge by the power elite. Until the arrival of Katrina, the most obvious manifestations of these dangers were reflected in the twin crises of the national security state in the post-9/11 United States, and the United States's invasion of Iraq and subsequent occupation since 2002. Despite its ferocious rage, Katrina is not solely responsible for the untold devastation that was visited on the poor people of New Orleans and the Gulf Coast region. She is only guilty of exposing the cynicism of an American political system that allows masses of the poor, especially the black poor, to endure lives of quiet desperation amid a land of plenty. As in all monumental events, Katrina has a context. Although we are mindful of the significance of more recent national and global trends, Katrina has a deeper context in the marginalization of the black poor in the history of U.S. public policy, as well as in the U.S. imagination.

The recent disaster in New Orleans and the larger southern Gulf Coast region has, in addition to inflicting incalculable horrors on the region in the form of death and misery, opened up the vortex of race, class, and citizenship that provides a backdrop to this unfolding national crisis. Sluggish federal response, a president lacking the political will to convey the breadth of the catastrophe, corporate media reports that characterized the black poor as savages while portraying their white counterparts as struggling innocents, and the Louisiana governor's hysterical threats to shoot "looters" bring these contradictions into sharp focus. Collectively, the masses of the black poor in New Orleans have waited much longer for government intervention than the agonizing hours and days it took to persuade government officials that the crisis was too overwhelming to ignore. The direct descendants of enslaved Africans, African Americans in New Orleans have lived and died, fought and struggled, and often waited lifetimes for help that never came.

The death and devastation in New Orleans, a city that is two-thirds black, with a poverty line that hovers above 30 percent (84 percent of whom are black), represents the contemporary face of racism. Hurricane Katrina's assault on the poorest and most vulnerable segments of the African American community throws into sharp relief recent debates over black poverty, civil rights, and individual responsibility triggered by comedian Bill Cosby's controversial comments that decried the decline of community values, family structure, and individual responsibility among the black poor.[1] In Katrina's immediate aftermath, federal officials echoed Cosby's indictment of the black poor. They also openly questioned why those left behind had stayed in their homes in the face of Mayor Nagin's evacuation order. Why didn't they leave sooner? They did not leave because they could not. In an economic climate where, despite soaring oil prices and middle-class anxiety, U.S. citizens consider the ownership of ever-expanding homes and gas-guzzling SUVs a personal right, it is easy to forget those left behind during these prosperous times. But for all too many African Americans, the denial of adequate public education and professional opportunities to participate in U.S. prosperity has a familiar ring to it. In an era where too many U.S. citizens congratulate themselves on the size of the black middle-class, the number of prominent black political figures, and the wealth of black entrepreneurs, the pitiful lives of the black poor goes rarely acknowledged and remains invisible.

African Americans in New Orleans represent the latest generation of blacks to live in shelter unfit for human beings, attend schools that do not educate, and often be viewed by black elites and white politicians as undeserving citizens. More than a century ago the great African American intellectual W. E. B. Du Bois, in his pioneering study *The*

Philadelphia Negro, investigated the miserable living conditions of blacks in Philadelphia and concluded that racist public policy, not racial malingering, conspired to trap blacks in the inner city.[2] Du Bois's intervention went unheeded during much of the first half of twentieth-century U.S. history, as waves of blacks migrated to big cities in the north, midwest, and west. Confined to racially and economically segregated "ghettos," black urban development during and after the First and Second World Wars was contoured by public policy (most notably the New Deal) that effectively prevented African Americans from enjoying the massive wealth transfers and subsidies (in housing, the GI Bill, and so forth) that facilitated the baby boomers' entrée into America's postwar middle class.[3] Of course, it was not just northern cities (or urban areas for that matter) that were shortchanged. Urban rebellions during the 1960s transcended regionalism. Although these upheavals are popularly remembered as having taken place in Harlem, Detroit, Newark, and Watts, the rebellions expanded the devastating nexus of race, class, crime, education, and poverty that would grip the 1970s. To add insult to injury, U.S. social scientists largely ignored the long history of racial discrimination and policy exclusion that (along with deindustrialization and globalization) led to urban crises during the 1970s and 1980s, and labeled the urban United States' most desperate residents as the "underclass." These are the African Americans who were left behind to die in New Orleans. In a different era, Black Power activists such as Huey P. Newton described this group as "brothers on the block," whereas Malcolm X characterized them as "Field Negroes."[4]

Perhaps it is fitting that one of the most eloquent defenses of black people—and by extension, of American democracy and the very meaning of citizenship—has come from rap artist Kanye West, whose improvisational critique during an NBC hurricane telethon ("George Bush doesn't care about black people") placed the spotlight on the media's hypocrisy and the White House's blatant callousness. Hip-hop, after all, was born out of the crucible of U.S. urban crisis, producing a generation of black and brown youth who know, against all odds, that their lives are worth living and saving. Although Katrina and Rita have unleashed a national crisis, this crisis also presents Americans of all colors with a tremendous opportunity.

If the nation ever needed to be reminded of what is at stake when we discuss "race relations," this is no longer the case. Chester Himes once said, "A fighter fights, and a writer writes." Now is the time for progressives, radicals, and humanists of all stripes to do both.

MY SISTER'S KEEPER: REFLECTIONS ON HURRICANE KATRINA AND BLACK FEMALE ACTIVISM

MARCIA L. DYSON

The sun blazed the mid-September streets of Houston as our small caravan made its way to the city's Reliant Center. I was part of a band of compassion called into being by the good folk at *Essence* magazine led by the remarkable Susan Taylor. Our charge was to minister to the courageous citizens of the Gulf Coast who were exiled in Houston by Hurricane Katrina's devastating fury. Many of these brave souls, mostly from New Orleans, were part of the overflow of hurricane survivors in Houston's Astrodome to claim shelter at the Reliant Center. It would be a stretch to suggest that they were being housed, because I heard too many stories of their discomfort, desolation, and despair from survivors in the Center and around Houston.

The Reliant Center looked more like a fort than a convention hall. A link fence separated us from the people who were sitting outside getting fresh air. We had to stay in groups as we were led into the building where thousands of folk slept, ate, and desperately searched for loved ones at computer banks. Katrina survivors also used computers to scour the meager listings for more permanent housing. The sight of a convention center transformed into a temporary shelter was frighteningly jarring: sleeping cots dotted the floor where major corporations had hawked their products and services, and where millions of out-of-towners had leisurely strolled.

The New Orleaners I saw that day were dramatically different from those ebullient folk that greeted us in their native haunts, close to the Superdome, during the annual *Essence* music festival. They were not dressed to the hilt; their hair was not freshly whipped or patted into place; chipped, broken nails replaced those adorned with stylish designs and unique air-brushing. The dazed look on the faces of young mothers and children mirrored those of aged men and women. A shy young boy spoke to me through his drumming on the gray concrete wall, not wanting to be disturbed again by yet another stranger.

I was momentarily stunned by the military presence roaming the halls with guns. Clearly, I had entered a makeshift reservation, not a place of refuge. The few belongings owned by the evacuees were bundled in corners, overstuffed into black plastic bags, and for the lucky ones, crammed into a suitcase bursting at the seams. "We are told when to wash, when to shower, and when to be back in this place," an irate mother of three told me. "They treat us like we did something wrong. They even tell us when to eat, and if we go out looking for permanent housing, or go buy something and we get back late, then they tell us, 'That's too bad, you can't eat.' They (officials) treated us nice when we first got here; now it's like we are a burden."

I ventured to the eating area where plates of corn and lima beans, unappetizing Salisbury steaks in thin gravy, withered salad, and cold rolls lay uneaten before a group of people renowned for their Creole and Cajun cuisine: red beans and rice; gumbo; dark, thick gravies; fried catfish; and boiled crawfish. I could not help thinking that if only the powers that be would allow folk into the kitchen, they might have a semblance of home. The bitterly displaced New Orleaners realized the truth of Dorothy's proclamation in the *Wizard of Oz*, that "there's no place like home."

This adage is perhaps as true of New Orleans as anywhere in the nation. Each year that I traveled to New Orleans, I felt I was on a pilgrimage to a holy place. That feeling has become even stronger in the aftermath of Katrina, especially since the Crescent City may never again be the same. This southern city, rich in African culture, is our Bahia de Salvador (Brazil) and our Santiago de Cuba, where the drumbeats of the motherland resound. New Orleaners have been our heritage keepers; we visit them often for their resonant music, flavorful cooking, spirited dancing, creative burying—and for just plain being. The Category 3 storm did more than blow away houses, flood the city, and wreak havoc on businesses and on the future dreams of New Orleans's poorest citizens. Katrina shredded the city's authentic African American identity.

What Katrina could not carry away in her mighty winds, however, or wash away in her torrential rains, is the legacy of racism and disdain for America's poor. These flaws are woven into the tapestry of America's history. Unlike the "tired . . . poor . . . huddled masses" from Europe that were welcomed to our shores by the beacon light held high in the right hand of the Statue of Liberty, blacks who made this country worthy of a transatlantic voyage are still given a left-handed slap in their faces when it comes to receiving aid from our government.

We are not given the hope of the words chiseled in the base of the Statue of Liberty. Nor are we offered the fulfillment of the words etched in black ink on the parchment of the Declaration of Independence, which purports, "We hold these truths to be self-evident, that all [people] are created equal, that they are endowed by their Creator with certain unalienable Rights, that among these are Life, Liberty, and the pursuit of Happiness." Frances Ellen Watkins Harper, educator, novelist, poet, and civil activist, captured the obligation of our nation to its beleaguered citizens when she wrote: "A government which has power to tax a man in peace, and draft him in war, should have power to defend his life in the hour of peril. A government which can protect and defend its citizens from wrong and outrage and does not is vicious."[1]

Two months after the storm hit the Gulf ports of Louisiana, Alabama, and Mississippi, the nation glimpsed the remnants of a slave culture laid bare by Katrina. Poor blacks were forced to live in regions against their will; unskilled laborers found it difficult to secure jobs in their new homelands; the uneducated and undereducated had their formal training even further undermined by stints in shelters and remote hotels, a situation often exacerbated by almost nonexistent transportation networks. And just as slave owners and missionaries justified slavery by contending that blacks were better off in the United States than in Africa, some observers have said that Katrina's gale force ushered black folk into superior living circumstances.

For instance, former first lady Barbara Bush infamously argued that poor black evacuees "were underprivileged anyway, so this [being exiled in Houston shelters]—this [she chuckles lightly] is working very well for them."[2] When Barbara Bush let those words slip through her lips like fine wine in a golden chalice, she was obviously intoxicated by her charmed Texas life. She could not possibly realize that if those who "have rule over us" did right by us, then we black folk would not have to settle for crumbs from the master's table. As I have talked almost daily to many folk forced away from New Orleans, another dimension of slave culture stands out: the glow they have inside their souls that gives them strength to continue believing in a God who, some say, like the Statue of Liberty, has turned his or her backside to a desperate people. I must confess that even I was a doubting Thomas as I visited the lost people of New Orleans in the Reliant Center and watched television reports about the chaos within FEMA, especially how the agency inconsistently rendered assistance to the most vulnerable. As I struggled to help those I met traveling, who sought me out by word of mouth, I shed many tears—not just over the storm, but over its brutal aftereffects, over the sheer calm folk were able to maintain amid such adversity.

At the same time, I forged strong kinship bonds with the folk I was privileged to serve. "Ma, my head hurts so bad," a voice cried to me over the phone. "I'm just so plain tired." When my husband overheard the plea, he asked if the voice belonged to our daughter. He was as surprised as I was—when I first heard the familial phrase uttered by women nearly as old as I am—to discover that the voice resonated from a beautiful woman, Joycelyn, who was battered but undefeated by her trials and tribulations, most of which had not begun with Katrina's fearsome flood. Like many other survivors, Joycelyn thought of me as her mother. I was greatly moved by the honor the title held, and by the affection the folk using it bestowed on me.

Joycelyn and her comrades in suffering called me "Ma" in the fashion and tone that could only be formed in mouths of "Nawlins" inhabitants: sweet, longing, and loving, even when gently moaned in pain. Joycelyn was joined in our kinship of necessity by a great cloud of survivors. These precious folk of New Orleans—citizens treated as refugees—are now dispersed across Houston and Dallas, Texas; Stone Mountain and Northcross, Georgia; on cruise ships in New Orleans; and in motels and hotels outside New Orleans. One survivor is living in her damp, moldy home in New Orleans. She received no assistance to move and had nowhere else to go.

I wake up every morning thinking about these folk, and about the folk who have no advocates. So many poor folk from New Orleans and from the Gulf Coast—and even some middle-class folk—are denied the dignity of their otherwise graceful bearing and movement and forced, awkwardly, into dancing in circles. This dizzying spin spikes blood pressures, deepens depressions, and instigates, in some cases, states of hopelessness. I heard it all in their voices, the way the fury and frustration lay barely beneath the surface of their words.

"Ma, call that landlord. You said when I got there he was going to let me have the place. When I got there, he had changed his mind." This scenario played out often when I attempted to secure someone an apartment or a better hotel. Many of the evacuees, despite the government's promise to pay for their rent, were turned away. They faced the bigoted distance that stretches between my formal speech and their quaint and resounding New Orleans drawl. This newfangled twist on an ancient prejudice, one captured in a Stevie Wonder song, laments how "you might have the cash, but you cannot cash in your face / We don't want your kind living in here." Once, I prevailed upon a dear friend—an aged, Jewish, southern gentleman of impeccable credentials from Atlanta—to drive Joycelyn around Georgia to help her deposit housing applications, and to stand there with her as I spoke with agents on the phone from my Philadelphia home explaining her plight, hoping to get her a place to live. I became sad and angry realizing that I needed a white proxy— almost literally, a knight in white-skinned, shining armor—to stand guard over this precious but durable black woman as we fought for her deserved place in the housing market, in the nation's quickly-fading consciousness.

Even after folk were placed in housing, they were not truly settled. FEMA often did a two-step dance on them, switching partners when Hurricanes Rita and Wilma came wildly waltzing on the shores of Florida and the gulf of Texas, leaving the folk of New Orleans and the Gulf to go solo in their pursuit of extended housing. To switch metaphors, as I found myself frustrated by the cavalry's refusal to respond to folk's needs, I headed to Washington DC to attend a meeting called by freshman Illinois Senator Barack Obama to address the crisis at hand. The meeting was also attended by the heads of FEMA and the Red Cross, and by other concerned members of the clergy, a couple of leaders from national organizations, and the president of the National Conference of Black Mayors, Edwin Dorn from Inglewood, California.

After spending two-and-a-half hours of rhetorical frolicking, I left with few answers, no clear sense of direction, and a gentle rebuke from our host (and my friend), Senator Barack Obama, who, spying my concern for the flock of faithful I came to represent, offered, "You are passionate about a hundred people, and we are addressing millions." The funny thing is that those millions are still frustrated about FEMA and the federal government's lackluster response. Nothing has come of that meeting; well, almost nothing. Senator Obama's comments spurred me to more intense action, but on a more systematic basis: I founded the Ida B. Wells-Barnett Initiative to amplify the voices of the hundreds I had already helped, through the voices and purse strings of millions of women I served in writing for *Essence* magazine—a network of women that is far larger and more influential than any single one of us is. Senator Obama had awakened in me a desire to coordinate all of my actions. He also awakened, if inadvertently, an intense passion of black women's social concern for our sisters and brothers hammered by Hurricane Katrina. If it was not quite a Sojourner Truth-meets-Frederick Douglass moment, it was a sufficiently instigating and inspiring moment of black female political awareness and activism.

The (re)birth of a new black female political consciousness provides links to our past struggle and to contemporary crises that must be placed in a broader racial, historical context. During the storm's early days, many observers compared the devastation felt by Katrina survivors to the devastation felt by the surviving family members of the victims of the terror of 9/11. But the comparisons soon stopped, and so did the cultural empathy and financial support for the victims of Katrina. As Dr. Martin Luther King, Jr. warned us nearly forty years ago, attention to black suffering in the United States is woefully episodic. Moreover, the nation seeks merely to paper over tragedy rather than address its roots. King wrote in *Where Do We Go from Here: Chaos or Community*:

> Negroes have proceeded from a premise that equality means what it says, and they have taken white Americans at their word when they talked of it as an objective. But most whites in America in 1967 [and even now in 2006], including many persons of goodwill, proceed from a premise that equality is a loose expression for improvement. White America is not even psychologically organized to close the gap—essentially it seeks only to make it less painful and less obvious but in most respects to retain it. Most of the abrasions between Negroes and white liberals arise from this fact.[3]

In the aftermath of Katrina, we have the opportunity to right significant wrongs and address the persistent poverty and social inequality that prevails among the poor. The same sort of political activism and social relevance that characterized the civil rights movement can galvanize our people via Katrina. The time is ripe for a spiritual rebirth to ignite our political and social advance. Just as Moses and his people had to first confront the wilderness while trekking from Egypt to the Promised Land, we, too, confront a wilderness of expanded economic opportunity for some, surrounded by crushing material suffering for many others. Some of us have taken the land, but some of that land, as in New Orleans during the reconstruction and rebuilding phase, is being snatched back by familiar culprits and erstwhile masters of our realm. We must organize to protect our assaulted brothers and sisters. In a palpable sense, what happened to our folk throughout the Gulf Coast could very well happen to any and all of us.

We saw some hard political truths amid Katrina. One of the most salient lessons we learned is that the government and the Bush administration seem only capable of moving quickly and effectively when the situation suits their ideological or strategic aims. The nation preemptively struck against Iraq in a war that has lasted far longer than the president predicted. Bush appears able to peek beneath the black holy dress of women ruled harshly by men in the Middle East and discern their future as an oracle of patriarchal compassion, and yet fails to peer beneath the suffering of dispossessed black women as the titular "father of the nation." Bush seems blind to these women's children who are not in school, or undereducated, and therefore underemployed, or disproportionately placed in juvenile detention centers, and subsequently, in prisons. Neither does he see other personal and social oppressions these women and their men and children face.

As with other quarters of black life, the women of New Orleans are often the heads of their households. Many of them, like Joycelyn, live with their "fiancés." The day after she celebrated finding a home—her daughter begged her, "Ma, let me just feel the keys"—Joycelyn suffered a stroke from her stressful ordeal, which was mainly finding an apartment after her two-month stay in a motel. I thought of Joycelyn as I traveled to address the Women Who Are Shaping the World Summit, hosted by *Essence* magazine in New York City, hoping to find a few sisters who also felt we are our sisters' keepers, to ask support for daughters of New Orleans.

Although the storm had subsided, the aftereffects of Katrina continued to spread. The media had ceased to cover the crisis as intensely as it had initially. As a result, most citizens did not know that many evacuees still had no housing, were still unemployed, and had not yet received help for their medical and psychological stress. The culture at large failed to see how the rebuilding of New Orleans would probably furnish the blueprint of how the government and all its agencies might respond to any black community in crisis at any given moment. I wanted to tell my sisters that Frederick Douglass once said that in order to measure the heights to which we have risen, we must first measure the depths to which we were dragged.[4]

I attended the *Essence* summit believing that my service to Joycelyn, at least, had reached a successful conclusion. But helping her gain housing was just the beginning. I had hoped that the apartment would please, and bring Joycelyn happiness, which it did for a while. But I forgot she had no furniture and had slept on the carpet floor of her living room. I was alarmed when I later retrieved my phone messages and heard Joycelyn's frail voice declaring, "Ma, you left me." I went to the summit to perform a victory dance that was premature. I bought Joycelyn bedroom furniture from my paltry personal funds, which I used to pay rent for as many evacuees as I could.

I was especially moved by Joycelyn because of the spectacular fashion in which she repudiated stereotypes of single black women. Contrary to the pernicious views of poor black mothers held by some critics, Joycelyn rose from her sickbed every day in search of elusive employment. She finally got a job at a nearby discount store. She must take a bus and walk a mile and a half—a prospect made more painful by a heel spur, which she told me she never had time to correct in New Orleans because she could not afford to take off from work to address her injury. Joycelyn expended all this effort on a part-time job, stocking clothes and other retail merchandise, only to earn a measly twenty-four dollars a day.

"It's better than nothing Ma," Joycelyn proudly insisted to me. "You can't do everything for me. I am used to working this hard. It's going to be OK." Joycelyn was happy to provide for herself. Her example humbled me, since I spend an average of forty-five dollars on one meal delivered to my home on days my other work will not allow me to cook for my husband and me. Joycelyn became my hero. She reminded me of my mother, the late Rosa Elizabeth Smith, who took any job—short-order cook, waitress, even numbers runner in the 1950s in Chicago—to feed her seven children.

****

Three months have passed since Katrina's lethal winds and waters descended. The bleak, cold, winter months bring the two holidays that remind us to spread cheer and count our blessings—Thanksgiving and Christmas. During Thanksgiving holiday, my family joined me to meet some of the New Orleans families I had the privilege to serve. We hosted a meal for nearly twenty-five folk. I enjoyed performing the wedding ceremony of two of the evacuees. Their witnesses were other evacuees I had worked with over the last several months.

We scrambled to decorate the reception hall on the upper level of Dr. Barbara L. King's Hillside Chapel and Truth Center into a wedding chapel. The small children pulled violet candles from windows and placed them on the floor under the crystal chandeliers as women dragged artificial trees to line the walkway where the bride would greet her groom. These are the New Orleaners I know—folk who work and pray together, who are willing to make everyone family.

And the bonds of community were strengthened as well. On this Thanksgiving Day in 2005, the village was healthy and was taking care of its own. After the festivities were over, and we returned the chapel to its original setting, we faced the bitter reality that the village beyond our walls was still sick, depleted, and in need of restoration. "Don't worry about your rent," I reassured the bride and groom as they came to my hotel to return the tuxedo and shoes. "These are going to get us good money. And, God is not going to let a love like yours go down in sorrow." I have to admit I fought back tears to utter these words of encouragement, because I was not sure myself if God would do what God proclaims, that if you delight yourself in the Lord, God will give you the desires of your heart. If anyone superbly translated this belief into action, it was this beautiful couple.

During the wedding ceremony, I prayed that their love and faith would move God's heart and provoke God's memory of the promise. I also pondered what our government would do for them. I was reminded of Dr. King's poignant words:

> The gospel at its best deals with the whole [person], not only [the] soul but [the] body, not only [the] spiritual well-being, but [the] material well-being. Any religion that professes to be concerned about the souls of [people] and is not concerned about the slums that damn them, the economic conditions that strangle them and the social conditions that cripple them is a spiritually moribund religion awaiting burial.[5]

I also kept King's words in mind as I finally visited the Big Easy for the first time since Katrina struck. On January 14, 2006, the day that I long awaited came when my husband and I boarded the plane bound for New Orleans. As we flew in the turbulent skies, I wondered anxiously about what I would see when we landed. The day was beautiful and the sky was clear. I felt nothing had changed until a host asked us if we had face masks when we said we wanted to visit the city's lower Ninth Ward. We had not brought such an item with us. I did not think or care about it. I wanted to see where I once celebrated the culture of the Crescent City; to see where Joycelyn once lived—where the infamous barge broke a levee, part of her home, and flooded the ward. I wanted to visit Darlene, another brave soul whose family I had served, as they came back to New Orleans from Houston, Texas—back because being away was too painful.

When I arrived at Darlene's housing complex, garbage still littered the streets; houses were boarded up or had for-sale signs hanging from broken porch railings. We climbed the outside stairway to the second floor of a mostly abandoned nine-unit complex, where only Darlene and another family resided. Inside her tiny, three-bedroom, one-bath apartment, I cried as Darlene and twenty-one members of her family greeted us. Boxes of clothing, baby items, food, and covered furnishings filled the unoccupied spaces of the apartment. Darlene's daughters, her son, nieces, nephews, and fictive kin all resided in this small space.

"Hey, I don't believe you came!" they gleefully shouted. Catfish lay seasoning on the crammed kitchen table; sweet potatoes that would soon be whipped into one of Darlene's delicious culinary treats boiled on the stove. I kissed babies, so many beautiful babies, who were held in their mother's arms, or who held tightly onto their mother's knees. "You all live here?" I asked in disbelief. "Yeah, Marcia, we do," Darlene happily responded. "When I left Houston, they all came with me. We are family and we stay together. It ain't easy, it ain't grand, but it is home. We are used to being together and that is what we are going to do."

Darlene explained how bad it was for them in Houston—not the housing, but the attitudes of those "fatigued" by hurricane victims' presence. "We never knew what would happen to or for us," Darlene said. "At least we know home. We will find jobs here and make it somehow in New Orleans." One of her daughters rose to turn on the hot water valve to wash one of the children. "The hot water leaks so we can't keep it on all the time," she offered.

I watched three generations of women, the oldest woman being forty-seven, as they worked together to prepare our Creole feast. They were constantly laughing, hugging, stopping to plant a kiss on my cheek now and then, and entertaining me with their stories of one another. These women, who were once employed, now lamented not having any work to do. Their compensation for contributing to the job market before Katrina was paltry, but their unemployment award was offensive. One of the women, who once worked as a patient caretaker, received only $46.78 a week for herself and four children; her sister-in-law, a former housekeeper at an upscale hotel, received only $51; and other mothers were getting a much smaller unemployment check.

"They got some work here for the men, not much for the women," Darlene told us. "We make it by pooling our money together. Long as we together, it don't matter." She paused briefly, fighting back tears, and forged on. "I am going to have a home of my own, one day, Mrs. Dyson," Darlene formally said, as she also announced plans of heading up a business. "We are going to find a way to take care of ourselves. Shoot, the government taught us real good that we better, because we sure can't count on them."

As they started serving the food, the smaller children were given chicken nuggets and fries while the older children and guests were served potato salad; catfish; and fried, seasoned shrimp. "When can I have shrimp?" a preteen boy asked. The women laughed and one responded, "When you get thirteen, just like it was with us." She turned to me to offer an explanation for the culinary hierarchy, an important rite of passage within the extended family. There were simply too many of us for him to have the small shellfish that symbolized maturity within the family and at the table. But, if for just a moment, I wanted to break protocol and offer the youngster a foretaste of glory divine. "You like hot sauce?" I secretly asked him. "Sure," he eagerly replied. I let him take the morsel from my plate and watched him as his face gleamed with joy. But his small portion, which made him so happy, will not do for the grown folk responsible for him. We need better allotments of funds for our people hit by disasters. What we generously give in foreign aid to other countries needs to be implemented on our own soil.

Since the formulation of the Ida B. Wells Barnett Initiative, we have purchased homes; started cottage industries for some of women; started tutorial programs for the less educated; and we continue to raise funds for future rents, mortgages, and business opportunities for our New Orleans folk. The future of the Crescent City, in relationship to its black citizenry, is still bleak; and the *daymares* they have about their day-to-day existence is frightening. The work to build a better New Orleans must be constantly renewed and affirmed. Katrina's winds remind us that although our "arms are too short to box with God," we can offer a hand to those who are knocked down by racism, inequality, prejudice, and governmental incompetence. As the classic gospel tune reminds us, God guides us even during storms and crises that challenge our faith:

Master, the tempest is raging! The billows are tossing high!
The sky is o'ershadowed with blackness, No shelter or help is nigh:
Carest Thou not that we perish? How canst Thou lie asleep?
When each moment so madly is threat'ning a grave in the angry deep?[6]

I still sing this song—but only this stanza—because we have not resolved the Katrina situation and have not yet found "rest on that blissful shore," referred to later on in the song. Peace has yet to be stilled in the hearts and minds of the dispersed folk of New Orleans and the Gulf Coast; their souls are still sinking. But I, and many others, hear the drumbeat of the master calling us to our task—spreading Godly love. Further, we understand what theologian Matthew Lamb meant when he argued that "the cry of the victim is the voice of God." Such a view conjures a paraphrase of the powerful scripture that features "the righteous" posing one of the most significant questions a believer—whether we are Christian, Muslim, Jewish, or another faith—might ask the God of the universe: "When did I clothe you? When did I feed you? When did I visit you?" What is the simple but profound answer? "When you did it to the least of these . . . you did it unto me." We must never forget these words as we attempt to love our sisters and brothers harmed by Hurricane Katrina.

Notes

1. Shirley Logan, ed., "Duty to Dependent Races" in *With Pen and Voice: A Critical Anthology of Nineteenth-Century African-American Women* (Carbondale: Southern Illinois University Press, 1995), 36.

2. *Editor and Publisher Journal*, page 1, September 5, 2006; *New York Times Online*, September 7, 2005, page 1.

3. Martin Luther King, Jr., *Where Do We Go from Here: Chaos or Community?* (New York: Bantam Books, 1967), 9.

4. See Frederick Douglass, *My Bondage and My Freedom*, chapter 5, p. 63; The Literature Network; http://www.online-literature.com/frederick_douglass/bondage_freedom/.

5. Martin Luther King, Jr., "Pilgrimage to Nonviolence," *Christian Century* 77 (April 13, 1960): 439-41.

6. Mary A. Baker, "Master, the Tempest Is Raging," 1874.

"The Sky Is Fallin', the Dam Has Broken": Violence, Chaos, and Oppression in Literature

Cheryl A. Kirk-Duggan

Throughout history, people—philosophers,[1] preachers,[2] and politicians—have expounded on why bad things happen in life. Often, we rationalize hurricanes, volcanoes, tsunamis, tornadoes, and earthquakes as a form of divine retribution.[3] In addition to the theodicy or why questions regarding the event itself, we seek to analyze larger society, its systems, its strengths and weaknesses. We note human complicity, such as global warming and ozone holes before, during, and in the aftermath of these natural disasters, as well as the theological and ethical implications of tragic, natural, human disasters. When such tragedy occurs, we ponder the dynamics of human behavior—the nature of circumstances when public and personal decorum remain above board versus when that behavior deteriorates—and seek the reason for the disaster. In other words, we seek to learn how the disaster could have been avoided or precluded, and what emergency management to have in place when it strikes.

Centered in Missouri, the New Madrid earthquakes, with more than two thousand tremors between December 16, 1811, and late April 1812, shook the Mississippi Valley and were felt from Canada to New York, New Orleans to Washington DC. Geographically, these quakes affected a million and a half square miles, destroyed towns, created an eighteen-mile-long lake, and even caused the Mississippi River to run backward temporarily. Politically, these quakes uncovered the cruelty of two of Thomas Jefferson's nephews and changed the course of the War of 1812 and the future of the new republic.[4] Less than a century later, another earthquake shook the United States, this time on the West Coast. On April 18, 1906, the earthquake in and around San Francisco tore up 480 blocks, wrecked 25,000 buildings, and disrupted gas mains and electrical power, which precipitated the fires that burned for three days leaving 250,000 people homeless and 700 people dead.[5]

In 1911, one hundred forty-six young immigrants, mostly women, lost their lives in a devastating fire in New York City's Greenwich Village when a fire quickly consumed a high-rise garment factory. Though workplace death was a routine hazard during this industrial boom, this disaster changed the United States, for the flames and the strikes against horrific working conditions changed the political machinery of New York City. The incredible speed of the fire, the tragedy, the terror, and the saving and deadly strokes of fortune all happened in minutes, because of locked doors, inadequate fire escapes, and delayed warnings.[6] On September 21, 1938, a maverick storm, like a giant Cyclops, moved up the Atlantic seaboard with its "eye" fixed on New England. Striking without warning, and going berserk through seven states in seven hours, this hurricane tore up the Atlantic City boardwalk, turned downtown Providence, Rhode Island, into a seventeen-foot lake, and flooded the Connecticut River Valley—the cost: the loss of about seven hundred lives; 1,754 people seriously injured; 20,000 buildings wrecked; and huge property loss, to the tune of $4.7 billion in twenty-first-century dollars. Geographically, new maps had to be created to reflect the new coastline. Politically and emotionally, with the winds and rains of that hurricane, the New Deal accelerated, those not harmed by the Great Depression were devastated, demand soared for air travel, and many young men who survived would shortly be going to World War II.[7]

On the cusp of World War II, midsummer, 1944, a fire erupted during a Ringling Brothers and Barnum and Bailey Circus performance in Hartford, Connecticut. The fire burned out of control with eight thousand people trapped inside, one hundred sixty-seven ultimately losing their lives. This fire occurred a month after D-Day, amid initial collective disbelief, followed by panic, and uncertainty as to how the fire began and who started it. Like Katrina, there was a great deal of miscommunication in the moments of crisis, and following it like Rita, the Port Chicago explosion and fire of the same year killed two hundred sixty-three persons.[8] What rationale can we find for tragedy of such massive proportions?

My essay explores the dimensions of so-called civilized behavior or respectability when this behavior disintegrates into chaos amid natural disaster, through the lens of literature. Using Archibald MacLeish's *J.B.*, William Golding's *Lord of the Flies*, and Thomas Hobbes's *Leviathan* as case studies, this essay first provides an overview of the stories and the issues concerning each particular disaster. An analysis of the related ethical and theological challenges that expose oppression follows. In the process, I note the issues of mimesis, violence, the levels of chaos, human complicity, and that left to mystery.

The Stories of Disaster and of Power

MacLeish's *J.B.*,[9] a poetic play based upon the biblical book of Job, signals MacLeish's response to the disasters of suffering and dreadfulness of two wars, including the Holocaust and the atomic bombings of Nagasaki and Hiroshima. J.B., a twentieth-century banker-millionaire, is a pawn between God and Satan. God lets Satan strip J.B. of everything, including his family and his wealth. Despite his great loss, including infirmed health, J.B. does not reject God. This play, with a prologue and eleven scenes, is set inside a circus tent. In the prologue, Nickles convinces Mr. Zuss to play God and Nickles plays Satan, as he is upset because of human suffering. These two old men play off of each other with gestures and rhetorical emotions, and both don masks; Zuss the white, lidded God mask and Nickles the dark, open-eyed Satan mask. The two of them play above the scene of J.B. and his family. J.B. is married, with five children. During the ensuing discussion, they discuss being grateful to God; offering thanksgiving; questions of luck and justice; the mysterious, undeserved goodness of God to humanity; and God's capacity to reward and punish. An interesting theodicy arises as Zuss and Nickles argue whether J.B. is a righteous man. When Nickles asks why J.B. must suffer, Zuss replies that one suffers to praise; Nickles counters that one suffers to learn. When the two Messengers visit we learn of the deaths of two of J.B. and his wife Sarah's children, as the Messengers continue off and on to ponder the theodicy question; the *why* question. Nickles argues, "God is where we all are—in our suffering" (84). An explosion destroys all of J.B.'s assets, but he is determined to continue. Besides, one should never give up, as Sarah and J.B. note; God is there in the midst of desperation (89). God gives up everything and everyone pertaining to J.B., except for J.B.'s life. All of J.B.'s children have died horrific deaths: raped and murdered, crushed by stones, and two killed by a drunk driver—they were smeared across the road. To wit, Nickles views such acts as indecent and disgusting (93). As four women and a girl watch J.B. and Sarah, like they are in a store window, J.B. wants God to let him die; Sarah doubts God will do J.B. that favor, because God is their enemy. Sarah questions the meaning of death and pain and God's justice, given the deaths of their innocent children. J.B. argues that either God is God, or we are nothing; if we are innocent, God is unthinkable (108-11). Sarah leaves and J.B.'s three friends, the Three Comforters, argue that J.B. must have done something for all of the punishment he is receiving; at least he is guilty because of original sin; he was born human. J.B. continues to interject that God is just. J.B. finally cries out to God for an answer. All is complete silence when a Distant Voice, the God voice, counters J.B.'s question with another series of questions about beginnings, power, and capacity. The Comforters wake up and leave; the women sit up and then leave. When the Distant Voice challenges J.B. to show himself as powerful as God, J.B. remains silent, then acknowledges the power of God and ultimately repents. In a twist from the expected, Zuss and Nickles angrily hold up J.B. in ridicule, doubt his sincerity, and critique the way the play, that is, the biblical story in the play, usually ends: God restores everything. Zuss and Nickles then argue the stupidity of J.B. accepting the restoration of his life, of living his life all over again. Neither Nickles nor Zuss can really figure out what has happened. Nickles moves to the stage and goads J.B., pushing him toward suicide and rejecting God. Nickles leaves when Sarah returns. Sarah says there is no justice in the world and that she left J.B. because she loves him and could not help him. J.B. says God does not love, God is. The play ends with the two of them together, without the complete restoration, with them alone without light in the universe, as they affirm that they will know.

Golding's *Lord of the Flies*,[10] an allegorical novel, concerns the plane crash of a group of English schoolboys on a deserted island. Initially, the stranded boys cooperate as they share and delegate the work of food gathering, making shelter, and building and maintaining signal fires. The boys choose Ralph to lead them. Piggy, Ralph's friend, also helps with resources, particularly his thick eyeglasses, which help them in lighting fires. Ralph appoints Jack as the leader of those who will hunt for food. After Ralph, Jack, and Simon explore the island, they decide to light a signal fire to gain the attention of passing ships. Unfortunately, they play and forget the fire and it burns out of control, presumably killing one of the youngest boys, who is missing. The boys enjoy not having to deal with grown-ups. Although Ralph tries to enforce order and delegate responsibility, many of them prefer to play, swim, or hunt the island's wild pig population. Soon they ignore Ralph's rules or they challenge him. One day a ship passes in the distance, but the signal fire has burned out. Jack, the redheaded leader of the pig hunters, becomes Ralph's fiercest opponent, and he manages to lure away many of the boys to join his band of painted hunters. Some of the other boys are now becoming afraid and they believe there is a monster or beast lurking on the island. Things begin to deteriorate as the semblance of civilization continues to fall away. Jack makes himself the leader and they hunt a pig, which they violently slaughter and decapitate, placing the head upon a stake as an offering for the beast—a head later covered with flies. Simon has a vision about the head where he believes he hears the head speaking: Simon can never escape him, because the "Lord of the Flies" exists in all people. They attack and kill Simon as he arrives back on the beach. Soon Ralph realizes that now he and Piggy are the hunted. The boys kill Piggy and Ralph barely escapes. Ralph hides and Jack and the others set fire to the forest to smoke Ralph out of hiding. When Ralph awakens, a British naval officer is standing over him. From the ship, they had noticed the fire. As the other boys reach the beach near Ralph, they stop when they see the officer. Shocked by the appearance of these savagelike children, the officer asks Ralph to explain. Ralph is so overwhelmed that he is now safe, and yet thinking about all that has happened, he begins to cry. The other boys also begin to cry. The officer turns away so that the boys can regain their composure. This novel explores the lines between human reason and animal instinct, amid adolescent competition.

Hobbes's *Leviathan*[11] is a book of political philosophy wherein Hobbes explains the beginnings of political institutions and defines these institutions' powers and limits, in response to his fear of the seventeeth-century century English civil wars. Hobbes creates an analogy between the art of nature, human productivity, and the productivity of the commonwealth. *Leviathan* argues for an absolute sovereignty, using a mechanistic view of the universe, where all phenomena exist as motion and matter, rejecting disembodied souls or incorporeal spirits. Hobbes believed that traditional philosophy offered no basis for truth claims. Hobbes saw civil war as the

ultimate terror—consummate fear. His answer to this fear and terror is
Leviathan, a way ultimately to end all controversy, war, and fear.
Leviathan, a metaphor for the state, suggests that by establishing a commonwealth through a social contract, one can create civil peace and
social unity. A commonwealth, where a large number of people agree to
the rule by a sovereign authority—a person or group of persons—is a type
of government designed to promote peace and provide for a common
defense. *Leviathan* is an artificial man; the sovereign is an artificial soul;
the states' officers are artificial joints; punishment and reward are nerves;
riches and wealth are strength. The artificial man is to ensure people's
safety. The state laws pertain to its reason and will; its health concerns
concord; its illness is sedition; and civil war is the state's death. Hobbes
argued against any sense of the infinite, for the infinite is something
where we cannot visualize boundaries; thus the notion of God pertains to
honoring something unfathomable, not to any supreme being. Since the
only universal things are names, Hobbes denies that objects share anything universal, and that reasoning, finally, is the addition and subtrac-
tion or manipulation of names. Since we can see everything in terms of
bodies in motion, our emotions are motions in the body. We obtain
knowledge through observance of fact, and conditionally, of science.
Religion, a human invention, is the result of human fear and ignorance,
and a vehicle that serves the desires of priests or clergy. Although people
are more alike than different, Hobbes posits that people often like or
desire the same thing. If they cannot both enjoy the same thing, people
become enemies and fight over the object. People fight because of glory,
reticence, and competition. To have peace, then, people agree to transfer
certain of their rights through a social contract under a sovereign in a
commonwealth: an aristocracy, democracy, or monarchy, with the latter
having certain advantages. However, if the sovereign ruler cannot protect
the people, they no longer have to be obedient. The rules of right and
wrong are civil law. Crime occurs because of misunderstanding or flawed
reasoning. Hobbes compares a general commonwealth with a Christian
commonwealth; he uses his exegesis of biblical texts to show that one can
obey both God and a civil authority. Whereas one must always obey the
sovereign, regardless of his religious sensibilities or lack thereof, no religious leader can ever rule the sovereign.[12]

J.B. and *Lord of the Flies* provide information of what happens when
civility falls apart; *Leviathan* shows one form of government that can be
problematic when dealing with disaster.

146

Ethical and Theological Challenges

J.B. explores the nature of justice, both human and divine. This question is one that was asked during the New York fires, the New Madrid and San Francisco earthquakes, and during Katrina and Rita. Theodicy, the traditional theological problem, states it as: if God is all loving, all powerful, and all knowing, and evil exists, how do we deal with the contradiction? Many theologians attempt to answer that question by exploring and trying to verify the existence of God. Two of the classical responses to this question are the Augustinian argument that says bad things happen because of human free will, that people have a choice; and second, the Irenean proposal, that human beings are like God but have not yet achieved God's perfected image. Thus difficult things happen to help mold us to be more in the image of God. Rabbi Kushner states the question elegantly and simply, "Why do bad things happen to good people?"[13]

Many people have tried to make sense of the tragedy that occurred in the aftermath of Katrina. In *J.B.*, the title character recognizes that he is not God, and that as human beings we are fallible and guilty. Whereas God is, we are weak; one can only repent. Yet, the play does not completely restore J.B., as does the biblical text. Further, if you follow the biblical text, innocent suffering occurs, and God does not answer the question of *why*, but rather implies *why not*, since God created magnificence and we have nothing to do with such reality on a cosmological arena. With Katrina and Rita, and the other catastrophes of 2004–2005—the tsunamis, earthquakes, and other hurricanes, and the tremendous loss of life and property—some are saying that we are being punished for being bad, for living a callous lifestyle. I have heard sermons where in an attempt to give people hope, preachers have scandalized the text by saying that bad things happen to glorify God. If such is true, what kind of God is this—a maniacal megalomaniac perhaps? Do we not have to consider the reality of global warming, wherein the waters on the Gulf are warmer, and with hotter water comes more hurricanes? What about the reality that, at least in the case of Katrina, the hurricane itself was not so bad, but the slow reaction time and the negligence of getting poor people help is what caused more harm? What about the fact that almost twelve weeks after Katrina there were more than two thousand people missing and one thousand dead? Why would anyone in their right mind rescue an elderly eighty-five-year-old woman without any identification, or information from the daughter who is nearby, and then not tell the daughter where her mother will be taken? Such unpreparedness and general disregard for human dignity is not a problem of the natural disaster itself, but smacks of gross negligence, human incompetence, and the flagrant, systemic oppression that allows a society to make poor people of African and Euro-American descent other. In the 1911 fire, the immigrants were dubbed other, so not only did they lose their lives unnecessarily, but also neither the state nor their families were able to prosecute the culprits who owned the factory and who had not maintained safe working conditions. Although the blame game does not bring back any of the dead, until we name the wrongs and work to right these systemic evils, we become complicit and part of the problem.

Lord of the Flies shows what can happen when civility shifts to chaos,[14] not unlike the popular song by the Pretenders that says, "It's a thin line between love and hate." Clearly, there is a thin line between civility and chaos. In the aftermath of many natural disasters, people often embrace a mob mentality. Just as the boys became savages, some during Katrina took on a criminal or a callous mind-set. Some who were trying to survive were criminalized. Over and over, a film clip portrayed blacks with bread and water from stores as thieves, and whites with the same kind of contraband as survivors, yet again marginalizing the poorest of the poor. Of course, there was a criminal element, but not everyone acted badly. People usually do not change because of a crisis; the crisis often exacerbates what is already in place. While people had to wait too long in horrific conditions those in charge seemed paralyzed and unable to make decisions, which cost some people their lives. Some police in authority, under orders, became violent with survivors. In the aftermath of Rita, some people were arrested for trying to check on their houses and being out after curfew. In many instances, the Ralphs, Jacks, and Piggys were not to be found. The president and many in FEMA and in local and state government were not prepared, or were untrained and not capable of commandeering resources quickly enough. The National Guard could not be marshaled to work because they were in Iraq. At the same time, there were many good Samaritans who came to help and made themselves available. They saw the survivors as neighbors whom they came to assist. Interestingly, in some cases the media tried to distance survivors even more by calling them "refugees."

Leviathan poses a type of government, of autocratic monarchical rule, as an answer to chaos, but the book does not deal with the problems of what happens with greedy rulers. Some rulers are greedy for power. Others want so much to be in charge, even though we are talking about a republic democracy, that they will not listen to those who may be better informed. In most of the disasters mentioned in this essay, the leaders—whether a mayor, governor, president, head of a company, or self-appointed leader—often did not act in the best interests of the public whose well-being and safety they were sworn to protect. In *J.B.*, neither Zuss nor Nickles protected J.B. God did not protect J.B.: J.B. was the pawn for their philosophical exercise. In *Lord of the Flies*, Ralph tried to look out for the best interests of the group, but Jack was bent on taking control and being in charge. Jack's thirst for power resulted in the loss of innocent life. Many innocent lives have been lost in natural disasters and those caused by human incompetence or callousness. Professing allegiance to a sovereign ruler, a *Leviathan*, can be problematic when the ruler is not empathetic and thinks he or she has the authority to make decisions that will affect people's lives in the long term, without being responsible for the unintended consequences of his or her actions. What else can we learn about civility and chaos from these stories?

Violence, Complicity, and Mystery

Violence is that which destroys, manipulates, defiles, corrupts, causes harm, and robs us of dignity and of true personhood. Violence involves thought and action within a sphere of the spiritual, physical, emotional, philosophical, and the psychological that oppresses and robs an individual or community of their gift of freedom, of their capacity to make choices. Violence is idolatrous in that violence destroys God's created order. Mimesis, to imitate, is central to the way we know and learn. Mimetic desire is that experience where two or more people desire the same thing, same person, same place, or same status. This desire leads to rivalry: several parties want the same object. For René Girard,[15] mimetic desire and its ensuing ritualized conflict is the process of resolving and containing the resulting violence. The scapegoat becomes the perpetrator, which affords a kind of calm, moving the given group of persons from a violent catastrophe into peaceful unification. This shift invokes a kind of sacred structure, rooted in sacrifice, which recreates communal, social solidarity. The success of the scapegoating process often hinges on the invisibility of the victim. The process of scapegoating usually releases dissatisfaction and internal violence, yet the violence and need for scapegoating seems to intensify. How do we resolve the conflict?[16] Extensive or collective persecutions of scapegoats are an ordinary kind of violence that can be "legalized," particularly when supported by public opinion, as people define themselves comparatively with one another. The dominant group can define themselves and find unity with one another by identifying a susceptible group as "other" or "outside." Those deemed other, because of differences expressed as gender, race, class, age, or sexual orientation, for example, must be vulnerable and visible. Heightened violence results when one cannot name someone(s) other; Girard refers to these conflictual rivals as "monstrous doubles." Creating differences, or being aware of the differences themselves, creates a definite kind of social order. Ultimately, violence occurs as people and groups struggle to be different; yet through their struggles they end up looking and acting more and more like one another. Lynching (or stoning to death in the ancient world) is the classic act of collective violence.[17]

In scapegoating and naming those who are different other, we become complicit in violence. When the violence spirals out of control, we have chaos: everything is in disarray. The theories about how life ought to be fall apart. Often when one person or group of persons insists on a type of monarchial rule that is incompetent, more devastation happens. In natural and human-incited catastrophes, all the rationale in the world has not helped the pain go away. Even with human mistakes after the fact, we are still left with the initial devastation of the hurricane, the fire, the tsunami, the earthquake, the tornado. Why does the weather become so devastating? Some will argue that bad stewardship—our mismanagement of our natural resources—has caused some of the global warming that intensifies hurricanes. Some wish to argue that God is punishing the planet for our bad decision making and our immorality. This theory does not wash, because there are a lot of bad things happening in places that have never been destroyed by bad weather. Further, in some places of tremendous catastrophe, some of the bars were left standing, whereas the churches were decimated. For some things the most enlightened and responsible answer that we can make is, "I don't know." Just as we cannot prove or disprove the existence of God with theory and philosophy, we cannot finally come to explain why some people die in tragedies and others do not. We cannot explain why some people are cured of cancer and others die. We can know that not every healed person is cured. We can know that our faith, however we construe it, can provide us with hope. Our communities can do a better job of preparing for disaster, particularly if we live near a body of water and over a major fault. Not having the answer to why things happen may not be such a bad thing, if we understand and accept each moment of this life as gift and we honor and cherish these moments, and cherish and respect the people who come along with us for the journey.

Notes

1. Consider Plato's story of Atlantis: "Atlantis—Fact, Fiction, or Exaggeration?" The story of Atlantis begins quite literally with two of Plato's dialogues, *Timaeus* and *Critias*. These accounts are the only known written records that refer specifically to a lost civilization called Atlantis. Many people believe the tale to be complete fiction, the creation of a philosopher's imagination used to illustrate an argument. Others believe that the story was inspired by catastrophic events that may have destroyed the Minoan civilization on Crete and Thera. Still others maintain that the story is an accurate representation of a long-lost and almost completely forgotten land.

2. Harold Kushner, *When Bad Things Happen to Good People: Twentieth Anniversary Edition* (New York: Schocken, 2001), is one of the older popularizations. Another is M. Tinker, *Why Do Bad Things Happen to Good People?* (Geanies House, Fearn, Scotland: Christian Focus Publications, 1997).

3. Scott M. Liell, *Founding Faith* (forthcoming). In a published sermon, the Reverend Thomas Church of South Church, Boston, Massachusetts, blamed the 1755 Cape Ann, Massachusetts, earthquake on God's displeasure at Bostonians' mounting of Franklin Lightning Rods. He saw this as meddling with God's usual mode of reprimand, and "attempting to control the artillery of heaven." "Shaking the Foundation of Faith," *New York Times*, November 18, 2005, A27.

4. Jay Feldman, *When the Mississippi Ran Backwards: Empire, Intrigue, Murder and the New Madrid Earthquakes* (New York: Free Press, 2005).

5. Simon Winchester, *A Crack in the Edge of the World: America and the Great California Earthquake of 1906* (San Francisco: HarperCollins Publishers, 2005).

6. David von Drehle, *Triangle: The Fire That Changed America* (New York: Grove Press, 2003), 1-12, 15, 37, 39, 126, 127, 159. The Triangle was the Triangle Waist Company, the largest shirtwaist or blouse-making manufacturing company in New York. This industry was a white-slave market in sweatshops, demanding long hours, eighty-four hours per week, and little pay. Immigrants provided cheap, abundant labor. Had the workers on the ninth floor been warned three minutes earlier, they may all have been saved. On the eighth floor, two hundred people were evacuated in seven minutes. The former reflects the callous attitude of the Triangle owners.

7. R. A. Scotti, *Sudden Sea: The Great Hurricane of 1938* (New York: Bay Back Books, 2003), 23, 24, 216, 225-32. This hurricane had the customary three factors going for it and an unusual fourth: vicious winds, extremely high waves, heavy winds, and surprise.

8. Stewart O'Nan, *The Circus Fire: A True Story of an American Tragedy* (New York: Anchor Books, 2000), 37, 67-68, 71, 197.

9. Archibald MacLeish, *J.B.* (Boston: Houghton Mifflin, 1956, 1957, 1958).

10. William Golding, *Lord of the Flies* (New York: Penguin, 1999).

11. Thomas Hobbes, *Leviathan* (1651).

12. http://sparknotes.com/philosophy/leviathan/context.html; Masterplots.

13. See Kushner, *When Bad Things Happen to Good People*, and Tinker, *Why Do Bad Things Happen to Good People?*

14. *Lord of the Flies* is also Golding's answer to Rousseau's hypothesis that humans in a state of nature are as perfect as God created them. Voltaire's *Candide*, as in Bernstein's stage musical of the same name, is also a response to Rousseau's perfectibility thesis. See also *Don Quixote de la Mancha* by Miguel de Cervantes.

15. See René Girard, *The Scapegoat* (Baltimore: Johns Hopkins University Press; reprint edition, 1989), and René Girard, *Violence and the Sacred* (Baltimore: Johns Hopkins University Press 1979).

16. Gil Bailie, "Cinema and Crisis: The Elusive Quest for Catharsis" *Image* 20 (1998): 17-20. See Girard, *The Scapegoat*. For further in-depth discussion, see chapter 2 in my work *Misbegotten Anguish: A Theology and Ethics of Violence* (St. Louis: Chalice Press, 2001).

17. Conversations with Diana Culbertson, Professor of Literature, Kent State University, Summer, 1995.

REGISTERING INDIGNATION AND INTIMACY: POEMS

Everything Is Wet and Gone

Cheryl Fries

Everything is wet and gone
she said:
the bed
where we made plain love and sometimes
something better than that
and the black Stetson hat that he
earned the hard way
in Vietnam
and all of the songs
that I hummed in the kitchen during all
of those meals I prepared
in there
and the locks of my babies' hair
that I snipped from their milk-scented heads
as they sat in my lap on the bed.
And the bed is gone.

Everything is gone, she said.
Everything is gone and wet.

I Weep on a Slanted Rooftop

Valerie Bridgeman Davis

Death is a part of the landscape;
No words, no priests, no prayers,
Only rampant and unfettered fear.
The faces of friends float by, flushed,
Waiting for you, waiting for God.

I weep on this roof aware
That we mesh cultures
In gutters rising
To our housetops and collapsing
Worlds and worries in the face of
Death in the air; we breathe it in;
It consumes us all.

Blame and dismay go hand in hand,
Kissing kin, and fateful friends
Behold our plight.
The blight of years of neglect
Floats up, blushed with our shame.
We cry together, me on a slanted
Rooftop.

Horror, shock, despair,
And there is no end to it in sight,
Just the certainty of my witness.
They will find my body, still
And clothed in this pain.

The fear, the horror, the frustration,
And my face pressed first in my hand
Then turned upward for answers;
My face streaked with the tears
Of many years of wanting
And waiting, of coping
And praying.

My back against loose shingles,
Collapsing under weight
Of grief and human pain—my own
And that of my two-year-old grandson
And seventy-six-year-old mother—
I weep on a slanted rooftop.

Water and woe climb steps
From windows and attic
And every deep cell in my body.
Wait for rescue and hope,
Wait for you;
Wait for God.

My shoulders jammed into a corner
Dangerous and dirty,
Filled first with the heat
Of noonday sun, the light
Of midnight moon;
A rooftop revelation of loss
And invisibility grabs me.

You cannot know how I longed to hold
Pictures of my mother that are now floating
In putrid rivers of sludge;
Mud and muck to roofline.
My throat constricted
In despair;
I weep on this slanted roof
And wait for you;
Wait for God.

EYES THAT DON'T SEE

CHERYL A. KIRK-DUGGAN

Life and death, juxtaposed
Seen and unseen forces
Bombarding reality;
A cacophony of fear and angst;
Confusion run amuck
When arrogant invincibility
Assumed veils of safety
That disintegrated in moments.
Lifetimes of culture,
Matrixes of hopes, dreams,
Thwarted in webs of tragedies
When, as a nation,
We lost our mythic innocence, again.

The bogeyman of disaster
Knocked down
Our imaginary doors of defiance,
Shattered windows,
Demolished houses,
Usurped civility,
Crushed human spirits,
Robbed bodies of existence;
All delivered death.

Mother nature imbalanced:
Angered by global warming,

Miffed by disrespected marshlands,
Baffled by disregarded barrier islands,
Upset at modern fragile ecosystems,
Threw a tantrum
Of catastrophic proportions,
Making mockery of our sensibilities
That tell us we are in control.

Humans, one among sentient beings
Gifted with capacities
To know, think, and create,
Have not been
Good stewards of planet earth,
Done in by that
Which nature did not destroy.

Human incompetence,
With blatant disregard for the poor,
Produced horrific cruelty;
Survivors warehoused inadequately
Made it through hurricane assault,
Died via human error.
Others still thwarted months later
With tension, disease, posttraumatic stress.

Our Gulf Coast citizens
Became disposable cargo
Torn apart, without tracking ID.
Relocated from their
Communal life in balmy climes,
Where beans and rice
And accessible public transport
Signaled getting by.
Their poverty hidden,
To scattered remote areas;
Their poverty now exposed.

Stormy weather
Made the hidden invisible visible.

Time passes by.
What happens to evacuees
When the glow of giving dims
And FEMA money is gone?

What then for these tired souls
Who have lost everything,
Who remain in shelters,
In tents, with family?
Though trailers stand ready,
"Not in my neighborhood"
Is the cry.

With deep poverty,
Classism and racism
Held firm by denial.
How is flourishing impossible?
Stormy weather exposed the lies;
Made black, brown, white poor folk visible.
The question remains:
Do we have eyes that yet refuse to see?

RIGHTEOUSNESS IN CONTEXT: SERMONS

"Wade in the Water": A Meditation on Race, Class, and Katrina

Alton B. Pollard III

A little more than a month has passed since the winds and water of Hurricane Katrina, swiftly followed by Rita, appeared along the southern Gulf Coast and aroused the national consciousness. The scenes of flooded communities; underwater homes; floating corpses; frightened people; stricken elders; separated families; lost children; stranded animals; makeshift M.A.S.H. units; military divisions; random acts of heroism; weary survivors foraging for food; the left behind on rooftops, highways, and in crowded convention centers; the destitute throngs seeking any way out of New Orleans; whole towns laid to waste in Mississippi; and an entire region yearning to breathe free are indelibly etched upon our collective memories.

There are memorable catch phrases and narratives too: "refugees," "evacuees," "looters," "finders," "incompetence," "too slow to respond," "out of touch," "body count," "death toll," "Third World nation," "our tsunami," and "this can't be America." There is the interview with Aaron Broussard, president of Jefferson Parish, who broke down and cried after criticizing the federal government on NBC's *Meet the Press*. There is New Orleans Mayor Ray Nagin, who in the early days of the crisis lashed out at federal officials, telling a local radio station, "They don't have a clue what's going on down here." There is Louisiana Governor Kathleen Blanco telling reporters that the National Guard have their M-16s "locked and loaded," and ready to shoot troublemakers on sight. There is

President Bush accepting the blame for a federal response that he deemed appropriate but "inadequate." There is federal housing secretary Alfonso Jackson (an African American) saying he believes New Orleans may never again have an African American majority since the displaced are predominantly poor and black with little reason to return. There is former first lady Barbara Bush on a tour of hurricane relief centers in Houston, referring to the poor saying, "This is working very well for them. And so many of the people in the arena here, you know were underprivileged anyway, so this—this [with a slight chuckle] is working very well for them." In the aftermath of Katrina, the early pandemonium and bedlam and the contradictory messages notwithstanding, in the public's inspiring willingness to see things differently and to act with compassion, at least for a time, there is hope.

But floods are also a time for moral and civic examination. Despite the mighty saga of Katrina, and the devastation born of this *natural act* (as scientists squabble over whether one of the most horrific hurricanes on record was really a Category 4 or a 3), I cannot help but wonder (social scientist that I am) if the *unnatural consequences* that followed in its wake—and the humanizing and democratizing lessons to be learned—will be so long remembered. Already, some of the national media attention is fading. Already, our interest is turning to higher crude-oil prices and climbing mortgage rates. Already, we are anticipating high drama on the Supreme Court while the president's political capital runs low. As a society we have been historically adept at concealing, especially from ourselves, the power arrangements we have made that manipulate and demean the life chances of many. Race, gender, and class are of no direct consequence to some of us, but they have always been matters of life and death for black children, women, and men in this country. Wholly unintended, the national media exposed the world to the ugly reality of poverty in the United States of America. The existence of a social undercaste historically premised on race, with gender and class in a virtual contemporary dead heat—permanent, invisible, in parishes and counties and inner cities—was made plain. Every thirty or forty years, it seems, "we the people" are forced to look at ourselves in the mirror and give an accounting for our acts. But even before we would do this we rush to put on rose-colored glasses.

More than forty years ago the great writer, brother outsider, American expatriate, and unsung theologian James Baldwin found himself back in the United States, awash in a sea of racism and the metaphysics of white supremacy. Black America, in the form of civil rights and black consciousness, was undergoing rapid and radical change, a radiantly dark collective bent on challenging the nation to live up to her professed creeds. Baldwin, immersed in the experience of his people, tried to reason with white people in the land of his birth to learn to "put yourself in the skin of a black person" (no less a poor person, a gay person, or any one of the multitudes of the nation's disinherited). There are many democratizing lessons to be learned from "The Fire Next Time," the title of which is in turn drawn from a prophecy recreated from the Bible among the community of Africa's enslaved children in North America: "God gave Noah the rainbow sign, No more water, the fire next time!"[1]

The meaning of the ancestral message from an antebellum and segregated United States of America in sad respects remains the same in the aftermath of Katrina. So much has changed; so little has changed. We have gone forward; we have stepped backward. We are in motion, and yet we are very much standing still. Somewhere, in between these polar assertions, these irreconcilable statements, these antithetical views, lies the sordid, shaded, and complex truth about the state of race, ethnicity, religion, gender, sexuality, and class in our country.

It has often been said that the measure of a society is found in how well it treats its most vulnerable citizens. The aftermath of Hurricane Katrina is thus an important time for us to take stock of where we are as a nation, a region, a city, and a community; and for the church to do a moral and ethical inventory; and to assess our public policies and priorities. The passing of Katrina has become a natural documentary on the fortunes of black, brown, and white; rich, middle class, and poor; the margins and the center; the children, the aged, and the infirm; and the haves, the have-nots, and the never-are-supposed-to-haves in this land. When the fierce winds of nature's fury joined with the gigantic tides of the Gulf to further erode the wetlands, and when the creaking walls of antiquated levees finally gave way in the city, unable to hold back the floodwaters any more, those who managed to survive in convoys, terminals, hospitals, hotels, dormitories, or wherever, and without benefit of outside aid for a time, gathered in places near and far with family and friends and strangers to celebrate the miracle that they are yet alive. The silver lining in the storm cloud, such as it was, is this: the all too tenuous and desperate lease on life had by the already poor and the newly made poor—the teeming whites and browns and blacks—appeared to find a momentary respite, a temporary haven in the land of the plenty, in our nation's psyche, philanthropy, and goodwill.

In truth, the race- and class-based abandonment of untold thousands to disparity, disease, despair, and death began long ago in prehurricane New Orleans. The whirlwind, with undeniable force, reopened the vortex of race, class, and citizenship that has always vexed this land. *We can begin by counting the social costs of Katrina.* Number one among the five cities with the highest concentration of urban poor in America (the city that I now call home, Atlanta, is also tragically on this list), the Crescent City is no different than any other United States urban enclave when it comes to a nation unwilling to live out the meaning of its creed. New Orleans is (was?) 67 percent black, with 50 percent of that 67 percent living below the poverty line. In this tourist-destination city, living wages are hard to come by for workers held captive to seasonal economies (Mardi Gras, the Sugar Bowl, the New Orleans Jazz Festival, and so forth) and service-driven industries. The average annual adult income in some wards of the city is eight thousand dollars. The city's submerged and 98 percent black lower Ninth Ward has long been ground zero for toxic exposure of people to the Mississippi River chemical corridor, also known as part of cancer alley.[2] Many of the Ninth Ward's residents are renters without resources. How will this Katrina diaspora restore their families, their communities, their lives? In the new New Orleans (also known as "New Orleans Version 2.0") and the real estate boondoggle that is sure to come, pariah developers and disaster profiteers will engorge without need of gentrification; the temporary poor and permanent poor are already exiles in their own city. To whom will the black poor turn? Where will they live? To what will they return? Perhaps, some privately but fervently hope, they will choose not to return at all.

New Orleans is also a city famously known for its black middle-class elite. The first literary magazine ever published in Louisiana was the work of French-speaking black poets and writers in a series called *L'Album Littéraire*. In the brutal shadow of sugar plantations and mills, the city boasted a prosperous class of free people of color, artisans, sculptors, business owners, and skilled laborers in all fields. Louis Armstrong is the best known in a long line of improvisational black musical geniuses. Rural blues and urban jazz permeate the Big Easy. Dillard University and Xavier University are their more formal educational counterpoints. But as every African American knows, the emergence of an Oprah Winfrey, Colin Powell, Bill Cosby, Clarence Thomas, or Condoleeza Rice does not for all "equality of opportunity" or "equality of conditions" make. The growth of a black middle class hardly means that racism has ended, but that our obligation to eradicate racial apartheid and black hypersegregation has only just begun. Nevertheless, there are some blacks who have "made it," and who are conveniently and comfortably ready to write off their own. Theirs is "the race to leave the caste."[3]

And what is the role and function of the church? The faith-based community cannot possibly meet the social and economic needs of the people on its own. Nor should we be expected to somehow miraculously remedy the nation's system of racial, gendered, and socioeconomic preferment. At the same time, white churches have only on rare occasion been willing to extricate themselves from the status quo. My sisters and brothers, often it is you who stand in the proverbial "belly of the beast." Work to transform society's institutions until the liberation of Latinos and Latinas, blacks, Asians, Native peoples, and all the dispossessed children, women, and men of this land is altogether bound up with your own. Ethically and theologically, to acquiesce in support of a system that denies the parenthood of God and the kinship of all peoples is to refuse to love. Similarly, if black churches do not commit to playing a more active role in the economic, political, and social transformation of the communities in which they are located, then they are derelict in carrying out their Christian purpose and responsibility. In sum, we, the faithful everywhere, are called to struggle for self-liberation and our common liberation, for our very lives and salvation depend on it. As Dr. Martin Luther King, Jr., stated: "Any religion that professes to be concerned with the souls of men [and women] and is not concerned with the slums that damn them, the economic conditions that strangle them, and the social conditions that cripple them is a dry-as-dust religion."[4]

If we will commit to intensifying our efforts, to investing fully in the utter sanctity of us all, the church that God intended will influence the private and public sphere, and in the process empower, enable, and encourage countless others to enter into their own process of liberation. The challenges are formidable and the opportunities immense. Some have ill-spoken of a divine hand behind Katrina; far more have somberly noted the absence of a human one. As believers, we acknowledge today that we do not always know when or where or how to move. But the biblical mandate, in the context of being as devoted to Jesus as slaves were to masters, understanding the import of privilege and responsibility, to move is sure: "To whom much has been given, much will be required" (Luke 12:42-48). "You will know them by their fruits" (Matt. 7:16, 20).

Politically speaking, whereas more than $156 billion has been spent on an unjust war in Iraq (at about $5.6 billion a month and counting), our government has scarcely approved one-third this amount for the entire Gulf Coast catastrophe to date.[5] Even worse, profitable rebuilding contracts for the region are finding their way into the hands of corporations that have preexisting federal contracts but no indigenous ties to the region. To people on the ground, this privatization of reconstruction is astonishing and beyond belief. Marketed as economic recovery, it is not local, not shared, and not us. Due in no small part to the growing chorus of protests, the federal government has been forced to rescind these no-bid contracts, at least in part. Our national predilection for disparity, our festering social inequities, our destructive environmental policies, our rotting infrastructure, our arrogant global politics, and even our abandonment of pretense about the common good have affected and infected Jefferson Parish, Biloxi, Moss Point, Pascagoula, Mobile, and thousands of communities from coast to coast. All of us, it appears, are but one disturbing saga away from disaster.

It has been said by many that better planning and response by local, state, and federal authorities could have lessened the severity of the hurricane's impact. Perhaps. But the just and moral exercise of power before the winds and waters came would have done far more to stem the disproportionate suffering. Greater redress and resistance against the terrors of tyranny on the part of blacks and browns, the poor and the working poor, and progressive-minded women and men are needed for such a time as this. Rapper Kanye West (who was recently featured on the cover of *Time Magazine* as "the smartest man in hip-hop") was right in his refreshingly candid assessment: "President Bush doesn't care about black people."[6]

At the same time, West's statement needs to be nuanced and complicated—the permanent black poor are but one of a number of communities that are devalued by our political process for lack of political capital. West did not set out to be a role model with his words, but like much of black America he was hurt and enraged that in 2005 it was still all right to denigrate and neglect poor people, the majority of whom looked like him. In the spirit of hip-hop, West improvised on the spot, choosing his principles over the long-term possibility of more money. Soon thereafter, Master P launched "Team Rescue" to assist evacuees. Sean "P-Diddy" Combs and Jay-Z donated one million dollars to the Red Cross, as well as clothing from their respective companies. With the advent of Katrina, one may hope that we will now see the emergence of a real and substantive hip-hop politics (although we still await a like response from the hip-hop community to West's indictment of the genre's homophobia).[7]

Meanwhile, even a politically conservative newspaper columnist such as David Brooks writes that "a joint race to the bottom" is taking place in the form of political grandstanding and partisan finger pointing by the Democrats and Republicans.[8]

In seasons of relative economic prosperity and peace, the persistence of racism can lie as subliminal and fallow as to escape clear and obvious detection by those who desperately want to believe the social fabric is not already rent. A former professor of mine was fond of saying that life has always been cheap in America, and black life is the cheapest of all, for what we value most in persons in this land is never their humanity, but their utility. We have artfully developed techniques in race- and class-relations management, deeming "unacceptable" large numbers of citizens, a disproportionate share of whom happen to be black and brown and poor. Self-assured that these poorer kith and kin are predisposed to inferiority, immorality, and lawlessness ("criminality"), white and black elites alike consign them to back alleys, street corners, underpasses, projects, ghettoes, halfway houses, alternative schools, shelters, jails, prisons, and other carefully controlled and shadowed spaces. Through every fault of their own this is where the unsaved and undesirable belong.

In a complex society like ours, it is well understood that no individual has power except to the extent she discovers a body of sentiment for her own ideals and values for which she can marshal further support. The Adolf Hitlers, Osama bin Ladens, Edgar Ray Killens, Eric Rudolphs, and Saddam Husseins are not solitary or exceptional examples of hatred, tyranny, or racism in our world. New Orleans is our Afghanistan. The Gulf Coast is our Iraq. Crime and violence were there before and during Hurricane Katrina because the very violation of people is fundamental to the origins of this land. In the human storm that followed the rainstorm, the very foundation of our civilization was shaken and the most elemental and feral in our human nature was revealed. The lurking ferocity of the environment, the labyrinthine response of bureaucracy, the uncertainty of humanity's ability to know and plan and control, has torn a hole in our soul. The tectonic plates have shifted, our moral compass has been thrown off, and our racial default setting—neglect—has once more been laid bare. This is the autumn of our discontent. The prophet Jeremiah had it right: "The harvest is past, the summer is ended, and we are not saved" (Jer. 8:20).

Some final reflections: The fierce and generally unacknowledged messiness of the continuing dynamics of race and class in our society is not lost on black America. The tragedy of our time is not whether one is personally a racist or not; that is increasingly inconsequential. Rather, it is society's "silent consensus," "neutral nonconcern," and "outward conformity" on matters of race, class, gender, sexuality, and more that institutionalizes hierarchy, division, and disdain, and is now the given that entraps us all. Justice and righteousness will have their day, and at the expense of an illusory domestic tranquility. Katrina has ripped the veil off the American dilemmas of race and class and hierarchy once again for the whole world to see. Believers, seekers, progressives, activists, countrymen and women of all colors, conditions, and creeds are presented with a clear and tremendous opportunity. As the floodwaters recede, we can raise our voices. No, let us do more. Let us dedicate our very lives to the creation of "a more perfect union," to remaking the United States again. In my mind's eye, I catch a glimpse of the possible in one of my favorite spirituals: "Wade in the water. Wade in the water, children. Wade in the water. God's gonna trouble the waters."[9]

Notes

1. James Baldwin, *The Fire Next Time* (New York: Vintage, 1963, 1992).

2. Ronald Roach, "Unequal Exposure," *Diverse Online*, December 1, 2005, http://www.diverseeducation.com/artman/publish/article_5145.shtml.

3. See my essay "W. E. B. Du Bois and the Struggle for African America's Soul" in *How Long This Road: Race, Religion and the Legacy of C. Eric Lincoln*, ed. Alton B. Pollard III and Love Henry Whelchel Jr. (New York: Palgrave Macmillan, 2003), 109-18.

4. Cited in Frederick D. Robinson, "Economic Empowerment through the Black Church," *Atlanta Tribune: The Magazine* (December 2004): 10.

5. "Military and Supplemental Spending," *Network: A National Catholic Social Justice Lobby*, April 2005, http://www.networklobby.org/issues/archive/military_spending.htm.

6. Kanye West, *A Concert for Hurricane Relief*, NBC telethon, September 2, 2005.

7. Hear and read the MTV interview, *All Eyes on Kanye West*, http://www.mtv.com/bands/w/west_kanye/news_feature_081805/index3.jhtml.

8. David Brooks, "The Storm after the Storm," *New York Times*, September 1, 2005, A23.

9. "'Wade in the Water': A Meditation on Race, Class, and Katrina" was presented for the Clark A. Thompson Lectures, Home Moravian Church, Winston-Salem, North Carolina, October 10, 2005.

STRONG AT THE WOUNDED PLACES (ESTHER 5:9-14)

VASHTI M. McKENZIE

One of the challenges in any life, in any age and at any time, especially in this postmodern twenty-first-century era, is to bring closure to issues and events that have damaged our body, mind, or spirit. We find it difficult to turn the page, complete the chapter, start another, and even close the book altogether!

We find it difficult bringing closure to traumatic experiences; closure to devastating incidents; closure to events that challenged our comfort zones and rocked our worlds. Many times it remains an open issue because it, she, he, or they may be finished with it or us—so the book remains open! Or, everyone has had his or her say but us, or we have not found the courage to let it go. For some, the saga of Hurricanes Katrina and Rita is over; they made a charitable contribution and now are getting on with their lives. And many survivors are still homeless, unemployed, and are, in the words of Fannie Lou Hamer, "sick and tired of being sick and tired."

At other times, traumatic experiences remain open, because we want a different ending, so we live with the hope that in spite of what has already transpired another benediction can be pronounced. And so, many remain hopeful and are working hard, months after Katrina, to come bring a different kind of closure for evacuees.

Then there are times the wound remains open simply because we are not ready to close it yet. So we pick at the scab until it festers; we remove the bandage too soon, exposing the wound to more germs and possible infection from the same source that wounded it. Sometimes this makes us "wanna holler," when people—you and I, and those in leadership, in government—get stuck in the minutiae, with no plan of action, as lives and spirits are wasting away, festering with the pus of confusion and weariness.

Then we fail to bring closure because others will not leave it alone. As far as you are concerned, it is over; but they (and ya'll know who *they* are) talk it up and around your social circle, post notes online, and remind you of every finite detail until it reappears on your emotional radar screen. And, before you know it, it starts making appearances in your thoughts and takes starring roles in your dreams—nightmares *and* daymares.

There are some of us who are crisis junkies—closure is not in our vocabulary! We just do not feel right unless there is a crisis going on! A day is not productive until there is an upset somewhere! We thrive on crises; we feed upon their tentacles that threaten to unravel our sanity or somebody else's. We relish a good crisis where we play the role of the victim: the wounded soldier; the perpetrator, wounded warrior, inflictor of pain; the prosecutor—the law and order of wound justice; or the problem solver.

In the medical field, to close a simple wound just requires a bandage or an appropriate covering, and disinfectant or ointments that promote healing. A more complex wound requires sutures or stitches to close it. The wound is shut tight and in a few weeks even the sutures themselves disappear. If the problem persists, then the medical technician reopens the wound, scrapes away the infection, drains away impurities, cleans, and recloses it. Reopening old wounds can be as devastating as the original wound. The replay button is pushed and everything carefully forgotten is again shown live and in living color. Not only did many on the Gulf Coast know the impending threat of the hurricanes, but after all the devastation, as they returned home, they relived the crisis; for they saw that where homes once stood, where pictures hung, where children played, and where families gathered for barbecues had been transformed into muck and mire, into cesspools of contamination and filth. It had become fetid, moldy, a hazardous waste zone.

Yet, opening old wounds sometimes becomes necessary. Unless the poison is removed, a greater problem could occur. What affected only one area could spread to others, contaminating other portions of your life. Wounds can be the womb through which stress-related disorders are born—the place where the sperm of anger meets the ovum of hatred, and rage is born, creating an unresolved life. There is nothing worse than an unresolved man or woman, unable to bring closure to anything—closure to past disappointments; closure to a poor decision; to rejection or refusal; to abuse, criticisms, or other unresolved trauma—and living out the pain of a wound; never healing, living in the past, reexperiencing the pain of the wounding, bleeding over everyone who gets close. Buried rage is powerful, and when that animal is loosed, writes George McKinney, it does not care a whit about consequences, only about retribution—ask Haman. Wounds can also be a source of healing—weakness converted into strength with the experience of becoming a source of strength, as when Jesus was wounded for our transgressions and bruised for iniquity—ask Esther. Ask those survivors who have had to relocate in distant places far away from the familiar. Ask those survivors who have had to start over, or those who returned to the Gulf areas trying to rebuild with minimal services amid maximum devastation.

Let's examine the text.

Exegesis

Esther is the undisputed heroine and Mordecai the hero of this book of the Hebrew Bible, where God is *not* mentioned in any verse or on any page. Haman is the villain of epic proportion, hands down. There is something, however, that both Esther and Haman share. They are both wounded. Their wounds have a history. One's wounds are obvious, and the other's lurk below the surface of a successful life. One wound was experiential—they lived it. The other wound was inherited—they were taught it.

Esther was wounded early in life by the untimely death of her parents. The child's most important relationship vanished. There was no provision under Mosaic Law for adoption; it was practiced by other ancient cultures and perhaps was adopted by the Jews during the exile. Wounded like Esther, many mothers were separated from their newborn babies and suffered for days, waiting to be reunited with the children torn from their arms in the aftermath of Katrina. Others were wounded watching dead bodies float by while waiting on rooftops to be rescued. Many elderly, separated from their loved ones and their medication, languished, wounded and waiting for relief.

Wounded, exiled far away from the familiar, Esther was placed in a harem, a place kept away from the public and outside world; a place of confinement and containment, albeit a luxurious one.

Wounded, Esther was stripped of her name, culture, heritage, and perhaps the public practice of her faith. What of those ripped from the Gulf Coast and relocated to Utah, California, and Idaho?

Wounded, engaged in a relationship not of her own choice, she could not be herself. She had to be transformed into what someone else wanted or needed, hiding who she really was from the man who shared her bedroom. Having complied, she then had to share him with the other women in the house.

Wounded, a queen with no real power, she was married to a king with too much money, too much time, too much power, and too easily manipulated. What of the citizens, with nothing but the filthy rags on their backs from wading in fetid water and from baking on rooftops, in a country many times with too much money, too much imperialism, and too much arrogance; a country that fancies itself the police of the world, yet overlooks its own people?

When the crisis of genocide knocked on the door, Esther could have hidden in her new identity. She didn't run for cover but reached through her spiritual weapons to grip with both hands the grace that led to victory.

Haman's wounds were not so visible. He was a man of power—who delighted to think more highly of himself. He bragged to his friends and wife about his riches, his promotion to second behind the king, the number of his sons, and how he advanced above the princes and servants of the king. George W. Bush has bragged that he is delighted to be part of the "haves and have mores."

On the surface it would appear that Haman was just another ambitious politician. He may have been driven by the thirst for power and for control, manipulating a powerful potentate who ruled from Asia to Ethiopia. Haman's wounds are revealed when he is introduced in chapter 3. Many times we miss the details by not paying attention to the genealogy. He is introduced to us as the son of Hammedatha the Agagite.

Agagite does not merely trace a family tree; it traces the coursing of a blood feud. The Amalekites were Israel's most hated enemies going back to the time of the Exodus (Exod. 17:14; Deut. 25:17-19). Agag, an Amalekite king during the reign of Saul, had warred against Saul, a member of the tribe of Benjamin whose father was named Kish. Mordecai is introduced in chapter 2 as the son of Jair, son of Shimei, son of Kish, member of the tribe of Benjamin.

Six hundred years ago, Haman and Mordecai's royal ancestors fought, and fought hard. Then add perhaps another two hundred years to that;

when Haman's progenitors attacked the Israelites, the progenitors of Mordecai in the wilderness. Now you see two representatives of two families and nations who have a history of battle and bloodshed that pitted the son of a king against the sons of Agag.

Haman's wound was simple—hatred. Hatred had the power to live beyond any specific memory and beyond one's lifetime, according to author John Indermark. Hatred was Haman's wound that sat in the background of his biography; it lived between the lines of his promotion and prestige. Hatred colored his character and fed his ego; it shadowed his self-importance, waiting for a spark or a crisis to ignite it, concludes Indermark.

Hatred, prejudice, phobias, ignorance, and fear fueled racism, classism, ageism, and sexism, which were uncovered by the winds and floodwaters of the hurricanes of 2005. Katrina, Rita, and Wilma were the sparks; the crises that revealed an ill-begotten evacuation plan that left out the poor, the elderly, and the sick. As the water receded, poverty was still alive and well and living in America.

The text says that when Mordecai, son of the king, failed to rise when Haman son of Agag came to the king's gate—Mordecai failed to give him deference when he did not move for him—Haman's woundedness prevented him from seeing the incident as just that. His woundedness made a big thing out of a minor deal, a mountain out of a molehill. An old wound reopened—one that festered between Saul and Agag, the Amalekites and the Israelites.

The hurricanes opened up old wounds that have never been acknowledged, that have never healed, which allow poor people, children, and the elderly to be objectified, discarded, disrespected, and ignored for four days on an ovenlike, broken expressway with no clean water, food, electricity, or toilet facilities.

Haman did not see Mordecai as an old man sitting down. He could not see that perhaps Mordecai was just being impolite, discourteous, or too tired to rise. Haman saw it as pouring salt into an old wound. He pushed the rewind button of family history and went right back to where it all started. The past and the present were remixed as the sore festered. What should have remained history was becoming today's headlines. What should have been a closed book became an active file. What should have been dealt with—such as an inferior levee system, poverty, clear lines of authority, and responsibility—was front and center. It was like the chicken coming home to roost.

Haman took up the blood feud and hatred as if it happened yesterday. Hatred rarely finds closure. Sarah's and Hagar's children were still having a hard time getting along. The promises of American democracy remained unfulfilled for most black people in America, according to Cornel West. Despite Dr. Martin Luther King, Jr.'s deep desire, many of the children of the twenty-first century are not yet judged by the content of their character. Hatred seldom finds courage.

- According to the text, Haman restrains himself.
- Haman thinks it is beneath him to confront Mordecai and the Jewish people.
- He manipulates the king with charges of how different these people are.
- He pays to have them killed—ten thousand talents or two-thirds of the annual income of the entire kingdom.
- Haman's wife suggests the gallows to rid him of Mordecai: "Ask the king when you go to the banquet tomorrow."
- And we know that the gallows he planned for Mordecai was the gallows from which his own body was hanged.

The roots of hatred blinded Haman with a single eye toward retribution. The wound remained fresh, surviving with a different name in a different history that came to the surface at the king's gate. Haman became so obsessed with revenge that he failed to see his own blessings. He had it all. He was at the top of the heap, the height of his game, and all he worried about was Mordecai sitting at the gate.

Here we see two wounded leaders. In a crisis, Esther rose to the occasion, risked her life, and went to see the king. In another crisis, Haman self-destructed. One bounced back and the other broke down. One rose to the occasion and the other fell from grace. One was strong in her wounded places and the other's wound became the stumbling block at the height of his success.

So what shall we say to these things? What lessons are here to help us bring closure to our own issues before they lead us toward our own self-destruction?

1. You may not be able to pick what happens to you but you can choose how you respond.

All of us have seasons where we are walking wounded. The hurricane hits. The house is gone. The ball drops. The friend betrays. The family member disappoints. The divorce is final. The baby died. The money is gone.

One of the characteristics of walking wounded is that you tend to feel sorry for yourself. The issues that wound us can make us feel sorry for ourselves. We may feel that our wounds handicap us. They interrupt the flow of life. The wounds become the reason why we do not, or cannot, act or why we do not have what we want. They are our "wound-excuses" that we wear like medals of honor. Sometimes they are visible to those who see us, or invisible because we carry the wound-excuses like scars on our hearts and spirits and in our minds.

People who have not been through what we have been through somehow live their lives better than us. Since they did not go through what we went through they somehow have an advantage. They never had to put up with what we put up with. They never struggled or sacrificed like we did. They were not uprooted from their homes and sent thousands of miles away to places where they knew no one and had nothing. They did not live through hours of fear while the wind raged or the waters rose.

The past and the present are remixed as we see how in a few hours what took a lifetime to build is destroyed. Life as we knew it no longer exists. We may begin to think nothing good is ever going to happen to us because since Katrina and Rita we have been stuck. This is it. We are marked and marred for life.

The wounds become a pair of sunglasses that we wear day or night. When something good happens our sunglasses darken the rush of good feelings that come; they cloud our vision to our own blessings, so instead of seeing the blessings we just see Mordecai sitting at the gate raining on our parade.

Instead of feeling sorry for yourself, seek favor like Esther. Before she made her request to King Xerxes—she sought his favor—she found favor at the banquet. She had already sought the favor of her heavenly king before she sought the favor of Xerxes—the favor of God changes the status quo. So even though she was a queen with no real political power, the tail became the head. The expected and the usual were interrupted. Like Joseph, who was sold into slavery and who found favor with God, so the one who was supposed to be servant was given the power to take authority over all of Potiphar's affairs. The prisoner in pharaoh's prison had charge of the prison. Favor, power, and authority were reconfigured. Power was transferred to those favored by God right underneath the noses of those in power and authority. David, one who found favor in the Lord, says it this way: "You prepare a table before me in the presence of my enemies . . . my cup overflows"; "yea though I walk through the valley of the shadow of death"; Mary, favored by God, a child betrothed, with no outstanding achievements on her résumé, is catapulted to being the earthly mother of God. Esther, an orphan among her captors, is elevated to queen.

Instead of feeling sorry for yourself, seek the favor of the King of kings and the Lord of lords; because you want God's favor, you want to put yourself into a position where God can reach you. David meditated day and night; Mary said, "Be it unto me"; Job refused to curse God and die; Jacob made an altar and worshiped God; Daniel prayed three times a day; Moses spent forty days and forty nights in the face of God; Elijah sought to see God face-to-face; Abram followed God's instructions; and the woman at the well dropped her pots and preached. Favor: pray, even if it is against the law; live holy, even if it costs you your life; trust God, even if you lose everything; worship, even if you are the only one; walk upright, even if it makes you a target.

2. You may not be able to predict what will happen next but you can determine your next steps when it is over.

The walking wounded tend to have two approaches, and we see this with Haman and Esther. The first is *jihad*, the Arabic word meaning attack, and the second is *hafrada*, the Hebrew word meaning separation or withdrawal.

Haman's *jihad* was with Mordecai. He later attacked an entire nation within a nation—all the Jews in the one hundred twenty-seven provinces of the Persian Empire—to get one man. When Esther was first approached with the genocidal problem, she withdrew until she became convinced that no matter what her title, it provided no protection against the decree.

We are wounded—we hurt and we want to hurt back. We get wounded—we hurt and we want to lick our wounds. What are you doing with your hurt from the devastation of Katrina and Rita? Do you attack those around you or do you retreat from life to lick your wounds?

Sometimes we fight little *jihads* with the people we live with, work with, pray with, are friends with, and are related to. We fight with acquaintances, or strangers on the street; and even with those whom we live with under the same roof. We may even fight those who are trying to help us. Others withdraw, that is, they are there but absent at the same time. We can be in the same room but somehow we become distant, disconnected, or no longer living in the moment. We are no longer active, present, and accounted for.

At the root of these two expressions is fear. All fear, says John Ortberg, is a lack of love, the violation of the one great commandment. All of our relational mismanagement is really a variation of these two tendencies of a wounded human heart. When we feel threatened, we want to hurt or hide. Haman could not reach beyond the wound of the past. Esther was able to reach beyond her wound to God; so instead of attacking others or withdrawing, she helped her people.

Let me share a story often told—an ancient Chinese story. A woman's only son dies. She goes to a wise man who says, "You will find relief when you find the house of a family who has not had pain." She keeps going; she hears the stories of great tragedies; she stays with a family, ministers to them, and in the end finds her relief helping others who are wounded. She did not attack. She did not withdraw. She helped. She herself was helped when she helped.

3. It may be difficult to keep your head above water when the worst that was predicted happens. There is One who can speak to troubled waters and calm the winds and rains in your life.

Walking wounded tend to think and act horizontally rather than perpendicularly. Haman was more concerned with working on his relationship with the palace potentate, whereas Esther worked on her relationship with God. Because of her relationship with God, when her life and lifestyle were threatened, Esther used it as an opportunity to find the solution to a difficult problem.

God did not cause the crises or the wounds, but God used them to help Esther and God's people. Sometimes God uses our wounds as a back door into our lives because the front door is barred. God did not cause Katrina to punish anyone. If you live near the Gulf, hurricanes come. If you live over a fault line, earthquakes may come; and sometimes people die. But there is a Christ in our crises. Katrina becomes the back door through which we can address long-standing problems and hurts in a more comprehensive manner.

Esther called her maids together. They fasted and prayed for three days and nights—and Mordecai asked the people to do the same. Now the text does not say Esther had Bible study, an institute, or a retreat to teach her maids the effectiveness of fasting or how to pray. There was no practice session mentioned, which leads us to believe that girlfriend had been doing it along.

The fast did not change the death sentence—the irrevocable decree of the king; it did not make the king send for her; it did not make Haman go away; it did not solve the problem or change the situation. In the fasting and praying, the old wounds did not reopen or fester; they did not block or become impeded—fasting and praying gave her courage. Fear was removed and confidence given so God could set the solution in motion.

With the relationship came providence. Charles Spurgeon writes that we believe in the providence of God, but we do not belief half enough of it. In spite of what we see, think, or feel about the events of human history, God's hand is still on our lives. We may be weary, worn, and wounded—old wounds and new ones; open or closed; healed or on the way. God's hand is still on our lives; it may be unseen, but working nevertheless. Sometimes God's unseen hand urges us forward; sometimes it holds us back—sometimes with a caress of approval and sometimes with a stroke of reproof; sometimes it corrects; sometimes it comforts; sometimes it opens a door; sometimes it closes one. The more we trust the sovereignty of God, the less we fear the calamities of daily challenges.

Walking wounded, we can become strong in our wounded places because our help is in the name of the Lord, the maker of heaven and earth. This is the fundamental truth of the Bible. God secures our lives and our future—God is for us. Haman's wounds could not abort the will of God for God's people. It is what Israel claimed in the postexilic period in Psalm 44. It is what empowered Jesus to bear the cross as a suffering servant. It is what empowers, and what will continue to empower us, so instead of being walking wounded we can become what Henri Nouwen calls "wounded healers"—strong at our wounded places. We can be resources of help and hope when old wounds open, new ones arrive, or one becomes infected or begins to fester, bleeding all over the place. We who are wounded directly or indirectly by Katrina and Rita can yet be there for others.

Remember how the apostle Paul put it in the midst of his own suffering? "If God is for us, who can be against us?" (Rom. 8:31 NIV).

> I was sinking deep in sin, far from the peaceful shore,
> Very deeply strained within, sinking to rise no more;
> But the master of the sea heard my despairing cry,
> And from the water lifted me, now safe am I.
> Love lifted me! Love lifted me!
> When nothing else could help,
> Love lifted me![1]

God's love will make us strong even in our wounded places. To Hurricane Katrina and Rita victims, the supporters, politicians, clergy, families, and friends: the love of God made me strong in my wounded places and God will and can do the same for you.

Note

1. James Rowe and Howard E. Smith, "Love Lifted Me," 1912. http://www.hymnal.net/cgi-bin/hymns/index?t=h&n=1070.

Natural Disasters, Unnatural Neglect: "It Be's That Way Sometimes" (1 Kings 19:11-18; 1 Kings 18:36-39)

Darryl M. Trimiew

Sometimes in the black community things go terribly wrong. Survivors of such catastrophes will observe sanguinely, "It be's that way sometimes"; which is the way some come to terms with tragedies.

What can be said about the tragedy of Katrina? How is Katrina a tragedy? More people have been killed in the recent Pakistani earthquake; thousands more died in the tsunami eight months earlier. Hurricanes come and hurricanes go. Earthquakes come and go. These disasters are not of human making and cannot be avoided through human efforts. From time immemorial, people have been killed because the earth is not a paradise but a crucible. Nevertheless, it would be inhuman not to mourn the deaths in New Orleans, Pakistan, and elsewhere. So we mourn and we help and, provided that we survive, we ask questions of theodicy. That is, since God is good and powerful, why do bad things happen, especially to innocent people? Why did these people have to die in this catastrophe at this time? We get at best God's answer to Job's query: "Where were you when I laid the earth's foundation? Tell me, if you understand" (Job 38:4). In essence, God tells us, "Who are you to ask me such questions?"

These answers are never satisfactory for nonbelievers and seldom satisfactory for believers. Where is God when these things happen? When God-fearing people die like dogs, where is God and what is God doing?

I have no new answers to these age-old questions and actually will not even try to answer them. Theodicy questions can never really be settled. What is important to us is another question: *How does God want the living to live together?* My answer to this question can be seen in the examination of two related texts in 1 Kings. The first passage is 1 Kings 19:11-18 (NIV).

> The LORD said, "Go out and stand on the mountain in the presence of the LORD, for the LORD is about to pass by."
> Then a great and powerful wind tore the mountains apart and shattered the rocks before the LORD, but the LORD was not in the wind. After the wind there was an earthquake, but the LORD was not in the earthquake. After the earthquake came a fire, but the LORD was not in the fire. And after the fire came a gentle whisper. When Elijah heard it, he pulled his cloak over his face and went out and stood at the mouth of the cave.
> Then a voice said to him, "What are you doing here, Elijah?"
> He replied, "I have been very zealous for the LORD God Almighty. The Israelites have rejected your covenant, broken down your altars, and put your prophets to death with the sword. I am the only one left, and now they are trying to kill me too."
> The LORD said to him, "Go back the way you came, and go to the Desert of Damascus. When you get there, anoint Hazael king over Aram. Also, anoint Jehu son of Nimshi king over Israel, and anoint Elisha son of Shaphat from Abel Meholah to succeed you as prophet. Jehu will put to death any who escape the sword of Hazael, and Elisha will put to death any who escape the sword of Jehu. Yet I reserve seven thousand in Israel—all whose knees have not bowed down to Baal and all whose mouths have not kissed him."

Here, in this passage, Elijah is on the run, evildoers in the land have put him to flight. He has been stalwart for the Lord and is not ashamed to tell God that fact. Elijah has been bold but now feels abandoned, observing, "The Israelites have rejected your covenant, broken down your altars, and put your prophets to death with the sword. I am the only one left and now they are trying to kill me too."

Some Christians in New Orleans were swept away; some survived; but many must have felt abandoned by God. People of many other faiths survived; and many others died. Survivors are left with the questions of Job and with Job's answers. Yet, Elijah's situation is more apropos.

If you are a survivor of life's storms, you will, from time to time, feel abandoned by God. In Elijah's case, the enemy of God was also Israelite royalty. Elijah survives a natural storm of wind, fire, and earthquake, yet still feels abandoned. Still, God comes to Elijah after all the storms have passed and reminds him that God is still in charge—but not in charge in a way in that none are ever killed or maimed. People were killed in Elijah's day and people are killed in ours. God is in charge *because God always preserves a remnant.* Seven thousand in Israel did not bow down to Baal and did not kiss him. And those are the ones who were preserved. You will notice that the trouble and death in this passage does not come from a natural disaster, but from idolatrous rulers. The wind and fire that come to Elijah are just to get his attention. He is invited to join a faithful remnant.

Yet this remnant is not home free; it is not invulnerable. That God still has God's eye on them does not give them immunity from natural storms, harms, or evil government. What was true for Elijah and the faithful in Israel is still true for us today.

The people of New Orleans and others could not stop Hurricane Katrina from coming. They could not stop it from being as powerful as it was. What can be said is that Katrina was simply a natural storm, but was unlike the great wind of Elijah. It blew things down. Fires broke out and floods did kill. Yet God was not in the storm of Elijah and God was not in the storm of Katrina.

God frequently comes to the faithful *after* the storm; at the same time God never forsakes us. God came to Elijah and God comes to us. God assures Elijah that he is not by himself, and God does that for us now. But we must be like the remnant of Israel. We must not bow down to Baal and we must not kiss him.

Who is the Baal of this age? Who is the enemy of God? Baal was a false god, an idol, luring the people away from the true worship of God to the lures of fertility. In the agricultural society of ancient Israel, fertility was the basis of wealth. For us today, the call of mammon—of unbridled wealth and consumerism, of wealth in collusion with unfaithful, uncaring government—still beckons us; still calls us to go astray.

The tragedy of Katrina is not the storm; neither God nor Satan was in the storm. The tragedy of Katrina is manifested in its aftermath. People who feel abandoned by God are not abandoned by God, but, unfortunately, frequently they were and are abandoned by their government.

Huddled in the Superdome, they were not supermen or women or children. In sweltering heat, with scarce and bad food and water and no electricity; with supplies delayed by a government that had incompetent management heading up emergency support services—a government that was more concerned with the unlikely possibility of human terrorism and more obsessed with security of private property over their welfare—they felt abandoned by God and government. God did not abandon them but our government did. We abandoned them; for in a democracy, where not all who can vote do vote, we left them months and weeks and years ago in our modern worship of Baal.

When Louisiana environmentalists and politicians asked for the preservation of more wetlands, which are God's natural sponge to minimize flooding, and were rejected by Congress so taxes could be preserved for the already wealthy, and we did nothing, we were kissing Baal.

When we allowed wetlands to be drained so that we could put up more condominiums and dig more oil wells and dredge up deeper riverways for import and export business, we were kissing Baal.

When we moved out of the Ninth Ward because it was getting too black and too poor, we were kissing Baal.

When we clucked our tongues at all the people who were trapped in their houses or in the Superdome because they had no private transportation and we had no adequate public transport, we were kissing Baal.

When newscasters characterized stranded people who were scrounging food, water, and clothing as "looters" and we cheered on the troops to restore order, we were kissing Baal. Just whose order do we want preserved? God's or Baal's?

When our government sent the most inept administrators in a castrated FEMA to simply preside over the chaos, we clearly bowed down to idols of fear. Human terrorism cannot be completely eliminated and we are bowing down to Baal when we make public policy as if such terrorism can be eliminated.

When the government can send out help on its own timetable in a way that scatters the poor to the winds without regard for their well-being and forgets to keep families together, clearly we are worshiping Baal.

When we allow New Orleans and other areas to be rebuilt without any provisions for low-cost public housing, economic work zones, relocation support, or adequate public schooling, we are in bed with Baal.

When we award exclusive contracts to rebuild devastated areas to fat-cat corporations with close ties to the government, we are kissing Baal.

When we allow our president to suspend minimum-wage laws so that a surviving remnant can rebuild New Orleans for the wealthy, but only if they are willing to do so at slave wages, we are no longer just kissing Baal—at this point, we are Baal.

And, finally, what do we remember about Baal, his prophets, his high places, and his priests? We remember once again, a passage about Elijah. Before Elijah experienced God, not in the wind, the fire, and earthquake, but afterward as a still quiet voice after the storm, he also experienced God elsewhere. In 1 Kings 18:36-39, Elijah again experiences God. That passage reads as follows:

> At the time of sacrifice, the prophet Elijah stepped forward and prayed: "O LORD, God of Abraham, Isaac and Israel, let it be known today that you are God in Israel and that I am your servant and have done all these things at your command. Answer me, O LORD, answer me, so these people will know that you, O LORD, are God, and that you are turning their hearts back again."
>
> Then the fire of the LORD fell and burned up the sacrifice, the wood, the stones and the soil, and also licked up the water in the trench.
>
> When all the people saw this, they fell prostrate and cried, "The LORD—he is God! The LORD—he is God!"

Here, in this passage, we do find God acting in the natural world. At the command of God, Elijah has built an altar and called for God to manifest Godself. God does so, demonstrating that when people of faith are willing to lay everything on the altar, God will come out of heaven and burn away what God wants consumed. God comes out of heaven when people act in faith, and God comes to show that false prophets and idols are of no avail. God's fire, like God's wind, serves God's purposes, burning and blowing away our idolatry.

We know as we continue to read Kings that Elijah slew all the false prophets, right after that theophany. We, however, do not live in a culture in which false prophets can be readily rounded up and killed by true prophets. We can and should thank God for that great mercy, since too often *we are the ones acting* as false prophets. Yet while God judges faithlessness and idolatry God also is merciful to a remnant that will not bow down to Baal and will not kiss him. Are we such a remnant?

We are such a remnant if we can do more than just give a charitable donation to the survivors of Katrina; even our false prophets of Baal will and have done that. We will be a faithful remnant if we remember that the long-standing poverty, homelessness, racism, classism, and environmental degradation in New Orleans were and are an American way of life. These circumstances have been tolerated and supported by our ongoing faithlessness. We should not rebuild New Orleans like it was before— a place of inequality and poverty. Nor can we let the priests of Baal rebuild it with high-rise luxury housing suitable only for the wealthy and tourists, relegating a dispirited remnant to return to the land as servants or slaves and not as citizens. To be faithful to God, we must insist that all the high places of Baal that we helped build be torn down. To be a city on the hill, a light to all nations, we must embrace justice and peace. We must give these values a chance to do so in the proper rebuilding of New Orleans for all.

Natural disasters occur: "It be's that way sometimes." Although tragic, disasters do not constitute tragedy until *we* prove unfaithful. "It be's that way sometimes," not because God has failed us, but because we have failed God, and thus God's people. Let us meet God in the stillness of the present time before another high wind comes. Let us hear God ask us just what it is that *we are doing*. But let us not just sit still idly by. We must fight for a new public policy for the abandoned.

Finally, let us remember that we are not isolated and not alone with God. God always has a faithful remnant. Let's find other members of that remnant and work together with them, starting today. If we do, then, "When the saints go marching in, oh, when the saints go marching in, [we will indeed] be in that number, oh, when the saints go marching in!" Amen!

After Katrina and Rita: What Must I Do to Be Saved? (Luke 10:25-37)

Melva L. Sampson

N ow before we begin this morning on our journey of enlightenment, I want you to pray with me. I want those of you who are
able to sit straight up in your seat, place your feet flat on the
floor, and now gently close your eyes. As you sit there taking careful
breaths, I want you to put one hand on each side of your head and repeat
after me. Say: "Mind, I give you permission to expand in knowledge this
morning." Now put both hands on your heart and say: "Heart, I give you
permission to experience love this morning." Together we pray that each
of us give ourselves to see and that others see us for who we really are:
Fragile, wounded, and in need of repair. Let each of us take permission to
love ourselves; and if you don't love yourself, I give you permission to at
some point during our time together ask the question, What must I do to
be saved? Amen! Come on, now open your eyes and give the Lord a
handclap of praise.

I'm going to make a general assumption here and say that most of us
want to be saved from some situation this morning, some habit, some
decision, some stressor that is weighing heavy on our hearts. Many
churches teach that salvation is the gateway to eternal life, and eternal
life is the gift that we receive when we confess with our mouths and
believe with our hearts that Jesus was born, crucified, and raised on the
third day—hence providing followers with the belief that resurrection is
also true for us. However, this reprieve from distress, discouragement, and

disdain is suggested to be otherworldly. That is, some suggest that salvation is something that we receive in the by-and-by and not today. Some embrace the song that suggests "one glad morning when this life is over, we will fly away" and then we will inherit this miraculous gift of eternal life.

Christians today inexplicably link eternal life with salvation. Salvation, or to be "saved," *soteria* in Greek, means to feel protected, to be whole, and to be preserved; for some it is synonymous, or we use it interdependently, with eternal life. Hence like the lawyer in our text, modern-day Christians want to know, What must we do to be preserved, protected, and feel like we are whole? Yet like the lawyer, wanting to justify himself, we have our own ulterior motives, which have more to do with personal piety than hopeful directives for our crucified communities here in the College Park section of Raleigh; in the Ninth Ward of New Orleans; the urban and rural 'hoods of East St. Louis, Illinois; East New York; the Sudan in Africa; Palestine; Afghanistan; and Iraq. Before Hurricanes Katrina, Wilma, and Rita, our questions of wanting to be saved or preserved had to do more with our individual interests of being ultraholy, sanctified, and fire baptized; with being an anointed worship leader, preacher, and/or psalmist; with eight thousand members; with being released from spending eternity in a lake of fire. Our question is asked with the hopes of response that relieves us as individuals. Justice does not mean relief is just for us! Although God is indeed concerned with our own individual experiences of natural disaster and mental anguish; and God is concerned with our emotional heartbreak and physical ailments; and God is concerned and will tend to our need to be saved from the negative effects of spiritual and moral bankruptcy, professional boredom, and vocational doubt; the message of today's text wants to move us beyond questions of personal experiences and piety to communal responsibility. The text asks us to move beyond ourselves to our community.

We enter this particular text with Jesus entertaining a question from a cocky young lawyer. Prior to the young lawyer's inquiry, earlier in chapter 10, Jesus had just blessed his disciples for what they had seen and heard during their evangelism mission. Through the work of the seventy or so disciples on mission, following Jesus' commission, the power of evil is broken and demons are cast out regardless of the fearsomeness of the opposition. Jesus' pronounced blessings upon his disciples not only affirm that they have power to survive with minimal to no material support, to heal and to cast out, but that their names are written in heaven—they shall receive eternal life. Knowledge of God has been revealed to them and they have seen and heard what prophets and kings desired to see and hear but could not.

According to some commentaries, although the lawyer is indeed test-ing Jesus, his question is readily understandable following Jesus' blessing of the disciples in verses 23-24 for what they have seen and heard. What if one has not seen and has not heard what the disciples were privileged to see and hear? Is there any hope for her or him? The lawyer asks the question that all who were not among the eyewitnesses would ask: "But what must I do to inherit eternal life?" Placed in contemporary vernacu-lar, the question reads: "What must I do to be saved, or more appropri-ately, how can I get down?" Jesus refers the lawyer to the law, where the lawyer recites the necessary requirements: to love God with all your heart, mind, and strength, and to love your neighbor as yourself. Living in this way ensures one the ability to obtain new vision and hear not with just one's ears but with one's heart. Jesus urges the lawyer to go and do likewise, but the lawyer, wanting to upstage Jesus, asks, "Who is my neighbor?"

As I reflect on the twentieth anniversary of Dr. Martin Luther King, Jr.'s birthday being deemed a holiday, I am compelled to ask the question as a point of critical reflection: What must Black folk do to inherit eter-nal life in 2006? What must black folk do to be saved from destruction within, from the serious condition of seeing and not seeing? What must we do to be saved from internalized oppression that prevents us from liv-ing in true community? What must we do to be saved from seats of com-placency and beliefs that we have arrived; from thinking that if we don't live in this neighborhood we don't have to worry about this neighbor-hood? What must we do to be saved from the notion that this is how it's always going to be?

The first thing we must do is resist the temptation to do nothing!

To illustrate his point to the young lawyer, Jesus asserts the story about three men who saw one man lying beaten, bruised, and bloodied in a ditch on a dangerous road between Jerusalem and Jericho. Three men, a priest, a Levite, and a Samaritan (considered racially impure and despised by the Jews), each saw the victim, but only one stopped to attend to the needs of this man. The text says that when both the priest and the Levite came to the place and saw a certain man lying in the ditch, each passed by on the other side. They did nothing. That is, they "may like"[1] they didn't see the man. You all know what "may like" means; that when you see someone you don't want to speak to, you "may like" you don't see her or him. You know, like when you see someone on the corner, bandaged and bloodied, asking if you can spare some change, and you are so hurried doing nothing you "may like" you don't see them. We "may like" we don't see the crack-addicted individual; we "may like" we don't see the entrepreneurial street-selling pharmacist. We "may like" all of these things. We "may like" the government is on our side when we go to those polls to vote. And so the Levite and the priest "may like" they did not see this man. We must open our eyes and see our surroundings and what is going on.

So they kept walking as if they did not see. It forces you to ask, "Why?" How could you walk past a living person and just keep on with the business of your day and not stop? So why did the priest and Levite do nothing? The text does not say, but many have speculated. One speculation suggests that it had to with their holy status.

Jewish Levitical law forbade both priests and Levites to touch a corpse within twenty-four hours of a ceremonial act; if they did so, they were considered unclean. In their minds, the person could not just have been badly injured, but was indeed dead, which would have required timely rituals and sacrifices for them to be made clean again. They walked past the man lying in the ditch to maintain accountability to the doctrine and traditions of their religious and social culture; sounds a bit contradictory, doesn't it? What must we do to be saved?

They probably also walked by because they were unable to see the humanity of one in need. Yet, if we were to reflect on our own actions critically, do we not walk by tragedy every day and do nothing? Do we not walk past the walking dead every day and do nothing? Do we not drive through neighborhoods that have all but lost their glory and do nothing? Do we not see them in need of repair and question the motives or the ability of those who seek to restore crack houses to wholesome homes; turn failing schools into Ivy League hopefuls; change street-corner pharmacists into legitimate and innovative entrepreneurs; and seek to garner state assistance for dependent men, women, and children to become independent land and business owners? The priest and the Levite committed a grave injustice: they walked past a situation that called for response. To not respond is sinful and selfish. What must we do to be saved?

Second, we must see and show mercy!

The ugliness of the priest and Levite's neglect appears sharply when surprisingly a Samaritan is introduced as the unselfish, concerned, attentive one; equipped with the ability to see human suffering and attend to it to the point of delaying his journey, expending much energy, and spending two days' wages with assurance of more. The Samaritan was living his faith. Ceremonially unclean, socially outcast, and religiously a heretic, this man saw the condition of his neighbor and showed mercy. Notice he did not look at his neighbor and shake his head with disgust. He wasn't bound to Jewish religious tradition that prevented him from assisting. He didn't just pray; he moved. With his eyes he saw the condition of this man, and the text says he got off his animal, poured wine and oil on the man's wound, bandaged him, and took him to an inn to heal where he gave the innkeeper two days' pay with promise of more upon his return if needed so that the man could heal and be restored. Prayer is good, but many times we need concrete assistance.

The Samaritan looked beyond his own status as second class. He could show compassion and mercy because he knew what it felt like to be overcome by the condition of powerlessness and vulnerability. The Samaritan may have experienced and remembered the dehumanizing and dismal effects of racism. The Samaritan may have recalled the hazardous conditions of nakedness and peril and being marred by the brutality of bureaucratic backlash. He may have suffered from the predicament of invisibility dictated by the religious intelligentsia and the intellectually prudent; that they cannot give us a good word. He could have been familiar with the conditions that could land one in such a ditch; conditions such as those that result from the crippling outcome of economic instability, furthering the calamitous effects of poverty.

The duty of neighborliness is an expression of love of God, love of others, and love of those who show mercy; of those who show that they belong among the heirs of God's reign. However, the duty of neighborliness transcends any calculation of reward. We do not do good acts so that we can get the reward; or ask, "When are you going to pay me back?" Helping others helps ourselves. The Samaritan did not expect any reward or repayment. One who shows mercy to gain a reward would, therefore, not truly be doing likewise.

Third, we must go and do likewise.

After clarifying the neighbor as the one who showed compassion and mercy, Jesus sends the questioning lawyer forth with the command, "Go and do likewise." We, too, must go and do likewise. The key to eternal life is not how loud you can speak in tongues; not whether you have the gift of interpretation; not whether you can tune really good; and not whether you get a shout and a praise every time somebody says the name *Jesus*; but the key as recorded by the author of Luke is standing in camaraderie with those who find themselves wounded and bruised by the blustering winds life will blow.

When I was a child, growing up in Pittsburgh, Pennsylvania, when we wanted to push a person's buttons or encourage them to do something that we were afraid to do we would enforce what was called a "double-dog dare." A double-dog dare was more serious than a regular or double dare; if completed, it carried far more weight and prestige. That is, if one completed a double-dog dare he or she reached star status in the 'hood. They were seen as brave, courageous, and as having heart. However, most of my little rag-tag, motley crew rarely accepted the challenge of the double-dog dare because it usually required a level of possible discomfort that we were unwilling to experience. To my childhood crew, who used to sneak in the funeral home in between Sunday school and church service to see dead bodies up close, the Samaritan's act was the result of an internal double-dog dare to be sensitive to human despair despite his own social status or position in class and religious hierarchy.

I have been trying to propose to you that our salvation is about more than our resistance of the usual sins: fornication, lying, stealing, and so forth; salvation is more about organized resistance to systems of oppression. We are called to the suffering in our community; we are called to do something about it. We should feel compelled to go and do likewise, to help our communities recover from lying in the ditch, and help the ones who, with their eyes wide shut, walk by the wounded. As a people, we have not arrived. On the contrary, regardless of how high-minded we become, how financially stable, how intellectually astute, how politically connected, how close we come to penetrating the holies of holies, how many firsts we've become, we are called to the suffering in our community and to do something.

As a people, we need to be recovered. We need to recover portions of not just our individual selves but of our communities that have been left for dead. We need to be recovered from crippling stigmas that have been used as tools to marginalize, exclude, and exercise power over those who show certain characteristics. In his final speech to a group of sanitation workers in Memphis, Tennessee, Dr. King reflected on the parable of the good Samaritan and specifically on why the Levite walked past the man. And using his sanctified imagination, Dr. King suggested that the two men asked themselves a question as they approached the situation: "If I stop to help this man, what will happen to me?" We can imagine the crowd nodding and saying amen. Then Dr. King said, "But then the good Samaritan came by. And he reversed the question: 'If I do not stop to help this man, what will happen to him?'" And so thirty-eight years later

I submit the same reflection Dr. King submitted to himself as he pondered whether or not he would keep walking past these striking sanitation workers or whether he would stop and attend to their wounds. The question is not: "If we stop to help people in need, what will happen to us?" The question is this: "What happens if a war, which was supposed to bring about democratic rule, continues to bring about body bags filled with American and Iraqi men and women?" If we do not stop this war and the increasingly high fuel and heating prices, inefficient corporate governance, ineffective and unscrupulous leadership that disproportionately affects the least of these, the question is not, "What will happen to us?" but, "What will happen to the others who have no voice?"

Our work, like the Samaritan's work, like Dr. King's work, like Sojourner Truth and Jarena Lee's work, like your own pastor's work, is to extend the divine invitation of human wholeness, healing, and affirmation to the "whosoever" of John 3:16. I double-dog dare you to reach beyond your need and be concerned about the whosoever community. I double-dog dare you to be concerned about the communities you worship and live in—the need for sustainable housing, quality education, and comprehensive health care for not just you, but for whosoever. I double-dog dare you to come out of the upper room and to bend down and care for the diseased and the dis-eased; those who live on the margins of the marginalized, who are the oppressed of the oppressed; the sexually battered and abused; the homeless and the bereft; the HIV/AIDS infected who are young and old, female and male, lesbian and bisexual, transgender and straight. Many of these people were victims of Katrina and Rita or their counterparts in your community. These are they, the children of God.

If you choose to accept this mission, *then* you will inherit eternal life. *Then* you will be saved. Inheriting eternal life and receiving salvation is not based on traditions and doctrines. True religion consists not of systems, written creeds, or rites, but in the ability to see. Eternal life has less to do with the highway to heaven, the by-and-by, and glory land, and more to do with living a quality of life characterized by resisting the temptation to do nothing; by showing mercy to those in need who are we ourselves regardless of what personal judgments we've placed on them; and by ensuring that our children's children will do likewise. What must I do to be saved? I must see my neighbor as myself. Being saved means being rescued from eternal blindness; it urges us to wipe the muck from our hearts, take the masks off our faces. You know how we like the mask: "How you doing this morning?" "Praise the Lord!" "How are things?" We shout, "Blessed and highly favored," when on the inside we are torn up and broken down. Salvation urges us to open our ears and lay down our religiosity and eternal permanent residence in "woe is me" victimhood and do something to create the type of world we want to live in.

I double-dog dare you to, as Dr. King explained in his philosophy of the power of nonviolence, live a maladjusted life. To be *maladjusted* is to be poorly adjusted. *Adjusted* means to conform, settle, or bring to agreement. In June 1957, King stressed to eager students in California the need to be maladjusted. He said:

> Now we all should seek to live a well adjusted life in order to avoid neurotic and schizophrenic personalities. But there are some things within our social order to which I am proud to be maladjusted and to which I call upon you to be maladjusted. . . . I never intend to adjust myself to the tragic effects of the methods of physical violence and to tragic militarism. I call upon you to be maladjusted to such things. I call upon you to be as maladjusted as Amos who in the midst of the injustices of his day cried out in words that echo across the generation, "Let judgment run down like waters and righteousness like a mighty stream."[2]

I double-dog dare you to never adjust to situations that prompt you to look over certain men and certain women, certain communities, whole nations, and certain generations that have been stripped, beaten, and left lying on the side of the road only to be talked about and told that they are worthless, letting the dream die, and contributing to the demise of the black community. I double-dog dare you to push beyond the niceties of piecemeal charity and into the realm of wholesale justice. I double-dog dare you to wreak havoc on sinful blindness and highlight the necessity of moral rightness that is accompanied by justice. I, like Dr. King, this morning call on you to be as maladjusted as some of you were during the Civil Rights movement; as maladjusted as you were when you heard that four little girls had been bombed in a church house; as maladjusted as you were when you saw the Rodney King video and others like it; and as maladjusted as you were last September when you watched your government leave thousands of U.S. citizens to fend for themselves during the worst natural disaster to be recorded in the United States. And if you have adjusted to this treatment, then I urge you to be as maladjusted as Jesus of Nazareth, whose mission and purpose was to reconstruct life in the face of domination and destruction. He never adjusted to religious politics and titles bestowed by the socially privileged. He answers our question, What must I do to be saved in action? He both figuratively and literally gives his life that we who believe likewise might gain our lives. The truth and power of the Resurrection in history is the result of never adjusting to injustice; never adjusting to the inhumane ways human beings treat and judge one another; never getting comfortable with the ways of a crucified world that is broken and suffering. What must we do to be saved? We must listen to our challenges. Although it is good to shout, every service is not a shouting moment. Every now and then, we must reflect on what we do and why we do it. You might say, "Rev., I'm concerned about the community and about making change, but I've got all of these debilitating things going on: a family member in jail, a child on drugs, and I just received a debilitating diagnosis."

The text says that we must love the Lord with all our heart, our soul, our mind, and our strength; and love our neighbor as ourselves. The problem is I can't love my neighbor as myself, because I don't know what it is to love myself; to be in relationship with myself; to attend to my own brokenness. Am I worthy of love? I'm broken, and I'm fragile with this mask on. I want to be like the Samaritan, not like the Levite or the priest. I want to be in right relationship. I've been that certain man, that certain woman, in the ditch on the road of hopelessness and despair; between being on the edge and going over the edge; in the ditch figuring out if I want to live or if I want to die. I want to live. So this morning I offer you an opportunity to experience true salvation; an eternal life not based on getting to the by-and-by. I offer you Christ, right relationship, this morning, so that our children's children will show mercy and do likewise! Thanks be to God.

Notes

1. "May like," in the idiom of black vernacular, is the code for "made like," acted like, or pretended to.
2. Martin Luther King, Jr., "The Power of Nonviolence."

Festival, and the Sugar Bowl. The city is renowned for its food, hospitality, and architecture. Xavier University of New Orleans sends more black students to medical school and produces more pharmacists than any other college in the nation. Martin Luther King, Jr.'s Southern Christian Leadership Conference was founded in New Orleans. The United States and the world will soon learn that New Orleans is more than parties and po' boys; it is more than good times and gumbo. Many New Orleans natives such as Harry Connick Jr., Bryant Gumbel, Louis Armstrong, Mahalia Jackson, Wynton Marsalis, Andrew Young, and Marc Morial have risen to influence this nation. And yet the question has been asked, Can anything good come out of New Orleans? Trouble makes us appreciate what we have lost.

Second, *trouble comes when we don't listen to warnings.* Before 9/11, FEMA listed a hurricane strike on New Orleans as one of the most likely disasters facing America. We did not listen. The United States cut funding needed to prepare for and respond to disasters. Since 2003, President Bush cut funding for the Army Corps of Engineers, the agency that works to protect cities from floods and reinforces levees. The disaster in New Orleans had been predicted for years. Just last year, an emergency response exercise showed that New Orleans would be overwhelmed by a major hurricane. Hundreds of regional and federal officials met in Baton Rouge for an elaborate exercise. A fictional "Hurricane Pam" left the city under ten feet of water and warned that transportation would be a major problem for one hundred thousand people.[2] Many experts warned that the city could not handle a Category 4 or 5 hurricane. Over and over, the United States was warned that the levees would break. The continual erosion of marshes and wetlands has devastated the Gulf region.

There has been a strong sentiment in Washington DC that it was a mistake to merge FEMA under the authority of the Department of Homeland Security. Graydon Carter of *Vanity Fair* magazine points out that FEMA director Michael Brown was a friend of Joe Albaugh, who had managed the Bush 2000 campaign. Was the warning that Michael Brown was unqualified to lead FEMA heeded? In fact, Carter further asserts that four of FEMA's seven senior officials under Brown had no legitimate natural disaster qualifications.[3] What about the issue of global warming? Recently, a group of scientists produced a study in the *Journal of Science.* Their research determined that over the past thirty-five years, the number of Category 1, 2, and 3 storms has decreased slightly. However, the number of Category 4 and 5 storms has climbed significantly.[4] Whereas in the 1970s, there were about ten Category 4 and 5 hurricanes annually worldwide, since 1990, the annual number has risen to eighteen. Category 4 and 5 storms have jumped from 20 percent of the international total to 35 percent. Atmospheric scientist Kerry Emmanuel of MIT has surveyed about four thousand eight hundred hurricanes in the North Atlantic and North Pacific over the past fifty years. Emmanuel discovered that the total number of hurricanes had remained the same; however, the wind speed and duration of the hurricanes has jumped 50 percent since the middle of the 1970s.[5] Clearly ocean temperatures have risen and our constant burning of fossil fuels encourages water vapor, which then increases the intensity of rainfall. Significant carbon dioxide in the atmosphere may also influence our weather. The U.S. business sector has consistently resisted efforts to reduce our dependence on foreign oil. Our nation must seek cleaner sources of energy such as solar power and windmills, in essence, nonfossil fuel. President Bush's rejection of the Kyoto Treaty magnifies our stubbornness in this area.

Third, *trouble comes when we do not listen to warnings, but trouble also makes us humble*. In 2003, the United States went to war with Iraq. We ignored the opinions of the United Nations and many other countries around the world. The United States acted like it did not care about the world. And now, after this catastrophic event, nations around the world (that we do not like) are offering us assistance. Nations such as Cuba, Venezuela, and Bangladesh have offered assistance. We say that the United States is the greatest nation in the world and yet we cannot respond to the needs of our own citizens. We ship tons of military equipment to Iraq and yet we could not deliver food and water to the Gulf Coast. The nation's poverty rate rose to 12.7 percent last year, the fourth consecutive annual increase according to the Census Bureau.[6] There are thirty-seven million Americans living in poverty and forty-five million without health insurance. These realities should make us humble.

Fourth, *trouble also shows us our shortcomings*. We have arrogantly fought a war against terrorism. The United States is the police officer of the world. Our leaders have told us that they are protecting us. And yet it is deeply disturbing that our nation could not respond more quickly than it has to the destitution of its citizenry. What will happen if a terrorist attack ever strikes a major U.S. city? And what about FEMA? On September 27, 2005, Michael Brown blamed a "dysfunctional" Louisiana for the crisis. Blame was assigned to Louisiana Governor Kathleen Blanco and New Orleans Mayor Ray Nagin.[7] Clearly there were failures of leadership at the federal, state, and local levels. Mayor Nagin surely could have utilized available buses to evacuate people out of the city. Although in his defense, Nagin probably hesitated to call for a mandatory evacuation because the city could be held liable for unnecessarily closing hotels and other businesses. The evacuations of tourists can also be very expensive.[8] Surely, Governor Blanco could have been more adamant and specific about her state's need for help from the federal government. There were failures all around, but we normally expect more from our presidents than from our governors and mayors. Is it acceptable for both Michael Brown (FEMA) and Michael Chertoff (Homeland Security) to have no previous emergency management experience? In an interview with National Public Radio, Chertoff was pressed six times about the twenty-five thousand people stuck at the New Orleans Convention Center. Chertoff said he had not heard about any of the problems.[9] Those problems were widely broadcast by the media. Why did it take four days for President Bush to make it down to the Gulf region? Why did President Bush praise Michael Brown for the job he was doing? Patrick Rhode of FEMA described the agency's performance as "one of the most impressive search and rescue operations this country has ever conducted domestically."[10] That is truly amazing. *Trouble* shows us our shortcomings. Does anybody really believe that if the hurricane victims were rich and white that things would not have been different? Did the United States respond so slowly because the victims were black and poor? If Hurricane Katrina had taken place in Texas or Florida would the response have been the same? George Bush's mother, former first lady Barbara Bush, said that there were "so many underprivileged anyway, so everything is working out well for them."[11] In 2004, FEMA paid thirty-one million dollars to residents of Miami/Dade County, an area that was one hundred miles south of a major hurricane.[12]

And, there has been much discussion about the looting that took place in New Orleans—people carjacking, and stealing food, televisions, and VCRs. We know that looting is wrong. Some people stole food and water because they were dehydrated and starving to death; but these people were not the only "looters." There was looting in parts of Miami for at least a month after Hurricane Andrew.[13]

There was also looting in Mexico after Hurricane Wilma. Black people are not the only ones who loot. Last year, Exxon Mobil Oil Company made twenty-five billion dollars. Yet, in the aftermath of Katrina they pledged only two million dollars to help the hurricane victims.[14] Gas prices were as high as six dollars a gallon in some parts of the country after

Katrina. Why should the average citizen have to pay so much? On September 21, 2005, eight democratic governors asked President Bush to investigate possible gasoline price gouging. A study by University of Wisconsin economist Don Nicholas found that for gas to reach three dollars a gallon, the price of crude oil would have to be about ninety-five dollars a barrel. Crude-oil prices have been holding around sixty-five dollars a barrel.[15] In the city of Fayetteville, North Carolina, one gas station made eighteen thousand dollars in one day. After Katrina, there was widespread anger in the black community about the federal government's response. And yet as of late October 2005, only 1.5 percent of the sixteen billion dollars in contracts awarded by FEMA have gone to minority businesses.[16] Additionally, the Davis-Bacon Act, which sets prevailing wages for government contracts, has been suspended. No-bid contracts have been issued to a select group of companies.

Although the president promised to make everything right, there has been no plan for "rescue, recovery, or return." Foreign workers from countries such as Brazil are being hired to work in New Orleans. Our government needs interpreters to communicate with these workers. What sense does that make? American citizens and New Orleans natives need jobs. *Are these things happening because the victims are black and poor?* People are receiving mortgage and utility bills even though their houses have been destroyed. How will New Orleans be rebuilt? Will the poor be able to afford to live in the new New Orleans? How will the nation pay for reconstruction? Can we pay for the war in Iraq, cut taxes for the wealthy, and still rebuild? Will we rebuild the Gulf Coast on the backs of the poor?

Fifth, *trouble makes us resilient.* New Orleans has known many troubles. New Orleans has been known as the "city that care forgot." In 1832, seven thousand people died in New Orleans from a yellow fever epidemic. In 1853, yellow fever killed more than eleven thousand people. In 1788 and 1794, two terrible fires swept through and nearly destroyed the French Quarter. In 1965, Hurricane Betsy hit New Orleans. In 1969, Hurricane Camille hit New Orleans.[17] People died during these storms, and yet through it all, New Orleans has stood the test of time. *Trouble makes us resilient.* New Orleans will rebuild.

And now as we turn to our scripture, Job is a man well acquainted with trouble. God allowed Job to be tested by Satan. The question is, Would Job curse God or not? In the time of trouble, will you curse God? The experience of Job teaches us three things: (1) *Trouble teaches us about our family and friends.* (2) *Trouble teaches us about our faith.* (3) *Trouble teaches us about our God.* Job lost his family, his material possessions, and he was afflicted with disease.

Trouble teaches us about our family and friends. In times of trouble people get impatient with one another and get stressed out. Yet in times of trouble families must turn *to* one another instead of *on* one another. In chapter 2, verse 9, Job's own wife says, "Why don't you curse God and die?" Job's own wife, who should have been his greatest support, discourages Job.[18] But remember, his wife is distraught because her ten children have been killed. Yet, even when we are troubled, we should comfort those who need our support. But far too often in times of crisis we lack support from family. What about our friends? There were three friends who came to visit Job in his time of trouble. They traveled a long distance to see him. They sat in silence for seven days and sympathized with him. But then they talked to him and told him that he had sinned against God. Why else would he have to endure such suffering? He must repent and get right with God. Job's friends did not understand. Life can be so painful in times of trouble when our family and friends do not understand. Sometimes the best way for friends to help is to just be with us and let us know that they care. In trouble, we want the support of family and friends. But we must also support others. I can tell you that during this time I have received support from unexpected places. I have gotten calls from Las Vegas, St. Louis, Kansas City, Miami, Tampa, Birmingham; from the states of Texas, California, and Maryland. In the mist of the support, I realized I needed to support others, so I began to call friends who also had family in Louisiana, Mississippi, and Alabama. In times of trouble, we may receive support from unexpected places. We may not receive support from people we expect it from. In chapter 42 of Job, God got angry with the friends of Job because they did not tell the truth about God. The Bible says Job forgave his friends. When we are hurt by those we love, there can still be reconciliation.

Trouble teaches us about our faith. When Job was tested, his faith was shaken. In chapter 3, Job cursed the day of his birth. He asked, "Why was I born?" Job accused God of abandoning him, and he questions God's justice. But then God questions Job. God asks Job if he could explain the creation of the world and oversee God's creation. Job is forced to admit the power and righteousness of God. During this time, my faith has been tested and there have been misunderstandings with family and friends. My mother did not leave New Orleans until Tuesday, after the storm. She tried to stay around to look out for two elderly friends who stayed, but as the city began to flood she realized that she had to leave. I was afraid for her life and safety. I had heard reports of shootings, killings, and carjackings. At one point I lost phone contact with her. I was afraid that she might be killed. My faith was tested. In times of trouble, our faith needs to become stronger. But so often in times of trouble we complain more, worry more, pray less, and trust God less. Trouble teaches us our faith is not as strong as we think it is. Trouble teaches us that we must always trust in the Lord.

Trouble teaches us about our God. In chapter 42, the Bible records that Job forgave his friends and the Lord made him prosperous again and gave him twice as much as he had before. If we trust God through our troubles, God will restore us. New Orleans has been a city with many problems and challenges. Perhaps this will be a new beginning for New Orleans and the nation. Perhaps the United States can have a new discussion about race and poverty in our country. As I watched the calamity on the television, I realized that I could have been stranded on the street. I could have been trapped at the Superdome or the convention center. I could have lost my house and my job. I could have been living in a hotel, separated from my family. I thank God, how God has blessed me. Our troubles teach us about the faithfulness of God. As Job said, "Naked I came from my mother's womb, naked shall I return" (Job 1:21). Adversity comes to make us strong. Adversity gives us new opportunities. The Gulf Coast will rebuild. And New Orleans shall rise again!

Notes

1. Ralph E. Thayer, "New Orleans," *World Book Encyclopedia* (Chicago: Scott Fetzer Company, 2004), 278.

2. James Carney, "Four Places Where the System Broke Down," *Time* 166, no. 11 (September 19, 2005): 37.

3. Graydon Carter, "Gone With the Wind—And the Rain," *Vanity Fair* (November, 2005): 88.

4. Jeffrey Kluger, "Global Warming: The Culprit?" *Time* 166, no. 14 (October 3, 2005): 44.

5. Ibid.

6. "Poverty Rate at 12.7 Percent, 4th Straight Rise," Associated Press, August 30, 2005, http://www.msnbc.com.

7. Lara Jakes Jordan, "Brown Blames 'Dysfunctional' Louisiana," America Online News, September 27, 2005, http://aolsvc.news.aol.com/news/article.

8. Carney, "Four Places Where the System Broke Down," 36.

9. Brian Bennett, "How Did This Happen?" *Time* 166, no. 11 (September 12, 2005): 59.

10. Ibid.

11. Carter, "Gone with the Wind," 90.

12. Carney, "Four Places Where the System Broke Down," 40.

13. Bennett, "How Did This Happen?" 59.

14. Derrick Jackson, "Big Oil's Big Time Looting," *Boston Globe*, September 2005, http://www.boston.com/news/globe/editorial-opinion/oped/articles/2005/09/02.

15. Todd Richmond, "Governors Seek Probe of Possible Price Gouging," America Online News, September 21, 2005, http://aolsvc.news.aol.com/news/article.

16. Hope Yen, "Minority Firms Getting Fewer Katrina Pacts," America Online News, October 5, 2005, http://aolsvc.news.aol.com/special4/article.

17. Thayer, "New Orleans," 279, 284.

18. Note that some scholars read this passage differently, ironically; that is, Job's wife was saying, "Job, you are always talking about your faith; now given your current difficulty, you have to walk the walk, not just talk the talk."

QUESTIONS, ENLIGHTENMENT, AND STRADIVARIUS

FERENC RAJ

I'd like to begin my teaching this Rosh ha-Shanah with the prayer that Jews all over the world offer upon entering their places of worship. Please repeat after me: *How goodly are your tents, O Jacob, your dwelling places, O Israel.*

I cannot help but remember, and I'm sure I'm not alone, our Chanukat ha-bayit dedication ceremony (dedication of the house) when hundreds of congregants, friends, and supporters of Beth El marched with our Torah Scrolls from Vine Street to this, our new sanctuary, here in Berkeley, California. In my remarks I tried to do the impossible—to put into words our feelings of joy and accomplishment, of hope and thanksgiving. That momentous Shabbat eve I began with yet another prayer: *How greatly we are blessed! How good is our portion! How pleasant our lot! How beautiful our heritage!* And I added to fit the occasion: *And how magnificent our Beth El!*

We have so much to be thankful for, as a community and as individuals. Yet, even during the moments of our greatest rejoicing, we are all keenly aware that we do not live in a perfect world. Only days before our opening Shabbat, Hurricane Katrina and the floods that followed swept away countless communities, separated families, and destroyed lives. Jewish tradition teaches us that when even one life is lost, it is as though we lost the entire universe. Today, as we sit in safety in this brand-new sanctuary with our families, our friends, and our community, enjoying many comforts, among them the air conditioning, I ask you to reflect upon the pain of those affected by Hurricane Katrina, those mythologized as looters when they were trying to survive and those made into refugees because of systemic racism, and the aftermath of looting and lawlessness that further devastated the already impoverished communities. Reflect upon their anguish as yet another hurricane, Rita, followed on Katrina's heels, further frightening and playing havoc in the Gulf communities. Reflect also on the myriad citizens of the globe who live in abject poverty, pain, oppression, and humiliation.

This Rosh ha-Shanah morning I will focus my remarks on some serious theological questions: First, how can we respond to natural and human disasters? What does Jewish tradition teach us concerning these difficult and timeless problems?

Surely human history has registered many natural disasters. Just to mention a few: the eruption of the Pompeii Volcano in 79 CE; the Lisbon earthquake in 1755; the Galveston, Texas, hurricane and flood in 1900; the San Francisco earthquake and fire in 1906; the Tangshan, China, earthquake in 1976; the Southeast Asia tsunami in December 2004; and most recently Hurricane Katrina. Although these were all natural disasters, "acts of God," if you will, we must acknowledge that, especially during the twentieth century, there were too many heinous intentional disasters committed by human hands: the Armenian genocide; the Holocaust; the atomic bomb attacks on Hiroshima and Nagasaki; the Three Mile Island nuclear power plant accident; the Chernobyl nuclear explosion; the Rwanda massacre; suicide bombings; terrorist attacks; and, in the twenty-first century, 9/11; and the Darfur, Sudan, genocide.

As we pray for forgiveness, fortitude, and courage, as we reach deep into our souls during this solemn ten-day period of introspection, there are so many daunting questions to be addressed. Don't worry, I will not address all of them today.

But, as long as we ask the questions, as long as we are shaken from our comfortable lives, there is hope of finding solutions. What are the theological and ethical implications of natural disasters? How can human intervention reduce or intensify those natural calamities? What are the theological and ethical issues of intentional, human-induced disaster? How much of human response is prompted by racism and classism? What are the issues concerning a disregard for ecology in the light of the theological notion of dominion versus stewardship, when the earth becomes a killing field or a cancer alley?

Our sacred texts can enlighten our understanding of divine providence and human responsibilities in the wake of natural or human-induced disaster. Early on, in the cradle of Jewish civilization, our people and the Hebrew Bible addressed many of these timeless questions. In the Holy Scriptures, it is crystal clear that the entire universe is under God's sovereignty and that we human beings are stewards, caretakers, and willing instruments of God's divine will. God said: "For the land is mine; for you are strangers and sojourners with me" (Lev. 25:23). And then again in the book of Psalms: "For the world is mine, and all that fills it" (Ps. 50:12).

In spite of this dependency on God, Jewish tradition emphasizes the extraordinary power with which human beings were endowed by their Creator. "And God said: Let us make human beings in our image. They shall be *custodians* of the fish of the sea, the birds of the sky, the cattle, the whole earth, and all creeping things that creep on earth" (Gen. 1:26). God or the laws of nature caused those earthquakes and hurricanes, the tornadoes and the tsunami, but we human beings have a substantial role and responsibility to take care of the environment and all that is in it. We decide where to build, how strong to build, what to repair and maintain, whom to evacuate—we set the priorities.

When the people Israel was born, our ancestors, like young children, needed a rather simplistic theology. The Pentateuch—the five books of Moses, especially the book of Deuteronomy—assumes that well-being and blessing result from faithful adherence to the covenant, whereas dire punishment and disaster are the wages of sin. Although the book of Job protests against this worldview, it does not offer any solution. Talmudic rabbis during the first five centuries of the Common Era found solace in doctrines of immortality, resurrection, and some form of afterlife in which justice would prevail through a system of reward and punishment. However, some of the rabbis such as Rabbi Yannai boldly stated: "We do not have an explanation either for the prosperity of the wicked or for the suffering of the righteous" (*Pirkei Avot* 4:15).

The Sky Is Crying: Race, Class, and Natural Disaster is an anthology that I am contributing to, to help us do critical reflection on such tragedy. In Louisiana and Texas, surely the sky was crying—God was crying—because so many of God's creatures were destroyed. Was it all God's doing? Racism and classism, in effect, human failure to respond, failure to live and act in God's image, turned a natural disaster also into a human-induced catastrophe. Why was one hospital evacuated in a timely way, and yet another too slowly for many of those who needed medical attention? We all know the answer. What can we learn from those events? Will we ever forget the images of the elderly people sitting on rooftops without food, without their medications, without shelter from the blazing sun, holding up signs that said: "Help us"?

Though our twenty-first-century minds can find scientific explanations for the physics and chemistry of natural disasters and we can comprehend the laws of nature that cause hurricanes, earthquakes, and tsunamis to happen, we are still puzzled and it eludes our understanding why certain people become victims and others escape. I, for one, refuse to occupy myself with the unsolvable problems of theodicy that vindicate God's justice in the face of human suffering. I find it more productive to focus my attention on the questions of *how* and not *why*: How will I go on in the face of disaster? How will I fulfill my obligation of the covenant with God that states, in the words of the Talmud: "I as a human being am one of the co-partners of the Blessed Holy One in the [unfinished] work of creation." I am a necessary link in the chain of tradition, upholding and fulfilling God's plans within my own small universe. My partnership with God gives ultimate meaning to my life. Yes, as Isaiah the prophet pointed out, I am, like other human beings, created in the image of God; one of God's witnesses. "You are my witnesses and I am God" (Isa. 43:12). There is a Midrash that boldly interprets this verse: "When you are my witnesses I am God, and when you are not my witnesses I am no longer God" (*Shoher Tov*, Buber edition, p. 255a).

In plain English, God communicates to us an all-important message: "I entered into a B'rit, a covenant with you. I implanted within you a divine spark of endless possibilities. I am always with you, but you must fulfill your mission here on earth. I have given you gifts, talents, and skills to accomplish your tasks and also the responsibility to get things done."

In George Eliot's poem "Stradivarius," the famous violin maker Antonio Stradivari said it so clearly when criticized for not playing the instruments he made:

> 'Tis God gives skill
> But not without men's hands: He could not make
> Antonio Stradivari's violins
> Without Antonio.

The great twentieth-century American Jewish theologian Solomon Schechter used to say: "Leave a little to God." We cannot fix everything. We are surely less than divine. But, we can do so much to repair the world and to right the wrongs. Solomon Schechter reminded us of our partnership with God, and of our responsibility to do our share. The early

Hassidic rabbis took the duties of partnership and responsibilities of Tikkun Olam, mending the world, so seriously that one of them, Rabbi Moshe Leib of Sassov, boldly declared: "If someone comes to you and asks your help, you shall not turn him away with pious words, saying: 'Have faith; God will help you!' You shall act as if there were no God, as if there were only one person in all the world who could help this needy individual—only you, yourself." I am asking every one of us in this sanctuary today: pray as if everything depended on God; act as if everything depended on you.

We all know that disasters do not only take the form of hurricanes and earthquakes, volcanic eruptions, tornadoes, and tsunamis. Often our disasters are individual and personal: illness and disease, loss, abuse, neglect, bigotry, pain, separation, and loneliness. Sometimes our disasters are small in scale and other times, monumental. Sometimes they pass quickly; sometimes not. Pray as if everything depended on God; act as if everything depended on you. We all have the talent and the skills to help others bear their burdens and to find healing and peace. We have the tools, if only we would use them.

As we enter the New Year 5766, let us enter it with the determination that each and every one of us is here to do our share. Calamities do happen. There is a Jewish way to face them: by asking not *why* but *how*; by searching for solutions as God's copartners in the unfinished work of creation. Let us realize that we are instruments of the Divine Providence, and God works through us.

> Work through us, God.
> Teach us to be Your messengers on earth.
> Wake us up, God,
> Show us how to help.
> Use us, God, shine through us,
> Inspire us to rebuild the ruins.
> Open our hearts so we can comfort the mourning.
> Open our arms so we can extend our hands to those in need.
> Shake us out of our complacency, God.
> Be our guide,
> Transform our helplessness into action,
> Our generous intentions into charity,
> Turn the prayers of our souls into acts of kindness and compassion.
> Amen. (Rabbi Naomi Levy)

PIMPING JESUS FOR POLITICAL GAIN: CASTING STONES AT OUR NEIGHBORS (LUKE 10:25-28)

CHERYL A. KIRK-DUGGAN

Thesis: Pimping Jesus or prostituting the gospel for political mammon destroys community and fails to follow the edicts of the ministry of Christ to the poor, the disinherited, the widow, the orphan, our neighbors.

Sometimes clergy, called by God, practice idolatry by making themselves God when they utter pronouncements wherein they demonize other persons or groups. Those making such statements remind us that these selfsame clergy forget and bankrupt the gospel message of Jesus the Christ. As one recent example, *The 700 Club* host Pat Robertson, during the January 5, 2006, edition of Christian Broadcasting Network's (CBN) program, posited that Israeli Prime Minister Ariel Sharon's recent stroke was because of Sharon's policy.[1] By returning control of the Gaza strip to the Palestinian Authority, Robertson claimed Sharon was guilty of "dividing God's land," basing his callous words on the book of Joel 3:2: "I will gather all the nations and bring them down to the valley of Jehoshaphat, and I will enter into judgment with them there, on account of my people and my heritage Israel, because they have scattered them among the nations. *They have divided my land*" [emphasis added]. Does not all of the land in the world belong to God? Isn't God then upset with the founders of these United States, since the Europeans came, stole the land from Native Americans, and divided God's land into political gerrymanders?

In the aftermath of the tragedy of September 11, televangelist Jerry Falwell and Robertson said that perhaps God allowed this debacle to happen in the United States because we deserve reprimand on account of the moral corrosion in this country; further, U.S. citizens need to repent before God and ask for divine protection. Falwell said, "What we saw on

Tuesday, as terrible as it is, could be miniscule if, in fact—if, in fact—God continues to lift the curtain and allow(s) the enemies of America to give us probably what we deserve." Robertson replied, "Jerry, that's my feeling. I think we've just seen the antechamber to terror. We haven't even begun to see what they can do to the major population."[2] Falwell named and blamed the following groups for this travesty: abortionists, feminists, gays and lesbians, the ACLU, and People For the American Way. Robertson responded with agreement.[3] To play the blame game is pimping Jesus. Jesus rarely blames; Jesus does ministry. All persons, in this country, have the right by First Amendment to speak their minds. When we preface our beliefs with words of divine justification, we glimpse idolatry. God is not a "board of education," a paddle to whip people into our desired shape. For months and years after this debacle, people will still be in need. People are in need before, during, and after tragedy. Blaming innocent people changes not the ways of the world.[4]

So, is it ethical that the innocent must always suffer for the guilt of others? What about all of the other sociopolitical areas in the world that are rampant with crime, pornography, gambling, sex trafficking, and yet no natural disasters have devastated their coastal lands?

These are the basic dilemmas of theodicy: (1) Why do bad things happen to innocent or good people? (2) Why do good things happen to demonstratively bad or evil people? (3) Why do good things avoid good people? and (4) Why do bad things avoid bad people?

When we distort the message of the gospel to use others for our own selfish gain, to feed our consumerism, to foster our prestige, to fortify our sense of power, and when we totally discount and forget Jesus' message of his fundamental option for the poor, we are pimping Jesus. In the aftermath of Katrina, when we, as a society, have defaulted on the common good and have determined that the only way to rebuild the Gulf Coast is to have the military or big corporations rescue New Orleans, we have abdicated the government's responsibility to "provide for the common defense and promote the general welfare." Carter G. Woodson, 1930s sociologist, who wrote the classic *Miseducation of the Negro*,[5] reminded us that we miseducate our entire society when we miseducate one group, in the school systems and in the church. Many churches are pimping Jesus; like corporations, they promote the common good, or the good of everyone, as long as someone greases their palms with a lot of dollars, whether it makes sense or not.

Our text from Luke 10:25-28 finds the story of a lawyer questioning Jesus about the individual's requirements to achieve eternal life. Jesus does not state: "Do good and avoid evil." Instead, Jesus agrees that God calls us to love God, love ourselves, and love our neighbors. This complex notion of love is interconnected. Love of God depends upon the mediating and sharing of love for our neighbor. This kind of love is inclusive, for ourselves and others; therefore we do not spiritualize love and forget its practice, for love is action. We are to love with our whole selves, all of ourselves: all of our heart, soul, strength, and mind.

Just as we have asked the *why* questions about Katrina and Rita, scholar and New Testament professor R. Alan Culpepper[6] reminds us that the lawyer in this story challenges Jesus. This lawyer knew religious and civil law, as there was no separation or distinction between the two. Only Mark 12:30 and Luke 10:27 name four qualifiers: love with heart, soul, strength, and mind. Matthew 22:37 names only heart, soul, and mind. The fourfold love of Luke is love of heart, to love with our whole being; to love with soul concerns our unique identity, our lives; to love with mind pertains to our cognitive, intellectual capacities; to love with our strength is to love with our energy, resources, vitality, and resolve. In the face of natural disasters, have we received a wake-up call reminding us that we tend not to love well at all?

1. Because grace is sufficient, even if each of us falls short, we ought not blame the poor.

The qualifiers about how we are to love speak to God's rule or sovereignty in our lives. We are to love God with all of our selves. Loving God includes more than participating in worship, daily devotions, and tithes, and engaging in ministries around our faith communities. Loving God connects with love of neighbor. If we do not love our neighbor, we cannot love God. All of us are made in the image of God, and all of us stumble and make mistakes. Sometimes we are able to love with our hearts, our beings, but not our minds. Sometimes we can love with our minds, but not with our strength or might. And, if we cannot love ourselves, we will have no love to give to God or to others.

In our daily lives, we often get caught up with trauma, drama, and blame. We exaggerate and blow things out of proportion. Sometimes we are well meaning, yet we try to control others and be in charge of things that are not our business. Several years ago, one of my prayer partners from Austin, Texas, taught me an adage that helps me not try to control everything and everyone. At the end of the day, a teacher shows her students a narrow-necked jar with a duck inside. The duck is much too large to remove via the narrow neck of the jar. The teacher asks her students: "How can I get this duck out of this jar?" The question is not how the duck was placed in the jar via some legerdemain,[7] but, rather, "How do I get this duck out of this jar?" The students are restless and unhappy at the end-of-school-day delay. Finally, from the rear of the room a hand shoots up in the air. Animatedly, the teacher says, "Yes?" The student says: "It's not my duck; it's not my jar; it's not my problem." Too often, other people's ducks, jars, and problems trap us; nevertheless, what about love of the neighbor? Or, when do we become our brother's and sister's keepers? When do the problems and afflictions of others become our problems and afflictions?

Loving our neighbors and controlling our neighbors are two different things; certainly distinct from blaming our neighbors for what happens to them. Many poor people could not get out of flooding regions on the Gulf Coast. That there was no efficient evacuation plan in place on the local, state, or federal level was not the fault of the poor. Many of them did not own cars. Armed deputies and a mayor who did not want them to cross the bridge into the deputies' parish blocked the passage on foot by some. The ministerial vision of Jesus embraced the poor. In recent years the slogan "What Would Jesus Do? [WWJD]" has become a popular query. Jesus would not have blamed the poor for not having transportation out of the areas of flooding, but would have gathered his team of disciples/deputies to help gather the people to move them out of danger.

In one sense, all of us are complicit when we disregard the poor. To ease our consciences, and to engender a feel-good emotion, we give food baskets for Christmas and Thanksgiving. Sometimes we collect clothing for our church's clothes closet. Often, we do not have a consistent plan of action in our churches or in larger society to assist the poor or to help the poor help themselves. Lyndon Johnson's "Great Society" with its subsidiary "War on Poverty" rapidly disintegrated into objects of parody when LBJ was faced with his Vietnam military attention and expenditures. Education and building self-esteem is critical. Just as racism and sexism are problematic in these United States, so is classism, the larger context of poverty. Classism or elitism is the kind of oppression that draws lines of separation that translate as "us against them," as if we are distinct, enviable, and unusual. Classism allows us to create walls of isolation where the wealthy, the middle class, and the poor do not interact. Classism allows us to view people as objects to use. The economics and clout that come with narcissism, affluence, and elitism often set up a false sense of reality, a way of thinking and being where we genuflect to a world of prosperity where everything has a price. Classism, like other forms of violence, trades on power, and ultimately denies the humanity of the poor.

Thus, four months have passed and victims of Katrina and Rita are still in tents. Lake Charles roofs are still covered with blue plastic. Many of the schools and businesses still have not reopened. Power lines are still strewn across the roads, as mold multiplies in the houses that some people want to reclaim—and they have yet to get any FEMA money to assist them.[8] If we are going to blame anyone, we each must blame ourselves for being content to have the poor remain invisible on a daily basis. If we must blame anyone, we must blame ourselves for allowing our country to not have affordable health care, particularly a health care system that would have sufficient mental hospital facilities available, reducing the number of homeless poor on the street. If we are to blame anyone, we need to blame ourselves for our worship at the altars of manifest destiny, consumerism, materialism, mercantilism, and capitalism that puts a dollar figure on everything, but shortchanges love.

2. Jesus' character is not subsumed by big business, consumerism, and scapegoating.

Throughout the Gospels, the picture of Jesus that emerges is pastoral, thoughtful, and caring. Jesus is an educator, a rabbi, a teacher who does not align with the Pharisees and Sadducees, or the Roman aristocracy. Jesus was the one who turned the tables of the money changers over in the temple. Jesus also taught, "Give . . . the emperor the things [or persons] that are the emperor's, and to God the things [or persons] that are God's" (Matt. 22:21). Jesus would not be schmoozing with the ancient Israelite jet set at Rehoboth. Many of his parables invoke an antithetical stance to wealth, power, consumerism, and scapegoating others. Jesus preached a simple yet demanding gospel of love.

Corporations are in the business of making profit and war, not love. Many twenty-first-century churches are also in the business of making money, a lot of it, without really caring about the poor or the disenfranchised. Many churches are built around a business-marketing schema, to the detriment of the well-being of all of God's children in that particular congregation and the community. They spend the earnings on their endowments, but never touch the principal. The stories that follow the lawyer's query—the so-called good Samaritan story and that of Mary and Martha—highlight and emulate the teachings of Luke 10:27, but the characters showcase love of God and love of neighbor. In ancient Israel, women were the property of their father or husband, and were not important except to function as a helper and to produce offspring, particularly a male to inherit the land. Women would not have studied with men, at the foot of their rabbi. The low-caste Samaritans were not good neighbors of the righteous. These stories turn that society upside down, and break the accepted rules of decorum. How can we live the gospel amid our own greed and callousness if we are to be neighborly?

In the United States, across the board, many of us have advanced degrees in consumerism. Up to the early 1960s, one could only make purchases through loans, direct cash, or by putting the object of one's desire on layaway. With layaway, people paid so much per month until the item was paid in full, then they would be able to take the purchase home. Today credit cards proliferate; we buy now and pay later. Interest accumulates and many of us end up in debt; many of us are only two paychecks away from bankruptcy or poverty. However, the laws have changed to benefit the moneylenders, and the clean slate of forgiveness via bankruptcy is much more difficult to pursue. Being gross consumers, do we also commit the sin of gluttony? Could we do better with less? Along with our thirst for more things has come our thirst for more individualism. Much of our individualism has become crass and filled with false piety. We think that we made it all by ourselves. No one can achieve without help from someone. Someone admitted us to a program, approved our hire, or trained us. We are made to be in community. However, there are so many solo, tiny boats on life's oceans that we collide against one another without meaningful interaction.

We adapt a cutthroat notion that "I've got mine; you can get yours the best way you can; and if you don't get yours, you are morally delinquent." Such attitudes infiltrate our classrooms, where often the task is not about being creative, or engaging in analytical, critical thinking, but about "What is the least amount that I can do to get a good grade?" "The competition is so steep that we all have to cheat." Such concepts are not foreign to many of our students from kindergarten to grade twelve and beyond. What could happen in business, in education, and in our religious communities if we really took the first-person-plural pronoun seriously?

The message of the gospel encourages us to avoid becoming anesthetized to others around us and to avoid becoming mesmerized by the glitter of success, fame, and fortune. That is not to say that it is wrong to have possessions and to enjoy life. Yet, life is problematic when we focus solely on acquisitions and materialism; when we forget about our neighbor; when we avoid contact; when our faith communities become docking stations where we tune in for a few moments to get a fix for the week, and nothing said or done during the service has an impact on us. We truly are caught up in our self-serving ways when we blame others for their plight, for our own mistakes, or blame them for things none of us can control.

French cultural anthropologist and literary critic René Girard talks about *scapegoating* as part of the matrix of violence and religion. He suggests that we learn from one another through mimesis or imitation, as in the mimetic triangle: the triangle consists of the subject, the disciple, and the object. The disciple or student wants to learn something from the subject. The thing to be learned is the object. In that process, sometimes we come to desire what someone else has. When that desire intensifies, it becomes rivalry. The rivalry can become so intense that lines blur and the triangle collapses into two, or doubles. Often the subject is no longer clear about what the disciple wants and vice versa. To diffuse the intensity of the violence, one needs a scapegoat. When Germany had to repay the debt of World War I, it became bankrupt. Times were tense and people were going hungry. Amid this kind of desperation, Adolf Hitler emerged, having produced his book *Mein Kampf*. *Mein Kampf* is Hitler's autobiographical work that he wrote while imprisoned in the Landsberg fortress in 1923. Hitler proposed his racial, political ideology of national socialism: his thoughts, values, and plans for the restoration of Germany. He argued that Germans belonged to the "superior" Aryan race, though he, and his inner circle, had none of those physical traits. The Hitler project was quite clear. He found a scapegoat—actually several scapegoats— persons to blame for Germany's plight. Those scapegoated included six million Jews, more than one million Roma (Gypsies), homosexuals, and persons with mental disorders or physical challenges, and more than three million Soviet prisoners of war. Murdering the scapegoats served as a safety valve so that the German society could prosper. In addition, war always stimulates the economy. With Hitler's charisma, the larger German public's desperation, and the rest of the chaos throughout Europe and Asia during the First and Second World Wars, sixty million people lost their lives.

What of the victims of Katrina and Rita? Was there some secret manifesto that stated people on the Gulf Coast needed to die to purge the level of poverty in the region? Had the standard of living been enhanced for those who achieved refuge in the Astrodome, as the former first lady and mother of the president asserted? That a Category 4 or 5 hurricane would ultimately develop was a known factor. Articles had appeared in a variety of places, including *Scientific American*, which stated that a Category 4 or 5 hurricane could wipe out the levees, particularly in New Orleans. Funding to some of these technical, engineering projects had been reduced or funneled elsewhere. By not having clear, direct plans, with sufficient vehicles for evacuating; substantial clean water, food, and electricity backup; and by not seeing and naming the poverty long before this, we have been complicit and we have scapegoated our neighbors. Who can forget the bodies floating in fetid water; the hundreds of stranded poor, vulnerable black people on rooftops and the interstate; the frustrated family members who have yet to find their children, their elderly parents, or friends?

3. Our need for answers is no excuse for pimping Jesus or pimping God's people.

In the hours, days, and weeks since Katrina, many have tried to make sense out of nonsense. Some have blamed individual and communal degradation for the poverty and death in New Orleans. Some have said that God was punishing New Orleans for its gross decadence, fast living, and partying mentality. If that is so, what is the most recent devastation to happen in Las Vegas? Atlantic City? Washington DC? If this God is so awesome, powerful, and loving, why would God need to exact such pain and destruction? Was the God of August 29, 2005, that came ashore with the winds and the water, a loving God?

One answer we can invoke without shame or doubt is, "We don't know." There are some things that remain a mystery. We can state as fact that the marshlands and outer land masses had been compromised through deep dredging and the building of numerous oil wells in the Gulf. We know that global warming had a definite effect. The Gulf of Mexico became hotter; the hotter the water, the more hurricanes. Hurricane season used to go from June to September. Now we are having hurricanes as late as December and January.

In our search for why bad things happen, there may be no answer that makes spiritual and logical sense. There is danger when we think that we can know God's experience of God's power and love for us, and how God moves and exists in this world. All our language for and about God is anthropomorphic. That is, we use human terms; ways of being, knowing, and experiencing life to talk about God. Though language is all we have, often it is so woefully inadequate when speaking about things of God, of the divine. To try to commandeer and shanghai God and Jesus to make our own points and to assuage our own guilt is another form of pimping the divine. We prostitute God for our purposes.

If we are to take the gospel message of Jesus the Christ seriously, if we are going to work to live out our covenant lives in relation, we need to rediscover who we are, whose we are, who is our neighbor, and our experience of God. Jesus teaches that we are to be in relation. Jesus became incarnated to show us how to love and how to be in relationship. His primary directive in community is the preferential option for the poor. In systematic practice, many of our faith communities and churches fail miserably at this task.

Life is incredibly complex. For many problems and challenges, there are no easy answers. When dealing with nature, we know that at some point rivers overflow. Volcanoes erupt and darken the atmosphere for months. Earthquakes shake things. Hurricanes come with the ecosystems of the southern Gulf Coast. There are many storms and hurricanes each year that blow out into the ocean. Other times they turn inward and do exhaustive damage. Part of the devastation of Katrina, in one sense, had nothing to do with Katrina. Katrina was the catalyst that unveiled a festering, long-standing problem of deprivation; of destitution; of abject poverty.

Katrina, and Rita to a lesser extent, exposed the depths of poverty on our Gulf Coast. The poverty uncovered is not of recent vintage, but has been long-standing. In the United States, we like to pretend that everyone has the same opportunity to succeed, but this is not so. Case in point: since historically our educational systems have been supported by property-tax dollars, people in lower income areas have always had inferior educational settings. In some instances, teachers have worked to help their students get ahead by transcending schools that have old equipment, used books, and aging buildings, but think of the toll this takes on everyone. Teachers are underpaid and overworked. Today's schoolteachers have to teach students to pass exams, or the teachers will lose their jobs. This is not education; this is indoctrination. Without a solid education, without a safe home environment, in home environments with cyclical issues of domestic violence, sexual assault, codependency, and other pathologies, children usually have no choice but to do as their parents do, unless someone steps in and shows them there are other options. What are faith communities doing about being good stewards to people in need?

The hurricanes exposed our poor stewardship when it comes to the tenuous, fragile ecosystem in that region. We got to see how many oil rigs exist in the Gulf, and the result of all the related petrochemical plants, for the region is also known as "cancer alley." That region has disproportionate cases of a variety of cancers, lupus, and severe allergies. Although God has given us brains to think and creative imagination, God has not demanded that we pollute the earth and in the process cause harm to the environment and ourselves.

The acts of terror, hurricanes, tsunamis, earthquakes, and coal mine disasters from 2001 to 2005 have reminded us that as citizens in the United States, we are not immune from disaster. As citizens in the world, natural and human-induced disasters occur. That these bad things happen does not give us license to be pimping Jesus, either to escape responsibility, to come up with simple answers that do not work, or to prostitute the gospel where we will succeed by any means necessary. Instead of pimping Jesus, we have an opportunity to revisit what it means to be Christian and live in community. We have an opportunity to begin to exercise our muscles of stewardship and relate better to our neighbors. We have a chance to love ourselves, our bodies; to not do anything that contaminates our beings, other beings, or the earth. If we continue to "turn tricks" and play games, and misuse and abuse the power and gifts given us by God, we will continue to scapegoat others; we will continue to perpetuate a gross division between the *have-nots* and the *haves* and *have mores* to the devastation of the very core of what it means to be human in relationship. Are we willing to pay that price?

Notes

1. http://mediamatters.org/items/200601050004.

2. http://www.beliefnet.com gives this partial transcript of comments from the September 13, 2001, edition of *The 700 Club*.

3. Ibid.

4. Following national publicity over the Robertson-Falwell interview, on September 14, 2001, Falwell issued an apology for his comments. Pat Robertson, on his website, distanced himself from the comments that he had agreed with at the time they were made.

5. Carter G. Woodson, *The Miseducation of the Negro* (Washington, DC: Associated Publishers, 1933, 1969).

6. R. Alan Culpepper, "Luke," *The New Interpreter's Bible: A Commentary in Twelve Volumes* (Nashville: Abingdon Press, 2001), 226-28, 232.

7. One can slip the component parts of the toy duck through the narrow neck, and then assemble the duck within the jar. This is how ship models are put into flasks. With a live duck, you're out of luck!

8. We note that Miami/Dade County received FEMA monies even though the Florida hurricanes did not touch Miami/Dade County. FEMA paid for more burials than the number of those who died as a result of the Florida hurricanes.

303.485

K591

116671